The European Academy of Legal Theory Series

MORAL CONFLICT AND LEGAL REASONING

European Academy of Legal Theory Series

General Editors

Professor Dr Mark Van Hoecke
Professor Dr Luc Wintgens
Professor Dr François Ost

Other titles in this series

Van Hoecke and Ost (Eds.)
The Harmonisation of European Private Law

MORAL CONFLICT AND LEGAL REASONING

SCOTT VEITCH
Reader in Law, University of Glasgow

·HART·
PUBLISHING

OXFORD – PORTLAND OREGON
1999

Hart Publishing
Oxford and Portland, Oregon

Published in North America (US and Canada) by
Hart Publishing c/o
International Specialized Book Services
5804 NE Hassalo Street
Portland, Oregon
97213-3644
USA

Distributed in the Netherlands, Belgium and Luxembourg by
Intersentia, Churchillaan 108
B-2900 Schoten
Antwerpen
Belgium

Distributed in Australia and New Zealand by
Federation Press
John St
Leichhardt
NSW 2000

Hart Publishing Ltd is a specialist legal publisher based in Oxford, England.
To order further copies of this book or to request a list of other publications please write to:

Hart Publishing Ltd, Salter's Boatyard, Oxford OX1 4LB
Telephone: +44 (0)1865 245533 or Fax: +44 (0)1865 794882
e-mail: mail@hartpub.co.uk

British Library Cataloguing in Publication Data
Data Available
ISBN 1 84113-108-3 (cloth)

Typeset by Hope Services (Abingdon) Ltd.
Printed in Great Britain on acid-free paper
by Biddles Ltd, Guildford and Kings Lynn.

ACKNOWLEDGMENTS

I am immensely grateful for the help, encouragement and advice, over a period of many years, of Beverley Brown and Neil MacCormick. Thanks go also to Zenon Bankowski, Emilios Christodoulidis, Adam Czarnota, Lindsay Farmer, Drew Fraser, Valerie Kerruish, Alison Mackay and John Touchie, each for their distinctive input and for ongoing debate; and to Mark Van Hoecke and Luc Wintgens for their help in the later stages.

Finally my thanks go to my family, and in particular to my parents. Without their support, in every way, this work would not have been possible.

CONTENTS

PART THREE

INTRODUCTION

(1)

My hypothesis is that liberalism, in the interpretation of it I will offer, and liberal legalism, defined broadly as the current role, rhetoric, and practices of legal institutions in contemporary liberal society, are incompatible. Further, it suggests, in order to hold true to its premises, such a theory of liberalism must challenge the institutional vesting it presently receives at the hands of the legal system. To explore why this might be so, I give a reading of liberalism which puts the social construction of morality at the heart of its critical concerns. In particular, how meaningful moral disagreement is conceived and articulated is of prime importance. There is great focus in moral and legal literature on how consensus is or ought to be achieved. But it is my contention that how disagreement or dissensus is constructed, and, what dissensus means, have been neglected. In a sense they might be thought of as two sides to the same coin: how to agree to disagree requires consideration of what we agree upon. But how we analyse disagreement can often be overlooked in the rush to create terms of agreement. How and why we disagree needs to be brought more clearly into focus.

Nowhere is this going to be more important than when courts assemble arguments applying "community standards" in justifying decisions. But I want to take a distinctive position when it comes to legal argument. Though I do consider how legal argumentation constructs standards which will be applied in cases that come before judges, there is much to be gained from turning away from this to a consideration of the role and position of law itself in the broader purview and construction of moral agreement and disagreement. Traditional legal scholarship, and certainly education, tend to view morality in terms of trying to understand what exactly its relation to law is: should law embody morality, or are law and morality conceptually distinct? This old, and no doubt important, question perplexes and re-perplexes old and new students in all jurisprudence courses. But there is a tendency to look at the question as an either/or issue. This in turn works to limit proper attention to questions of morality themselves, which may become homogenised in aspects of content and form since the focus of lawyers and legal philosophers is usually, "how should law (or lawyers) respond?" Once again, this is an important question, but the vantage point—of argument and analysis—is a legal one, and its ultimate destination (law's response) works to obscure the genesis and construction of moral problems in the first place.

In order to explore my hypothesis I concentrate far more on moral theory than many jurisprudential analyses do. But I also follow a suggestion in the work of Alasdair MacIntyre that law is implicated in the way in which we conceive, construct and deal with moral questions. As such it is important not only to consider how moral disagreement is constructed, but to see what role techniques of law, and more particularly the contemporary institutional dependency on law, play in how we deal with moral problems. It is in exploring these issues that I come to suggest the practices of liberal legalism damage and distort the premises of the liberal theory I advance.

(2)

"The values of Liberalism should not to be reduced to nought simply because their practice has historically been so shoddy."[1] There is no shortage of critiques dwelling on such shoddy practice. Critical scholars who often share little else are usually at one in their demonisation of liberalism. But is this an overreaction? What are these values that ought not to be overlooked? Liberals will themselves dispute what these are as they will also dispute their implications. Martha Nussbaum has recently given a succinct three-fold definition of liberal values that will serve as an introduction: first, "that all, just by being human, are of equal dignity and worth, no matter where they are situated in society"; secondly, "that the primary source of this worth is a power of moral choice within them, which consists in the ability to plan a life in accordance with one's own evaluation of ends"; and finally, that "society and politics . . . must respect the liberty of choice, and must respect the equal worth of per-

[1] Elizabeth Fox-Genovese, "The Many Faces of Moral Economy: A Contribution to a Debate", *Past and Present* 58 (Feb. 1973), 168.

sons as choosers".[2] An apparently minimalist position, and not itself uncontested, it is one, I will argue, that has radical consequences when delineated in a certain way. The way I choose here is taken from the work of Isaiah Berlin and represents what John Gray has termed Berlin's "agonistic liberalism".[3]

In interpreting some of the aspects alluded to in Nussbaum's definition, I argue that it is important to situate that aspect of "moral choice" she refers to in a specifically constructivist sense: that is, one that focuses primarily on the contextual and constitutive relations between self, identity and values, and which draws out the implications of these relations both for a theory of liberalism and for a liberal theory of law. As Nussbaum and many others note, one of the major criticisms of liberal theory or, more precisely perhaps, its "shoddy practice", has been that liberalism has assumed an unjustifiable and harmful methodological individualism. Additionally, it has been taken to link such individualism, or atomism as it has been called, with a specific, though universalised, notion of rationality. Examples abound, but here are a couple that are indicative of such critiques: "liberal theory insist[s] on positing individuals as rational, self-interested, and pre-social ethical beings"[4]; and again, "the denial of dependency on the social other presupposed in the market conception of rationality is present in the original liberal account of the individual and of society and the state . . . [which] denies the social and connected nature of the self".[5]

I argue that such criticism is mistaken. Concentrating on Berlin's version of liberalism, and touching on the moral theory of Adam Smith in whose name—or rather against whose name—much criticism of individualism has been directly or indirectly invoked, I show that individual moral choice, while still a clear value of liberal thought, can only be understood in a contextual manner. The effect of this is to suggest that critiques of liberalism along the lines of the two above set up a straw man. The liberal theory I delineate here challenges these criticisms, and does so by concentrating on the way in which a theory such as Berlin's depends upon the embedded nature of self and values, as well as on the limitations of reason. To do so I once again concentrate on the

[2] Martha Nussbaum, "The Feminist Critique of Liberalism," Lecture at Oxford University, Feb. 1996, excerpted in the *Times Higher Education Supplement* as "The Sleep of Reason", Feb. 1996, 17.

[3] John Gray, *Isaiah Berlin* (London, HarperCollins, 1995), chap. 6.

[4] Allan C. Hutchinson, *Waiting for CORAF: A Critique of Law and Rights* (Toronto, Toronto UP, 1995), 95.

[5] Val Plumwood, *Feminism and the Mastery of Nature* (London, Routledge, 1993), 152.

construction of moral judgement and the settings and meanings of moral conflict for such a liberal theory.

I should note that this has two implications. The first is that I refuse to draw a strong distinction between morality and politics. The tendency to locate moral problems in the realm of private autonomous individuals, whilst political problems are deemed merely to concern issues of public welfare or redistribution, has been one of the misunderstandings of both liberal proponents and their detractors. Such a separation is, I suggest, not a necessary component of liberal theory. This is not to deny that liberalism is concerned with the extent of state or any other forms of authoritarian imposition in what may be thought of as private matters: clearly it is. However, I suggest that to hold on to a morality/politics or private/public distinction when posed in this way fails to recognise both the constitutive nature of identity within social forms, and that commitment to values cannot neatly be separated across such divisions without misunderstanding the source and meaning of such values. It is thus in this more expansive sense that I use the term morality in the book.

Secondly, the implications for the role of law I see in this type of liberalism may go further than many liberals, even "agonistic" ones, would themselves endorse. But given the aspirations and meanings of the liberal theory I delineate, it is necessary to make this further conclusion which challenges the current role of law in contemporary society. De Sousa Santos has suggested that "the absorption of law in the modern state was a contingent historical process which, like any other historical process, had a beginning and will have an end".[6] Though I do not get into quite such grand arguments, the more limited point I do want to make is nevertheless similar in vein. That is, that to hold to the worth and values of the type of liberalism put forward here, a more fundamental challenge has to be made to the present positioning of law and particularly the courts, than many liberals, or for that matter their detractors, have so far made.

Such a challenge follows not simply a recognisably liberal argument about the fears of an intrusive state, but further points to an analysis of how the common law, as part of what has been "absorbed" into and in fact bolstered the law of the state, continues to be an obstacle to the goals and values of the liberalism I describe. The common law has had, at least since the time of Sir Edward Coke, extraordinarily powerful

[6] See his *Toward a New Common Sense: Law, Science and Politics in the Paradigmatic Transition* (London, Routledge, 1995), 94–95.

integrating, unifying and consequently excluding, effects on the shaping of community, and has used the rhetoric of its, in Coke's words, "artificial reason" to mythologise and mystify the standards according to which it works. Moreover, the logic, if not the outcomes, has remained remarkably static over time. "Once the facts are proved", wrote a recent Chief Justice of the Australian High Court in a negligence decision, "all that remains for the court to do in determining the standard of care is to apply community standards".[7] The question this challenge is concerned with, then, is how, given the liberal premise of tolerance towards *incommensurable* values, the common law can operate so smoothly to produce the "community standards" by reference to which it justifies its decisions. And the issues that need addressing are not simply how the judges produce such standards (the problem to which traditional legal scholarship devotes so much of its time), but what is the meaning and significance of their doing so? In particular, what effects do the institutional setting and dynamic of law within the community have in turn *back* on the varied values and social forms of that community? Again, to explore these concerns it is necessary to focus more determinedly on the construction of these values and forms themselves, before considering the legal viewpoint.

(3)

The book is constructed in three broad parts. The first provides an in-depth analysis of the recent work of Alasdair MacIntyre in moral theory. It charts his historical argument about transitions in thinking about morality from Aristotelian to current models, and in particular draws out his critique of liberal moral theory. He suggests that we are witnessing a new Dark Ages, and that this is the result of the necessary failure of what he calls the Enlightenment project. I focus in particular on the way in which he sees moral debate taking place in liberal community, and how the conception of the self informs this debate. To complement this analysis I consider the liberal theory of Richard Rorty which, I argue, though it celebrates some aspects of what MacIntyre treats as a failure, nevertheless essentially replicates MacIntyre's description of liberalism.

I spend some time delineating these arguments because of what they have to say about the role of law in contemporary society. MacIntyre's

[7] Brennan J, in *Gala v Preston* (1991) 172 CLR 243.

analysis of liberalism provides a way of seeing how the use of law and the position of legal institutions impact and in some sense depend upon the meaning of moral conflict in the broader community. Using a four-level model drawn from his work, I suggest that though MacIntyre may be incorrect in his diagnosis of liberalism and its conception of the self (the full critique of which does not emerge until the second part), he does provide important insights into the role of law in liberal community, and in doing so opens out the possibility for challenging the legitimacy of law in the liberal legal order.

The second part examines, and in part develops, a theory of liberalism drawn from the work of Isaiah Berlin. Here I consider the version of liberalism alluded to above, and one that is clearly at odds with the picture of liberalism usually portrayed by its detractors. I concentrate on the way in which he treats the meaning and significance of moral conflict, and how this depends upon the constitutive relation between self and values and the limited role that reason has to play in resolving such conflict. Here I draw on the helpful analysis of Joseph Raz which I treat, particularly in its notion of "constitutive incommensurabilities", as a more subtle though indirect development of the arguments Berlin is making. Finally I extrapolate from Berlin's liberalism some tentative conclusions about the role of law, and do so by way of comparing this theory with MacIntyre's.

The third part draws on two strands of critique in recent theoretical developments in order to address how they conceptualise responses to liberal legal institutions. These strands are taken from feminist analysis and from postmodern critiques based on what has been called the "ethic of alterity". In considering several elements to these positions I look at two things: first, whether they correctly identify problems with liberal theory, or whether they tend to set up the "straw man" of liberalism while attacking instead its "shoddy practices"; and, secondly, what a genuine countering of the practices of liberal legal institutions might involve. In order to explore this, at this stage I consider both how legal justification takes place in contemporary institutions and some of the often unexamined dimensions to this process (including for example what Judith Shklar calls the "ideology of agreement"), and some of the sociological significations of this process, such as the effects of legal professionalism.

Here I will argue that in order to give full expression to the incommensurable values and social forms that liberalism identifies and seeks to respect, and with which, I suggest, recent critiques espousing difference and "otherness" may seem to be remarkably at one, fuller attention to the stifling effects of common law reasoning and its institutional power is required. When postmodern theorists, in particular, overlook that institutional dimension, they fail properly to grasp the structural and constitutive effects of law. Where they talk then of exploring forms of "partial" or "local" justice, such arguments, I suggest, can only make sense within a more global critique of vested power and the institutional dynamics of law, an approach that has historically been one of the core concerns of liberal thought.

Throughout and underlying much of what follows is a view of morality or moral rationality, and of the self, which challenges the view of liberalism as being committed to a rule-based individualism, whether that interpretation is given by its adherents or its critics. But not enough has been done within liberal thought to see how such a view relates to the role and impacts of justificatory practices of law when these practices endorse a commitment to a universalism at odds with that initial position. The Scottish institutional writer Erskine wrote that because of "the depravity of men's minds", civil powers add to the laws of nature positive laws "that so all members of the community, instead of being left to their own partial reasonings, may be tied down to a set of laws that speak the same uniform language to every individual".[8] This is in many ways emblematic of the liberal legal argument about law's aspiration to impartiality; to raise law above those "partial reasonings" that exist beyond the legal realm. But what are the status and nature of these partial reasonings? Erskine himself believed them to be rooted in a theology of original sin, in the "depravity of men's minds". Others, including the two critics mentioned above, see them as allied to an instrumentalist self-seeking market rationality. Alasdair MacIntyre thinks they exemplify an emotivist set of preferences to be fulfilled. I want to explore a conception different from all three, and one that in turn has implications for the perceived legitimacy of law and legal reasoning.

The relation between law and "partial reasonings" is of prime concern. Erskine suggested that law should "speak the same uniform language" to all individuals. For him, law's partiality itself was not put in question. A century earlier Hobbes had given perhaps the most powerful argument to defend law's legitimacy, partial or not. Addressing the same issue as Erskine, he noted that, "Law can never be against Reason,

[8] John Erskine, *An Institute of the Law of Scotland*, (1773, 5th edn., Edinburgh, Bell and Bradfute, 1812), I.17.

our Lawyers are agreed . . . but the doubt is, of whose Reason it is, that shall be received for Law".[9] Hobbes's answer, of course, was that "[i]t is not Wisdom, but Authority that makes a Law".[10] Here was a striking answer to law's relation to "partial reasonings", and one that has remained remarkably resilient.

For Hobbes, Erskine and others, the role of law is integrally related to how our "partial reasonings" are conceived. In a sense, I agree. But what happens when such reasonings are reconceptualised, when "partiality" is seen as integral to social forms within which meaningful values and identities are constituted and maintained? If law is to speak a uniform language, as Erskine suggests, or is to apply "community standards" as Chief Justice Brennan would have it, how is this singular voice construed, and what effects does this have on the language and meaning of the partial reasonings by which we live our lives outside the formal legal arena? These are the kind of questions the book seeks to explore.

Erskine's contemporary, David Hume, though himself committed to "general and inflexible rules of justice", nevertheless observed that, "there is a principle of human nature, which we have frequently taken note of, that men are mightily addicted to general rules, and that often we carry our maxims beyond those reasons which first induc'd us to establish them".[11] I contend that such a "mighty addiction" has had a hold on the mind-set of liberal legalism and has edged it to the place where the aspirations for its institution—the values and concerns of liberalism—may now be being done a disservice by the continued devotion to a bureaucratic legalism at odds with the radical spirit of liberal thought. To address this problem requires a focus on the institutional vesting of common law reasoning and the paraphenalia of power and expertise which supports it, but above all requires an investigation of the worth and meaning of those "partial reasonings" without which we could neither make sense of ourselves nor the commitments and values which we hold so variously and so dearly. With this in mind, let us begin.

[9] Thomas Hobbes, *Leviathan* (ed. C. B. Macpherson, Harmondsworth, Penguin, 1968), ch. XXVI.7.

[10] Thomas Hobbes, *A Dialogue Between a Philosopher and a Student of the Common Law of England* (ed. J. Cropsey, Chicago, Chicago UP, 1971), 55.

[11] David Hume, *A Treatise of Human Nature* (2nd edn., ed. L. A. Selby-Bigge, Oxford, Clarendon Press, 1978), 551.

PART ONE

1: The Dark Ages of Liberalism

Amongst other things, the phrase Dark Ages conjures up a time of cultural loss, a loss sustained most dramatically as a result of the virtual disappearance of the classic texts of the past. The loss could be considered as a double one in the following sense. First there had occurred the fragmentation of a once more whole body of knowledge and, secondly, the means whereby the fragments that remained could be brought back together under a new cohering unity had also been lost. Irreparable damage would thus have occurred. Described very simply in these terms we might be somewhat quizzical when we hear the suggestion that contemporary society is experiencing a new Dark Ages. What, we might ask, is the loss we are alleged to have suffered? And does not the idea of irreparable damage cut across the grain of our culture of possibility and innovation? Apart from the run-of-the-mill prophets of doom, is not loss, in the sense of fragmentation, most often experienced in the form of an idealised nostalgia for a more simple and just past, a nostalgia, as Lyotard puts it, of the whole?[1] Often it can be. But the purpose of this chapter is to outline and assess a serious and challenging reconstruction of a part of philosophical history which points us precisely towards this "new Dark Ages" conclusion.

In focussing particularly on moral discourse Alasdair MacIntyre attempts to show how we should see our contemporary moral vocabulary as little more than a series of fragmented survivals from a once more coherent past. He suggests that "the contemporary vision of the world . . . is predominantly, although perhaps not always in detail, Weberian".[2] Yet his argument is at once more specific and dramatic than the Weberian description of disenchantment. Disenchantment, which Weber saw somewhat nostalgically as a loss, but nevertheless as an inevitable price to pay in the rise of modernity, is for MacIntyre a key symptom of fundamental flaws and a prefiguring of our contemporary malaise. Contemplating the Weberian universe, where on the one hand

[1] Jean-François Lyotard, *The Postmodern Condition: A Report on Knowledge* (transl. G. Bennington and B. Massumi, Manchester, Manchester UP, 1984), Appendix, "Answering the Question: What is Postmodernism?".

[2] Alasdair MacIntyre, *After Virtue: A Study in Moral Theory* (2nd edn., London, Duckworth, 1985), 109. Note that page references, in brackets, in this and the following two sections of the text are to this book.

we find a moral world without objective foundations and on the other the rise of an instrumental rationality at home in an efficiency-driven formalism, is for MacIntyre to contemplate an arena of despair. Entering contemporary moral discourse with MacIntyre is like finding oneself in the familiar territory of a Shakespearean tragedy. Here we find a dialogue riddled with unsustainable dreams and burning ambitions, fatal flaws and doomed revolutions. And of course, dead bodies.

For Weber "disenchantment" was, literally translated, "demagification", the world "robbed of gods" and mystical spirits through which people had once understood the world and their place in it. It meant:

> that principally there are no mysterious incalculable forces that come into play, but rather that one can, in principle, master all things by calculation . . . One need no longer have recourse to magical means in order to master or implore the spirits, as did the savage, for whom such mysterious powers existed. Technical means and calculations perform the service.[3]

These "technical means and calculations" Weber identified with the processes of rationalisation which had developed specifically in the West largely since the Renaissance. Though they had many distinct manifestations—in natural science, architecture, law and government, for example—a commonality could be traced. As Gerth and Mills have put it:

> The extent and direction of "rationalisation" is measured negatively in terms of the degree to which magical elements of thought are displaced, or positively by the extent to which ideas gain in systematic coherence and naturalistic consistency.[4]

It may be considered to be one of the paradoxes of modernity that at the same time structures of thought and organisation worked to improve the efficiency of means available to humans—the more they helped us to predict and therefore to control the future "by means of increasingly precise and abstract concepts",[5] the more disenchanted the world became.

Moreover, for Weber, the success of these techniques had finally driven a wedge between the normative and the scientific. Where for the pre-modern world a harmony of man and nature had meant the possibility of a theological unity—where knowledge came with obligation, so

[3] Max Weber, "Science as a Vocation" in H. H. Gerth and C. Wright Mills (eds.), *From Max Weber: Essays in Sociology* (London, Routledge, 1991), 139.

[4] "Introduction", *ibid.*, 51.

[5] Max Weber, "Bureaucracy" in *ibid.*, 239.

to speak—the modern world could not sustain such a unity. Yet what the modern world shared with the ancient, though not with the Christian, was the release of a plurality of lesser, secular, gods and demons. But their context and status had clearly changed. In modernity we returned to "polytheism", but with this major difference: the "various value spheres in the world stand in irreconcilable conflict with each other. . . . According to our ultimate standpoint, the one is the devil and the other the God, and the individual has to decide which is God for him and which is the devil."[6] Here we see the link between disenchantment and value pluralism. In a world "robbed of gods" the individual alone could decide his or her moral obligations, for there could be no rational resolution of such conflicts as arose. And it is in this sense that MacIntyre sees the modern world as "predominantly Weberian".

However for MacIntyre the current state of moral fragmentation can ultimately trace its origins back more precisely to the eighteenth century, which for him not so much consisted in enlightenment, but was instead, as Lord Grey was later famously to say in another context, like the lamps going out all over Europe. But in true tragedian style the main protagonists did not know, nor perhaps could ever know, the consequences of their plans. It was for them a time of brilliant confidence, of belief in the idea that new and lasting work could be carried out in the science of society just as the previous century had produced such stunning results in the natural sciences. One need only think of the social-scientific remit that David Hume, perhaps the pre-eminent sceptic of his time, gave himself in the *Treatise*—"to introduce the experimental method of reasoning into moral subjects"—to witness an enlightening confidence not at all out place in the intellectual climate of the times. But MacIntyre sees this in quite a different way. He describes these times as displaying "a peculiar kind of darkness in which men so dazzled themselves that they could no longer see" (at 92). In setting out to find a new, rational foundation for moral discourse, the "Enlightenment project", we are told, not only failed but, according to its chosen method, was bound to fail.

In unfolding this particular narrative which in this chapter relies heavily on an appraisal of MacIntyre's thesis, the "Enlightenment project" will come to appear in two different senses. In the first it will be seen as an attempt finally to demolish what were seen as the numbing effects of the many illusions and deep-seated despotisms of a localised

[6] Max Weber, "Science as a Vocation", *ibid.*, 147–8.

and insular traditionalism. Continuing a process already partly in train—and using, as Weber had made clear, some of the techniques honed in older disciplines—collapsing the hegemonies formerly in place meant completing what was essentially a destructive task. But to do so was also to enhance and experience a liberation, since this transition, this very destruction, was intended to allow, in MacIntyre's words:

> the emergence of the individual freed on the one hand from the social bonds of those constraining hierarchies which the modern world rejected at its birth and on the other from what modernity has taken to be the superstition of teleology [at 34].

Thus in completing a liberation from what were perceived to be the particularly debilitating effects of the past we may consider the project in its second sense; one which is essentially that of rebuilding, discovering and creating anew grand solutions to moral and scientific problems. But it is precisely as a result of the success in the completion of the first, destructive task that MacIntyre will find that the price of the failure of the second, reconstructive one, is a largely irrecoverable loss. Increasingly seen as failures, the solutions proposed brought with them, he suggests, a series of problems which carry around them an air of insurmountability.

In understanding this argument we will, following MacIntyre, trace first how moral injunctions were deprived of the context that had been provided for them by the teleology of Aristotelian philosophy, and the immediate effects that this was to have. In turn, the consequences of the (failed) alternative attempts to provide a rational foundation for ethics will be seen ultimately as coming to deprive moral injunctions of even the formalist, rule-based criteria which, for a large part of Enlightenment thought, had sought to replace Aristotelian teleology. The result of this is the emergence of an "emotivist self", a self whose sense of morality, seen to be independent of either of these contexts, is to be treated as merely reporting desires or preferences, themselves subject to no independent or even interdependent rational scrutiny. It is in the concept of this emotivist self that we will find reason to believe in a certain, though serious, experience of loss. For in this modern figure exists the embodiment of the loss allegedly symptomatic of the new Dark Ages.

In bringing out the problematic of the Enlightenment project I hope to situate more precisely the notions of disenchantment brought out in Weber's description. Yet even in its most extreme form, this position—

which has led some to proclaim the demise of philosophy as it had been known for over two millennia—can be seen by some as a cause for celebration. The work of Richard Rorty will be explored to this end later in this Part, for although he sees immense possibilities opening up with the end of traditional philosophy, and particularly epistemology—we can now stop scratching where it does not itch, he says—his position is fundamentally at one with the critique of Enlightenment MacIntyre supplies. Thus I will consider along with MacIntyre's critique elements of Rorty's theory of liberalism, since even though there are clear discrepancies between the two positions, I will argue that the grounds for Rorty's optimistic endorsement of post-traditional philosophy are largely the same as those which lead MacIntyre to despair. And with Rorty, we will come to the relation between philosophy, the self, and the restatement of liberalism. But this is to jump ahead. We must first go back to MacIntyre's narrative.

The Rejection of Teleology

We have touched briefly on how Weber saw, in the processes of rationalisation, the onset of disenchantment and the loss of an identifiable telos in human endeavours, and how this might explain the irreducible plurality of contemporary morality and moral theory. But MacIntyre attempts to locate the problem more precisely than Weber. Its essence lies in the demise of the Aristotelian tradition which had provided for a shared belief in a *summum bonum* for humanity, and which had provided "morality with a point and a purpose, in virtue of which the moral life could be treated as an intelligible pursuit for a rational being".[7] A moral life in a community imbued with purpose, with a goal, with a shared idea of the good was thought achievable, and had at its centre a coherent account of the virtues. But it is the loss of this teleology provided by the Aristotelian model in which MacIntyre locates the seeds of the failure of subsequent moral philosophies.

Aristotle had provided a schema whereby three distinct elements were interlinked. The first of these was a conception of a state of untutored human nature, of "man-as-he-happens-to-be". This state was original—in the sense of primary as well as basic—and consisted of the natural

[7] Alasdair MacIntyre, "Moral Philosophy: What Next?", in Stanley Hauerwas and Alasdair MacIntyre (eds.), *Revisions: Changing Perspectives in Moral Philosophy* (Notre Dame, University of Notre Dame Press, 1983), 9.

desires and emotions of the uncultivated human being. But this state was considered to exist not simply as such (basic, primal), but to exist in or as a state of potentiality. That is, untutored human nature was seen as a primary state in the logically relational sense that there is a further state in which it can exist. That further state is precisely that of the "essential nature of man", the state whereby an initial potential is fulfilled in the sense that its goal has been worked out and reached, in other words, that its given telos has been achieved.

The mechanism which enabled this transformation to take place and thus provided the linkage between these two states was provided by ethics. In proper relation therefore, the Aristotelian model provided:

> a threefold schema in which human-nature-as-it-happens-to-be (human nature in its untutored state) is initially discrepant and discordant with the precepts of ethics and needs to be transformed by the instruction of practical reason and experience into human-nature-as-it-could-be-if-it-realized-its-telos [at 53].

The study of ethics was therefore the study of the techniques through which the fulfilment of given ends was achieved. Thus the catalogues of vices to be shunned and virtues to be extolled which were the common currency of pre-Enlightenment moral theory existed precisely to actuate the potentiality that each human being had. As MacIntyre puts it, "the whole point of ethics was to enable man to pass from his present state to his true end" (at 54). Furthermore, this also meant that as a consequence of the location and as a function of their role, moral directives were therefore "testable" in the sense that they could be evaluated in terms of the likelihood of their being able to achieve those pregiven ends.

It is clear that this Aristotelian schema is concerned essentially with transition from potential to fulfilment. It is only by understanding the overall functioning of the three elements and the relationships that exist among them that we can properly understand them as forming constituent parts. We find a similar set of relations in Christian ethical thought too. Again the notion of movement from one state to another is primary, albeit with variations in the content of the intermediate directives. Of course what these directives were formed much of the practical deliberation of both theologians and practitioners alike. But in all the intricacies of natural law doctrine we never lose the sense of actuating the potential of humanity toward its natural telos. We find a memorable formulation of this in the opening passages of Stair's presentation of the laws of Scotland where it is unquestionably given that "Law is the dictate of reason, determining every rational being to that which is congruent and convenient for the nature and condition thereof".[8] Stair assumes the ends of such nature to require and include being "humble, penitent, careful and diligent for the preservation of his self and his kind" and sets law within the framework of how these, amongst many other given ends, are to achieved.

But during the later sixteenth and seventeenth centuries—indeed by the time Stair was writing—this model came under great strain, according to MacIntyre, in the sense that the questions with which it was faced became increasingly difficult to answer from within that teleological paradigm. As Christian theology came under secular attack and where the Aristotelian version was rejected on scientific as well as philosophical grounds, the effect ultimately was that "moral injunctions became deprived of their teleological context" (at 55). Of course this was also true in matters concerning not just questions of morality. Indicative of, if not part of, the inspiration for these broader developments—though of course still working within the Christian tradition—was the work of Descartes. And although it was distinctively with the eighteenth century that the decisive break with the past was made, it was Descartes who was in large part responsible for the creation of a particular methodological mind-set which was to influence the aspirations of successive generations of philosophers. In promoting the notion that the *form* in which truth came—as being clear and distinct ideas—was essential to its status as truth, and moreover that the foundations which philosophy could supply necessarily provided unity to the body of knowledge, Descartes aided the move away from teleological thinking towards a new type of epistemology. In particular, the role of reason came to represent the change in a move away from a context of teleology as it was envisiged by Aristotle and later natural law theorists. As Lloyd puts it, "Descartes' method transformed Reason into a uniform, undifferentiated skill, abstracted from any determinate subject matter".[9]

Taking this into account, and as a preface to MacIntyre's argument on Kant, we should rehearse briefly just what have been taken to be the central strands of Enlightenment thinking, aware that it is a simplification though one which has been, and remains today, particularly influential (and noting here only in passing that its depiction of the role of

[8] James Dalrymple, Viscount Stair, *The Institutions of the Law of Scotland* (1693, ed. D. M. Walker, Glasgow and Edinburgh University Presses, 1981), I.1.i.

[9] Genevieve Lloyd, *The Man of Reason* (London, Methuen, 1984), 50.

reason is one that is clearly at odds with the Scottish tradition of Hume and Smith, and before them of Hutcheson).

Significant elements of the new Enlightenment attitude in moral philosophy had sought to challenge the (teleological) Aristotelian reasoning that had preceded it. The release which this provided was thought capable of creating new spaces, and with that came a certain tolerance and encouragement of diversity. It meant opening up new avenues of possible knowledge under a new umbrella of rational proof. Metaphorically it meant not just shedding new light on old beliefs, but seeking out and searching with that light in hitherto unexplored areas. As Diderot had said in the *Encyclopedie*: reason is "a torch lit by nature and destined to enlighten us". However these guiding thoughts did not lead to an immediate fragmentation; on the contrary, what was important was the belief in unity, the idea that all that was found in the new searches would form a coherent body of knowledge, though in a now differently-conceived sense. The role of reason here was paramount: as Habermas has put it, "reason was validated as an equivalent for the unifying power of religion".[10] To this end, Windsor notes, the Enlightenment promoted "a new, autonomous reason which could provide an ultimate court of appeal, based not on the end inherent in the phenomenon but on the internal consistency of the system".[11] Disagreement or apparent incommensurabilty could be resolved or overcome for, in the end, truth (which was still a single truth) would out. And why would this be so? Primarily because of the domination of a method in which unity was presupposed. This is not as tautological as it sounds: if it was the aim of the project to uncover law-like generalisations then it would uncover those or nothing.

We can consider two levels to this. First is the notion of the unity or coherence of all possible knowledge worked at a meta-level. As a kind of epistemological tale of the unfolding of truth in and about the world it worked as an over-arching grand narrative which situated particular and often discrete areas of enquiry. At the second, working level however we find the use of particular techniques and forms through which knowledge is uncovered and stored. These techniques which aimed at attaining objectivity through form included primarily the rigorous appli-

[10] Jürgen Habermas, *The Philosophical Discourse of Modernity* (transl. F. G. Lawrence, Cambridge, Polity, 1987), 84.

[11] Philip Windsor, "Reason Becomes Contingent in History: Can History become Reason?" in Philip Windsor (ed.), *Reason and History: Or Only a History of Reason?* (Leicester and London, Leicester UP, 1990), 23.

cation of the concept of reason and its attendant techniques, such as universalisation. The function of this second level therefore could be thought of as constitutive of knowledge, the creation of law-like generalisations within disciplines. In distinction, the function of the first level would remain that of legitimating and situating the results obtained at the second, more a regulative than constitutive function.

MacIntyre is thus correct in suggesting that the most common form of explanatory work in the eighteenth century was of the type that assumed unity as its working hypothesis. Of course however, it is naïve to think the Enlightenment on this count as merely expressing a philosophical optimism. In practical terms there was associated with this—to varying degrees—a struggle against the perceived tyranny of a state-sponsored theology. The spirit—the autonomy and professed merit—of enlightened reason was often put up against traditional sources of authority and hierarchy in an attempt to undermine that authority, initially in philosophical but then also in political terms. In the latter case it could be expressed in the form of hostility towards tradition, towards the constrictions of an ongoing and still-pervasive feudal present that could be overcome only as a result of being able to show the existence of a form of political equality (or a legal equality in the form of rights) based on precisely the alternative conceptual schema that deemed itself to be adequately coherent and unified. Consisting, so to speak, of a "move inside", a move into the universalising system of reason, and one rooted in the desire to challenge a particular social and political context, this understanding was to fire a significant portion of Enlightenment thought and, most importantly as we shall see, to release and promote the value of an autonomous, rational subject.

If we return to the question of teleology, we find that it is one of the facets of already-existing philosophical thought that in the eighteenth century was found ripe for rebuttal. Not only had it been consistently weakened by the rise (and the rise in the prestige) of the new type of scientific thought, but simultaneously there appeared what seemed like better answers to the thorny questions that had come to be asked of the Aristotelian schema. What MacIntyre's analysis seeks to show therefore is the unintended effects this had, and to do so by arguing that the method whereby the old theory was superseded by a new one gave birth to a new creature that was inherently and fatally flawed.

As a result of the critical onslaught on the notion of a final state or telos to which human beings by their nature aspired, the function and idea of ethics were fundamentally altered. Instead of following through the dynamic of the Aristotelian schema, the rejection of Aristotelian teleological thought resulted in attempts now being made to found universal moral principles on the state of humanity as found in the first, uncultivated state. However, as MacIntyre reminds us, the earlier two notions of human nature—as potential and telos—were "expressly designed to be discrepant with each other" (at 55) and as such were not intended as separate, nor indeed separable, entities. Furthermore, as adverted to earlier, they only existed in so far as they formed a coherent schema in which transition through ethics provided the sense of dynamic relation: the three-fold model could only be sustained as precisely that. Once one part—here, the essential telos—was removed, the other two remained in bizarre irrelation.

The effect of this was to be felt most acutely on what had formed the central element in the old schema, namely in ethics. Any attempt to base a new morality on human nature in its primary state was clearly going to be problematic given the way in which that state had been functionally constituted. Thus as MacIntyre puts it:

> Since the moral injunctions were originally at home in a scheme in which their purpose was to correct, improve and educate that human nature, they are clearly not going to be such as could be deduced from true statements about human nature or justified in some other way by appealing to its characteristics [*ibid.*].

Moral injunctions therefore, and indeed the very language of morals itself, were designed for and justified within a framework of transition, namely that of tutoring towards a given end.

Thus where the primary state had, for Aristotle, "strong tendencies to disobey" the educating moral injunctions, it is in retrospect absurd, MacIntyre suggestes, subsequently to attempt to build an ethical theory on that (by definition) errant state. Even attempts to refine the notion of a primary human nature did not aid the fact that they, the Enlightenment moral philosophers, had "inherited incoherent fragments of a once coherent scheme of thought and action" (*ibid.*). Yet this is precisely the mistake that according to MacIntyre they did make, though which, in their blinding optimism, they could not see. Moreover, the nature of the mistake meant not simply that the project somehow got underway on the wrong footing; worse than that, argues MacIntyre, it was as such, *conceptually*, doomed to failure. It is in this sense that we find MacIntyre describing the Enlightenment project as relentlessly in pursuit of the impossible.

Earlier in this chapter I put forward the idea that we should think of the Enlightenment project in a double role: that of demolishing or escaping from a dark past, and that of rebuilding bright and coherent futures. The case of the rejection of teleology is a part of that dual strategy. Put in terms perhaps overstated, the Enlightenment "shattered all previous communities and objective moral systems" and attempted to introduce in their place, "an abstract universal standard which would allow one to choose between those systems".[12] This formulation however displays the ambiguity of the project: namely whether such "shattering" was the natural consequence of the attempt to build new structures of thought or the deliberate series of moves required before rebuilding could begin. At the risk of appearing to fail to say which, I will leave this ambiguity to run in so far as such a double role is not in itself an incoherent possibility, if not yet a fully articulated and attractive one. But with the break from classical teleology being established, it is now appropriate to look at one of the attempts to refound moral theory in the new era and which, according to MacIntyre, sows the seeds for our contemporary emotivist malaise.

An Enlightened Alternative

O'Hagan suggested that the Enlightenment project shattered all previous "objective moral systems". To an extent this was true. Importantly, however, it was generally not the case that a problem was perceived in the ideal of objectivity *per se*. Indeed part of the reason the project might be seen to fail is precisely because it tried to attain "the objectivity of theism without the embarrassment of theistic doctrines, and an objective moral code without God as its author".[13] We might think then of a move away from objectivity as signifying a content inherent in nature, to an objectivity discoverable through form. Perhaps best known of the attempts to rebuild ethics on such a rational foundation is Kant's, where objectivity was provided primarily through the formalist structures (and strictures) of reason. The use of such a technique was not at all out of step with the spirit of the times; as Habermas notes with reference to Rousseau as well as to Kant, as ultimate justificatory grounds—in the sense, for example, of classic teleology or religious cosmologies—were

[12] Tim O'Hagan, "Searching for Ancestors", *Radical Philosophy* 54, Spring 1990, 19.
[13] *Ibid.*

seen as no longer plausible, and the formal properties of reason in particular gained predominance, the result was that "the formal conditions of justification themselves obtain legitimating force".[14] That is, *formal* conditions for the acceptability of grounds or reasons became important in the sense that it was no longer the substantive reasons themselves which were convincing (for Habermas, which provide legitimation), but instead the *kind* of reason. Significantly, the level of justification has become reflexive: "[t]he procedures and presuppositions of justification are themselves now the legitimating grounds on which the validity of legitimations is based".[15] In order to trace this development in the context of the present analysis it is necessary to see where this solution fits the dynamic of decline towards the emotivist self in MacIntyre's telling of the Enlightenment story.

Hume and others in the line of Francis Hutcheson in early and mid-eighteenth-century Scotland had developed a highly sophisticated theory of morality based on a moral psychology of the passions and of their relation to reason. But the notion that, in Hume's terms, moral distinctions were not derived from reason but from a moral sense gave cause for a grave fear in many intellectual circles, a fear that if Hume were correct then there could be no true objectivity in moral judgements. Moreover this would have a knock-on effect. So in a critique of Hume by Thomas Reid for example, Reid suggests that if we were to adopt the openly "anti-reason" suggestions of Hume we would have to refer to judges not by that name, but instead as *feelers*, for according to Hume's theory that is all they would be![16] Kant, like Reid, therefore, sought to respond directly to this description of morality.

According to MacIntyre, Reid and Kant shared two features in their moral philosophies. First they believed that the will could be determined by rational or nonrational motives. Secondly, they believed in "moral judgement as an expression of conformity to an objective moral law".[17] However in order for this second feature to be correct, Hume (and therefore also Smith) had to be wrong about the source of moral injunctions, for a moral psychology based on the passions was antithetical to the notion of an objective moral law. What was significant however, says MacIntyre, was that, by and large, Kant *did* believe Hume's account of

[14] Jürgen Habermas, *Communication and the Evolution of Society* (London, Heinemann 1979), 185.

[15] *Ibid.*

[16] Thomas Reid, *Essays on the Active Powers of the Human Mind* (1813–15, Cambridge, Mass., MIT Press, 1969), 474.

[17] Alasdair MacIntyre, n. 7 above,10.

the passions. Therefore, as far as Kant was concerned, if Hume's account of the passions was correct then because of the consequences for objectivity, he was forced to conclude that morality "could not be a matter of the passions".[18] As such, the considered attack that Hume had made on the objectivity of moral judgements had to be spurned, for it was nothing less than subversive. For Kant therefore, morality's proper domain had to be shown to lie elsewhere.

A "rational being", said Kant, had to have the freedom to choose the morally good way of acting. Either that or—just as a plant might fare poorly under extreme weather conditions—they would be determined by factors external to them. As rational beings, persons could make rational choices, yet humans are not, for Kant, perfect beings, they cannot always do the morally good thing without thinking; doing so is, for rational human beings, an act of will. However we do know, he continues, that a morally perfect being would act in a morally good way all the time. The only way we have then of approximating to such perfect consistency is for us to act according to the same principle on each occasion. Our desires and subjective purposes may vary according to the situation we find ourselves in or according to our own constitutions, but these cannot be determinative of the morality of the way in which we act, precisely because of that variation.

When called upon to justify our actions we instead use what Kant calls a maxim, which will count as the principle according to which we act. That is, a person's maxim will be a general rule which they choose to follow in their actions. Clearly we do not have to be fully conscious of this maxim or principle each time we act, and more than likely we will only consider it when asked. Nevertheless maxims play a central role in assessing the quality of an act. But they alone however do not account for the morality of the act. In order to achieve that status the maxim must conform to a further test, that is, the test of objective morality. This is not another maxim but is itself a purely formal criterion. Only by applying this test can we discover whether the maxim is moral or not. The test is whether or not the maxim on which we choose to act should at the same time, through the application of our will, become a universal law. The answer was either yes or no, and had to hold at all times and in all situations, for all people. As Kant puts it: "[t]he supreme principle of the doctrine of morals is, therefore: Act on a maxim that can also hold as a universal law. Any maxim that does not

[18] *Ibid.*

so qualify is contrary to morals."[19] Reason and the universal could not fragment: if it was morally wrong to lie, then it would still be so even if by telling the truth we put another's life at risk. For Kant there could be no possibility of contradiction. Objectivity could not propose yes on some occasions and no on others.

In full then, this is Kant's schema:

> A maxim is moral if it accords with the moral law, if such exists. It is not moral because it lies in the desires, purposes, or consequences of the act, of the doer. The morality of an action, is therefore nothing but conformity to law in general. My action is moral if and only if I can will that my maxim should become a universal law.[20]

There is no direct link therefore with either the desires of the actor or the act in itself or its consequences, and their moral quality. That quality exists only as a function of an abstract testing of the maxim, and its application is a matter of the rational agent's will. Such an application will not add anything to the *content* of the maxim but is purely formal; it will only tell the agent whether the maxim—and so the act—is, objectively now, moral or not.

Let us consider two effects of this. First, the idea of the role of the passions and of their relation to reason espoused by Hume and followed by Smith in their moral psychology was effectively disempowered by Kant's theory. The former's relational view of moral judgement, dependent as it was on those "desires and purposes of the doer" as they could be reconstructed within a theory of a thoroughgoing and contextually-situated moral—or, as we might say now, social—psychology, was rejected as being incompatible with maintaining a belief in the existence of an objective morality. We might usefully suggest then that what has happened is that the idea of the proper "ends of man" Aristotelian-based teleology is replaced by the ability rationally to know and to try to obey the moral law. But the way in which this occurs under Kant's influence is that the context-based reasoning—such as was put forward by Hume—is likewise negated by the belief that objectivity could only be asserted by an abstract and universalising formalism. Thus not only do we see the teleological context of moral injunctions being lost, but also discover that the attempt to provide for a sociopsychological one is dismantled.

[19] Immanuel Kant, *The Metaphysics of Morals* (transl. M. Gregor, Cambridge, CUP, 1991), 51.

[20] Stephan Korner, *Kant* (Harmondsworth, Penguin Books, 1955), 134.

The net effect of this was to make morality a matter of following the right rules. This we should consider to be the second effect of Kant's analysis. The form of justification is prescribed in order that one knows when one is acting according to the moral law, but it is this form itself which becomes important. Rules and abstract principles become the common currency of moral deliberation. The technique of universalisation, although of course in evidence pre-Enlightenment, gains a new kudos in the Kantian moral universe. But there is also an important flip side to the way in which this kind of moral theory is constructed. What is integral to Kant's description is not just the universal form which a moral injunction is supposed to take, but that the rational agent be able to "will that my maxim should become a universal law". If, as will be shortly suggested, the drive for a consistency or objectivity which was thought providable by universalisation, wanes as a result of powerful critique, then what is likely to be left in its place is simply that vital will or power, retained significantly in the locus of the individual. MacIntyre suggests therefore that once the will to provide a universal law is seen as more powerful than that law, or, what in effect may be the same thing, that universal law is held to be merely the expression of an arbitrary will, then since the contextualisation of a certain type of psychology had apparently been done away with, the individual, decontextualised as it now was from a teleology and further abstracted from social responsiveness in the rigorous search for rules, begins to appear as a lone, isolated, yet nonetheless centrally powerful, figure in moral theory. This will be the topic of the next section, but before that it is time to make a brief summary.

It had in the nineteenth century—as was documented by both Weber and Nietzsche—become abundantly clear that the Enlightenment's attempt to provide new, rational foundations for morality had failed. Faith in the idea of an objective morality had been consistently weakened, notably according to MacIntyre, by the types of doctrine espoused by Hegel and Mill. Dreams of a moral Esperanto had led straight back to Babel. The reconstructive aims of the Enlightenment project had thus failed to deliver their promise, but had nevertheless in the process of deconstruction dealt a fatal blow to those philosophies, including Aristotle's and Hume's, that had gone before them. But the price of failure was high and the consequences far-reaching. This at least is MacIntyre's interpretation:

> the morality of our predecessor culture—and subsequently our own—lacked any public, shared rationale or justification. In a world of secular rationality

> religion could no longer provide such a shared background and foundation for moral discourse and action; and the failure to provide what religion could furnish was an important cause of philosophy losing its central cultural role and becoming a narrowly academic subject [at 50].

Leaving the last, albeit significant, point aside, we should now move on to the inexorable conclusion to this drama which MacIntyre believes consists in an emotivist ethics rooted in the figure of the emotivist self. For as the Enlightenment project had begun from a set of "fragmented survivals", so, he argues, have we inherited its fatal flaws. Since then, we might put it, we have merely continued along a similar line, strengthening as it were, our weak, emotivist culture.

The Emotivist Self

> We are selfish men:
> O! Raise us up, return to us again;
> And give us manners, virtue, freedom, power.

This was Wordsworth's plea to Milton's spirit in "London, 1802". Yet its sentiments are recognisable as those also of MacIntyre writing today. Both writers look back to a better past, finding what is contemporary to them singularly unattractive in its indulgent, selfish outlook. For MacIntyre, it is the state of contemporary moral disagreement which holds the key to understanding our culture as an emotivist one. What is so striking, he says, about our current moral discourse is both that "so much of it used to express disagreement" and that the debate which ensues is "interminable in character" (at 6). These two features point to the conclusion that our moral world and its vocabulary are in chaos, and, as much symptom as cause, so are its emotivist underpinnings.

MacIntyre defines emotivism as follows: "the doctrine that all evaluative judgements and more specifically all moral judgements are *nothing but* expressions of preference, expressions of attitude or feeling, insofar as they are moral or evaluative in character" (at 11–12, original emphasis). Emotivism, most closely associated in the earlier half of the twentieth century with A. J. Ayer and the American C. L. Stevenson, has become located within a framework which sees morality as essentially concerned with the subjective emotions and urges of human beings. For MacIntyre, the point about the character of contemporary moral disagreement is consequently this: how could any rational resolution of a dispute occur when all we are giving vent to in the first place is a matter of our own taste? Our moral attitudes would exist in the same way as our attitudes to what dressing well involved. That I might disagree with the latest fashions, call them absurd and fanciful and suggest that things were better in my day, would not mean that I could show by argument that they were worse than the old style. There would be, as the phrase goes, no accounting for taste. And this would be as true for morality as it would be for dress. As Wachbroit puts it, "[i]f moral assertions are seen as mere expressions of approval, there can be differences of opinion, but no contradictions".[21] It is precisely as a consequence of this that moral debate cannot terminate, since there is no rational way of deciding what that termination point would be. In order fully to understand how this situation has been reached, it is vital to understand the role played by the construction of the self in this picture and the way in which the concept of self has become radically altered over time.

The sense of movement or transition that was central to Aristotelian moral theory had clear implications for the self. In its teleological framework the self was conceived of as always "at a point on a journey, moving or failing to move, towards a certain destination, pursuing a trajectory which form[ed] the object of ethical evaluation".[22] The idea of fulfilling or completing life in such a way that its success may be judged at the end is clearly at one with this picture. The image that the emotivist self conjures up on the other hand is that of something static and unchanging, a fixed point in distinterested surroundings. (That is why, says MacIntyre, the ancient Greek proverb "Call no man happy until he is dead" is so eerily out of place in an emotivist's vocabulary; how could you ever possibly express this?)

As suggested above, the demise of such a teleological framework was historically taken as a signal of liberation. But the emergence of the emotivist self is not made complete until the Enlightenment project's—represented above by Kant—attempt to recreate new certainties through the formulation of a universalist ethics, is itself discredited. Deprived of these two former justificatory contexts—teleology and universalisation—the self emerges isolated, without either externally imposed or internally formulated standards. Turning away from such possibilities and so competely in upon itself, the individual self becomes—as Nietzsche

[21] Robert Wachbroit, reviewing MacIntyre's *After Virtue*, in "A Geneology of Virtues", 92 *Yale Law Journal* (1982–3) 564–76 at 565.

[22] C. Beveridge and R. Turnbull, *The Eclipse of Scottish Culture* (Edinburgh, Polygon, 1989), 103.

predicted—the unchallenged locus of all judgement. The individual self has shed the varied contextualism of previous cultures, and the possibility that the self be defined in different ways as a member of different groups drops away. It instead becomes a self stripped bare of all context, now supposedly revealing the true desocialised, dehistoricised self underneath. The net effect of such change is that morality itself increasingly becomes a separate domain, cut off from broader public concerns, introspective, losing thereby its former anchoring meanings. In these moves, the emotivist self, joyously one supposes, retreats into the private realm. Released from the stringencies of its former contexts it sets up in an area beyond public scrutiny.

Ultimately in fact this self becomes separated off from even social concerns. For if all that our linguistic moral utterances report are the feelings or preferences we have, how can rational public debate on these even begin to take place? As MacIntyre says:

> to be a moral agent is, on this [emotivist] view, precisely to be able to stand back from any and every situation in which one is involved . . . and to pass judgement on it from a . . . point of view that is totally detached from all social particularity [at 31–32].

We find therefore that individuals' "moral" statements, and the processes whereby they come to moral conclusions, are placed in an inscrutable realm, one not subject to debate, since such conclusions are taken to exist to the side of any debate.

What is most significant of all of course for MacIntyre is the apparent loss entailed by this new-found "privacy". Coming hand in hand with the separation off of the self is the spectre of a radical subjectivism and, with that, the idea of attaining a common or shared standard through moral discourse or debate becomes quite empty: "I cannot genuinely appeal to impersonal criteria, for there are no impersonal criteria" (at 24). This is the crucial point, since any such discourse is now no more than "the attempt of one will to align the attitudes, feelings, preferences and choices of another with its own" (*ibid.*). Moral discourse is, in other words, little more than spare, superficial, and inorganic, as genuine a compromise-producing technique as a game of snap. Yet, says MacIntyre sarcastically, for contemporary morality the "ultimacy of disagreement is dignified by the title 'pluralism'" (at 32).

This "privatised" self, becomes then "liberated" from historical and social context and, because it has apparently successfully turned its back on these, is now at ease to "choose freely the composition of its moral world".[23] Moreover, the immediate question of how to deal with competing choices is not at any point considered problematic at the *moral* level. This second "move inside" has neatly surmounted—by avoiding completely—the question of resolving moral dispute.

Unsympathetic reviewers might see this emotivist self as simply selfish, even although in practice such selfishness has never really appeared without some price attached. Indeed if we consider the view of the self as it was championed in the existentialism of Sartre, as MacIntyre does,[24] we find that though it attempted to break out of what we might in the present context think of as the dead hand of old philosophies, it was a self continually strained by having to make its own genuine choices. Though able to apply its own, pure will, it was a self that was, ultimately, condemned to be free. To consider how this was so we can think of Sartre's own example.

A young Frenchman during the Nazi occupation is faced with the choice of helping the free French forces in Britain or staying at home to look after his mother. Whilst the former is more obviously an attempt to contribute to the common good of the nation, the latter attends to the wishes only of one individual. The point that Sartre emphasises is that no ethical doctrine can be simply applied to this situation and an answer to the problem read off. Such a possibility does not exist, and so all the man can do is to make a decision in good faith; that is, by being true to himself. "So when Sartre was consulted by this young man, he said merely 'You are free, therefore choose'."[25] What we might take from this is Sartre's point that no philosophical doctrine can externally provide a prescription for the way the man should act, that no doctrine can provide us with a calculus by which we can compare the possible benefits of one "nation-inspired" action and one "family-inspired" action. But what is particularly apposite to the present discussion is the very way in which this problematic is set up.

[23] *Ibid.*

[24] MacIntyre notes that he is talking of the "Sartre of the thirties and forties" (n. 2 above, 32). This squares with other commentary on Sartre's work identifying a shift between the earlier and later positions, a shift which Warnock argues "allowed the individual to be swallowed up in the group, and existentialism to be swallowed up in Marxism" (Mary Warnock, *The Philosophy of Sartre* (London, Hutchinson, 1965), 134). For present purposes I take the extreme position of the earlier Sartre which Warnock puts in the following terms: "[a]ccepting values from another rather than knowingly and deliberately adopting one's own values in choice, indeed, accepting any general rules for behaviour, must be Bad Faith" (Mary Warnock, *Existentialist Ethics* (London, Macmillan, 1974), 48).

[25] Quoted in Leslie Stevenson, *Seven Theories of Human Nature* (Oxford, Clarendon Press, 1974), 86.

Sartre's denial of any objective values by which action could be guided leads him to assume a self alienated from *any* prescriptive—be it individual *or* community-based—authority: the moral agent "is himself the source of all values".[26] So it is not just that Sartre cannot advise the young man to care first for someone close to him and secondly for an ideal of his nationhood (or vice versa), but that, because of the fundamental alienation or distancing of the self from anything in any way social or public, no inroads to this problem can ever be made. The problem, given the nature of the self and its relation to the social, is forever intractable. And this incompatibility is precisely the problem for contemporary moral theory in its emotivist condition.

I will return to Sartre later, but for now MacIntyre's analysis of what the nature of moral disagreement signifies for contemporary society should be clear. The effects of this on both the self and the public realm need now to be drawn out, since such effects consolidate for MacIntyre the very problematic of contemporary liberalism.

The Emotivist Compromise

To begin to do so, the *optimistic* endorsement of the description of contemporary morality as an emotivist morality is a position we should now consider. By looking at the work of the prominent postmodernist philosopher Richard Rorty, we will see how MacIntyre's diagnosis of contemporary moral debate might be at once condoned and celebrated. In a way quite different from Sartre and MacIntyre he argues that, with the liberation from teleology and Kantian formalism, we ought now to be able to make the philosophical point of not taking ourselves too seriously, in the public arena at least. Rorty argues that there is a realm for self-creation which need not be considered selfish, nor necessarily angst-ridden, and one that is not dependent upon nor yet a detrimental imposition on, the public realm. But for Rorty, the realisation of the freedom of the self to choose its own destiny comes only as a result of realising the situated—historically and socially—contingency of the self. As far as Rorty is concerned, the self has now, in contemporary Western liberal democracies, attained the conceptual ability, and increasingly the secular willpower, to sustain a separated private and public (or political) programme. This is to be done, no less, by trying to redefine our idea of

[26] Mary Warnock, *Existentialism* (London, OUP, 1970), 125.

morality and political obligation in the light of the claim that "traditional" (that is, most previous) philosophy has been consistently misguided in following Plato's "attempt to fuse the public and the private".[27] What is most interesting about Rorty is his refusal (when we compare it with MacIntyre's analysis) to see this development, this separation of public and private, as necessarily problematic.

At the core of Rorty's analysis is a theory of language. In a post-referential, linguistic account of philosophy, truth is only a property of sentences. If we accept that our language is purely contingent we will see it not as a medium between ourselves and the world, a filter through which we can discover better or "more adequate" descriptions of the world as it "really is", of what reality or being human is "really like",[28] but as a tool at our disposal. Any and all the truths we build up of ourselves, our communities and our moral beliefs are constructs of the language games we invent, sustain and change, and within which we invent, sustain and change ourselves. It is in this frame of mind that we ought now, Rorty urges, to face up to the contingency of our selves and our beliefs, if only because we are aware of the contingency of the language in which we are situated. This is at once liberating—since our imagination becomes the boundary to our worlds—and awesome—since we are forced to recognise the responsibility we now have for ourselves.

Central to Rorty's treatment of how we should consider language is his use of the term (and concept of) "vocabulary". Its role is significant in both practical and philosophical pursuits, and its position in Rorty's theory makes it possible here to consider his thesis as, in a certain sense to be drawn out, supportive of an emotivist position. Clearly echoing the later Wittgenstein's category of the "form of life", vocabularies are essentially ways of "describing, evaluating, judging, and even acting".[29] But once we give up the idea that one of the core purposes of language—or even philosophy—is to represent or discover truths about the world as it really is, we must simultaneously give up on the idea of "getting the picture right" through our use of language, as if language was like a television aerial whose function is to pick up the best picture from the signals available. Instead language should be considered as a way in which continually to redescribe ourselves and our concerns that makes

[27] Richard Rorty, *Contingency, Irony, and Solidarity* (Cambridge, CUP, 1989), p. xiii.

[28] See for example his "Introduction", *Consequences of Pragmatism: Essays 1972-1980* (Minneapolis, Minn., University of Minnesota Press, 1982), p. xxxvi.

[29] Richard Bernstein on Rorty, in his *The New Constellation: The Ethical-Political Horizons of Modernity/Postmodernity* (Cambridge, Polity Press, 1991), 262.

us better able to cope with our worlds. So for Rorty, the most important aspect of our vocabularies is that they are all:

> even those which contain the words which we take most seriously, the ones most essential to our self-descriptions—are human creations, tools for the creation of such other human artifacts as poems, utopian societies, scientific theories, and future generations.[30]

Having got rid of the notion that language ought to provide us with a picture of how the world, or the self, or justice or morality, really is, we can now only put forward competing suggestions as to which vocabularies we ought to adopt on these matters. But since there is no external—outwith language—picture against which we might test or judge our vocabularies, what criteria can we possibly now have for choosing which vocabulary to adopt? How are we to know whether one description is more valid than another, or show that one person's vocabulary is immoral and another's sound? The answer Rorty gives to these questions is crucial and paves the way for seeing *his* vocabulary as emotivist. For what Rorty's reflections about language, vocabularies and selfdescriptions inexorably lead him to is this conclusion: that "anything can be made to look good or bad by being redescribed".[31] For Rorty, the only constraints on choosing vocabularies (for we are no longer constrained by "truth" or "reality") are conversational ones. Those who ascribe to this notion will see themselves as "ironists"; that is, people for whom:

> nothing can serve as a criticism of a final vocabulary save another such vocabulary; there is no answer to a re-description save a re-re-description. Since there is nothing beyond vocabularies which serves as a criterion of choice between them, criticism is a matter of looking on this picture and on that, not of comparing both pictures with the original. Nothing can serve as a criticism of a person save another person, or of a culture save another culture—for persons are, for us, incarnated vocabularies.[32]

Continual innovation is thus played out at the level of adapting and inventing vocabularies. Change is merely a function of re-description, nothing more, though nothing less either.

The import of this is exemplified by Rorty's approach to philosophy, in the way he wants to write himself. So in his *Contingency, Irony, and Solidarity* he announces that rather than "offering arguments against the

[30] Rorty, n. 27 above, 53.
[31] *Ibid.*, 73.
[32] *Ibid.*, 80.

vocabulary I want to replace", he will, instead, "try to make the vocabulary I favour look attractive by showing how it may be used to describe a variety of topics".[33] The suggestion that this would turn our linguistic (and our philosophical and scientific) practices into mere talking shops is not denied. Stemming back to Rorty's view of language generally, if we have given up on the idea of "getting things right" through language or philosophy, then all we can hope to do is to keep talking. Rorty makes an analogy of language and evolution: we adapt our linguistic practices to suit our needs, and in so doing we press on "not to accomplish a higher purpose, but blindly".[34]

To see debate in this way has a particular significance when turned to moral or social issues as we shall soon see. And though Rorty will not deny that this is so, his primary target, his primary suggestion for the putting in place of a new vocabulary, is philosophical. For him, because of the very fact that we are situated in and by our language and could never have been not so situated, that redescription through changes in the vocabularies we adopt is the only form of change we have, he seeks to elude traditional philosophical issues by taking them inside language:

> Once we realize that progress, for the community as well as for the individual, is a matter of using new words as well as of arguing from premises phrased in old words, we realize that a critical vocabulary which revolves round notions like "rational", "criteria", "argument" and "foundation" and "absolute" is badly suited to describe the relation between old and new.[35]

This has implications for the way in which argument (if such it can still properly be called) itself takes place. But it would also appear immediately to raise relativist objections concerning the use of vocabularies as way of seeing ourselves and the world. Rorty however, very much aware of this possibility, faces it straight on. He points out that to take on board the ideas about language and self-description he has presented to us is to realise that one no longer has to engage with the charge of relativism. This is because epistemological arguments along the lines of "*how do you know* such and such to be true or just or rational or whatever?" are now redundant. Rorty's intention here is thus "neither to praise nor to blame epistemological philosophy but to bury it".[36] A

[33] *Ibid.*, 9.
[34] *Ibid.*, 19.
[35] *Ibid.*, 48–9.
[36] William M. Sullivan, "After Foundationalism: The Return to Practical Philosophy" in E. Simpson (ed.), *Antifoundationalism and Practical Reasoning: Conversations between Hermeneutics and Analysis* (Edmonton Alberta, Academic Printing and Publishing, 1987), 22.

philosophy which searches for foundational criteria for knowledge ought to be abandoned, even if this means the end of philosophy as we knew it.

With this background in mind we return now to issues of the self and questions of morality. It should be noted that Rorty does not treat morality or moral philosophy as a separate entity in the way MacIntyre's analysis did, though this will not detract from my treating what Rorty does have to say as being essentially emotivist, as should become clear. His primary division is instead between the public and the private realms. For him there is always a conceptual gap between the private and the public. This gap cannot be bridged, not by philosophy or politics, metaphysics or epistemology. There is no social or theoretical "glue" to hold the two together: "There is no way in which philosophy, or any other theoretical discipline will . . . let us hold self-creation and justice, private perfection and human solidarity, in a single vision."[37]

Returning to the notion of "ironism" mentioned briefly above, Rorty suggests that in the private realm the "ironist" self will "face up to the contingency of his or her own central beliefs" and, most importantly, give up on the "idea that those central beliefs and desires refer back to something beyond the reach of time and chance".[38] Having given up on teleology and metaphysics, any sense of movement for such a self is quite different from that which might be described as an unfolding trajectory. For the ironist self, life "cannot get completed because there is nothing to complete, there is only the web of relations to be rewoven, a web which time lengthens every day".[39] But like painting the Forth Bridge, the unending character of the job does not detract from its worthiness; it is (dare one say it?) just the way things are. All that a person can do is constantly to revise their "final vocabulary", that is the set of words they employ variously to "justify their actions, their beliefs, and their lives" and in which they formulate their "deepest self-doubts and highest hopes" and tell "the story of [their] lives".[40] But what is fundamentally "ironic" about this person's "final vocabulary" is their awareness that no other vocabulary could possibly underwrite these beliefs or doubts or hopes. And what is "final" about it is not that it is ever complete, but that there is "no noncircular argumentative recourse" to be had which will finally justify these words.

[37] Rorty, n. 27 above, p. xiv.
[38] *Ibid.*, p. xv.
[39] *Ibid.*, 42–3.
[40] *Ibid.*, 73.

I suggest that such an analysis remains at heart emotivist when it comes to dealing with moral issues. Part of the reason for this extends out from the role of language in Rorty's theory. Rorty quotes with approval Michael Oakeshott on rules and principles of moral deliberation:

> What has to be learned in a moral education is not a theorem such as that good conduct is acting fairly or being charitable, nor is it a rule such as "always tell the truth", but how to speak the language intelligently.[41]

We have here a clear, if implied, rejection of the type of moral theories—Aristotelian, Kantian—charted above. Any account of morality which is non-linguistic, which attempts to assert a deeper or a-contextual grain of moral knowledge or action is denied.

Let us consider two aspects to this as they relate to the "ironist self": first that the individual self is the source of moral inspiration, and secondly that changes in one's moral beliefs come about through changing one's self-description. These rely primarily on being situated within Rorty's more general linguistic framework where truth is not discovered but created, but also further require the proviso that the ultimate arbiter of what is true about oneself is oneself. Not only does this unashamedly self-centred vision demand of us that we give up any and all claims to "morally privileged" arguments, but also that in so doing it commends to us the essentially emotivist position that our moral convictions are nothing but the expression of the urges or preferences that we might have, and, more significantly, that any ensuing moral "debate" is no more than a matter of urging those expressions on other people.

This "flattening" of the conceptual landscape attempts to de-problematise conventionally troubled concepts by putting them on the same plane and thus making them all equally open for negotiation. What is particularly reminiscent of MacIntyre's description of the contemporary culture of emotivism is where Rorty's thesis takes us to when coming to describe the debating and choosing of competing "vocabularies". The situating of the self and its moral choices on the level plane of language entails the loss of the possibility of any hierarchical or external structures of justification. In this picture there "will be no higher standpoint to which we are responsible and against whose precepts we might offend. There will be no such activity as scrutinising competing values in order to see which are morally privileged."[42]

[41] *Ibid.*, 58.
[42] *Ibid.*, 50.

And it is this position which is at the heart of Rorty's enlightened, secular, vision of liberalism. All or any non-human forces which previously humanity has thought itself responsible to, or directed by, drop away in the completion of the "process of de-divinisation". Given this, what the emotivist compromise, as I have called it, consists in becomes apparent. To live with others, individual self-describing selves must make a compromise by entering a new public vocabulary which is quite different from any private vocabulary. But this public vocabulary is not so much shared, as developed as an aggregate.[43] The reason for this is that no necessary extension can be made from one's privatised desires to the public vocabulary; no philosophical foundations for the public vocabulary can be based on one's ability and desire for self redescription. As Rorty puts it, "our reponsibilities to others constitute *only* the public side of our lives, a side which competes with our private affections and our private attempts at self-creation, and which has no *automatic* priority over such private motives".[44] The self-aware "ironist" self is to be considered freed to choose the patterns of obligation within which s/he is situated. Obligations for private self-description are therefore to be thrown in together with public duties, with no formal pecking order either available or desirable. Talk of compromise necessarily enters at this stage, but, just as was seen in MacIntyre's description, this compromise will always be thin and superficial. The reason for this in Rorty's case is his insistence on holding the public/private distinction firmly in place. No "higher set of obligations" could ever bring the two aspects together under one unifying principle; moreover, previous attempts have been shown consistently to fail. Without any theoretical "glue" to hold the two together the public and private realms remain distinct, and the relation between them a bare compromise. As Rorty stresses in the most telling fashion, "[a]ll that is in question is accomodation—not synthesis".[45] Thus in terms reminiscent of MacIntyre's description of our emotivist culture, all that is achievable, says Rorty, is that—and this, given his earlier post-epistemological urgings, is as much a definitional point as anything else—there be "enough overlap" amongst competing private desires to sustain a basic public solidarity.

[43] Cf. Bentham: "The interest of the community is, what?—the sum of the interests of the several members who compose it", quoted in Philip Selznick, *The Moral Commonwealth: Social Theory and the Promise of Community* (Berkeley, University of California Press, 1992), 536.

[44] Rorty, n. 27 above, 194 (original emphasis).

[45] *Ibid.*, 68.

Since there can be no question of a rationally superior agreement, this is the best one will be able to do.

To accept this is, however, as I put it, to accept the emotivist compromise. Rorty's "self" must compromise in that as an individual coming together with others in the public arena they must contribute to the "social self-description" that any group requires to be able to make communal life viable. But of course being faithful to the insight that there can be no external "trumping" criteria—such as appeals to natural justice, inalienable rights, etc.—to override competing claims, here again there can be no criteria of "success". So just as Rorty tries to imagine rational argument giving way to the interplay of old and new vocabularies in the private realm, so in the public realm redescription rather than any type of foundationalist debate is to remain our guiding metaphor. As he says:

> We should see allegiance to social institutions as no more matters for justification by reference to familiar, commonly accepted premises—but also as no more arbitrary—than choices of friends or heroes. Such choices are not made by reference to criteria.[46]

And here then lies the essence of the emotivist compromise, since:

> There is no "ground" for such loyalites and convictions save the fact that the beliefs and desires and emotions which buttress them overlap those of lots of other members of the group with which we identify for purposes of moral or political deliberation.[47]

The only duty we can sensibly speak of is the duty to keep the conversation with others going and to keep it open; success can be nothing more than continuance, whatever that might mean.

There now arises a particular issue which Rorty must face and which springs from his assertions about vocabularies at both the public and private levels, an issue that MacIntyre we could imagine would find deeply problematic. The awareness of the contingency of even our most cherished beliefs is seen by Rorty as releasing the self from the possible intrusions of a publicly imposed morality, since possibilites for change come only through self-redescription. But as this is true for the private, so too must it be for the public sphere. To be consistent, in other words, with his philosophical point, there can be no external constraints on public debate except conversational ones, again no "trump" arguments

[46] *Ibid.*, 54.

[47] Richard Rorty, "Postmodern Bourgeois Liberalism" in *Philosophical Papers: Volume I* (Cambridge, CUP, 1991), 200.

which can be introduced into the political debate. This means that even, perhaps especially, in liberal societies we cannot condemn public political arguments with which we disagree by asserting foundational or essentialist claims about what it really means to respect being human. The philosophical argument that there are no timeless justifications for present practices but only new and different ways of redescribing what to make of them must be applied across the board. The effect of realising this is crucial. In terms of politics and the institutional order, it even means:

> giving up the idea that liberalism could be justified, and Nazi or Marxist enemies of liberalism refuted, by driving the latter up against an argumentative wall—forcing them to admit that liberal freedom has a "moral privilege" which their own values lacked. From the point of view I have been commending any attempt to drive one's opponent up against a wall in this way fails when the wall against which he is driven comes to be seen as one more vocabulary, one more way of describing things.[48]

This is precisely MacIntyre's emotivist nightmare, the sure sign that we are going though a new Dark Ages. But for Rorty the lack of criteria which would allow one to say "I refute the Nazi because I know s/he is wrong" is an advance for philosophy for the very reason that it skirts traditional (and especially epistemological) problematics which have singularly failed in their task to come up with such criteria. But rather than continually trying—and failing—to produce rational criteria through philosophical theories that would detail what rational moral and political debate should be like, Rorty urges us to adopt vocabularies which create solidarity amongst like-minded people, with no in-built criteria for success except furthering our ability to cope. What Rorty suggests is that we turn, in the realisation of our contingencies, away from traditional philosophy and theory towards narrative, towards the "edifying" philosophies of the "strong poets". In line with his stress on the concept of vocabulary, "edification" is to be taken as the "project of finding new, better, more fruitful ways of speaking", and "edifying philosophers" those who "are reactive and offer satires, parodies, aphorisms" rather than "building for eternity".[49] Like poets they can create and cause a sense of wonder through exploring the notion that there is "something new under the sun, something which is not an accurate rep-

[48] Rorty, n. 27 above, 53.

[49] Richard Rorty, *Philosophy and the Mirror of Nature*, (Oxford, Basil Blackwell, 1980), 360, 369.

resentation of what was already there, something which (at least for the moment) cannot be explained and can barely be described".[50]

But what Rorty is essentially doing—and this move is reinforced rather than challenged by his division between public and private—is signalling the withdrawal of the possibility of rational debate, for fear that it might invoke rationalist or essentialist or foundational assumptions. (It is no coincidence that elsewhere Rorty has written that "moral progress has, in recent centuries, owed more to the specialists in particularity—historians, novelists, ethnographers, and muckracking journalists, for example— than to such specialists in universality as theologians and philosophers".[51]) It is not my purpose to question his intentions for so doing, but the consequences of his position have, I hope, become clear: that there can be no *a priori* notion of a distinct form of social communication which is more than a mere aggregate of self-styled desires and final vocabularies. This is for Rorty a success, a victory for a new type of "self-creating" philosophy, a victory for the "strong poets", and the death of an impossible project of fusing the public and the private: "[m]y 'poeticized' culture", he writes, "is one which has given up the attempt to unite one's private ways of dealing with one's finitude and one's sense of obligation to other human beings".[52]

At both levels—public and private—this picture is emblematic of what MacIntyre sees as the loss of the ability to carry on rational debate. The main reason for this lies in the emotivist type assumptions which such a vision has at its heart. In effect, the turn towards narrative (self-) re-description champions the criteria-less renewal of vocabularies over and against the production of "better arguments". As Bernstein has put it, "[t]he 'logic' of Rorty's strategy comes down to making the adoption of a vocabulary a matter of taste about which there can be no rational debate".[53] Yet the loss MacIntyre finds in the demise of an Aristotelian *summum bonum* becomes in Rorty's hands a celebration. It is a liberation of the self, a liberation from the dead hand of old philosophies, and the acceptance of the most meagre form of community which is the emotivist compromise:

> human solidarity is not a matter of sharing a common truth or a common goal but of sharing a common selfish hope, the hope that one's world—the little

[50] *Ibid.*, 370.
[51] See his "On Ethnocentrism: A Reply to Clifford Geertz" in n. 47 above, 207.
[52] Rorty, n. 27 above, 68.
[53] Bernstein, n. 29 above, 278.

> things around which one has woven into one's final vocabulary—will not be destroyed.[54]

Meagre indeed.

Initial Problems with the Emotivist Self

Such a conclusion is unacceptable to MacIntyre. Moreover, Rorty's thin version of community fails, I suggest, to treat the consequences of the separation of private and public seriously enough. His optimism is unsustainable where, in the public realm, the chances of achieving solidarity turn out to be no more than an expression of faith. Additionally, his uncritical endorsement of the potential of liberal structures of contemporary America to support such solidarity, it has also been argued, flies in the face of a multitude of empirical counter-examples.[55] This naïvety is compounded at the theoretical level on the grounds that Rorty fails to acknowledge the difficulties faced by the vision of separate but co-existent realms of public and private. Where MacIntyre would argue the definitional point that "a self for which . . . regard [for others] is problematic could only be a self which had become isolated from and deprived of any community within which it could systematically enquire what its good was and achieve that good",[56] Rorty denies this as a problem at all while nevertheless celebrating its spirit. Without realising it, Rorty's consistent denial of a common good and his faith in the separation of public and private therefore reinforces MacIntyre's diagnosis of emotivism. In this section I want to explore difficulties with both writers' analyses and in so doing pave the way for a different theoretical understanding of the problems of the self and its community.

At this point let us return to MacIntyre, and in so doing raise an objection. We recall that in MacIntyre's narrative the fragmentation of once whole moral doctrines resulted in our inheriting a moral vocabulary comprised of fragments of concepts initially designed to exist within particular conceptual frameworks. The charting of such developments

[54] Rorty, n. 27 above, 92.

[55] See, for example, from a feminist perspective, Nancy Fraser's "Solidarity or Singularity?" in Alan R. Malachowski (ed.), *Reading Rorty: Critical Responses to Philosophy and the Mirror of Nature (and beyond)*, associate ed. Jo Burrows (Oxford, Basil Blackwell, 1990).

[56] Alasdair MacIntyre, *Three Rival Versions of Moral Enquiry: Encyclopaedia, Genealogy, and Tradition* (London, Duckworth, 1990), 193.

resulted in the emergence of the emotivist culture within which we allegedly find ourselves. The primary feature of this is that we have no rational way of resolving moral disputes or weighing moral claims, because, to use his image, we have lost the scales. Such inability to resolve moral disputes is in large part the consequence of the fact that the *language*—which Rorty does not problematise but leaves merely at the level of contingency—in which such discourse takes place excludes resolution because it is thought merely to express our preferences or desires which are themselves not subject to rational scrutiny. In so far as this picture further suggests, and indeed demands, arguments about liberal institutions to which I will next turn, I will concentrate briefly on the linguistic point.

What MacIntyre sets up as one of the fundamentals of the emotivist self gives, I suggest, too much credence to an incoherent idea. There is a sense, that is, in which the breakdown of contemporary morality cannot be complete. The progress of the argument saw a dropping away of certain types—teleological, universalistic—of contextual constraints, resulting ultimately in an alienated, albeit supposedly liberated, self. Prominent amongst the characteristics of this self was its capacity "to evade any necessary identification with any particular contingent state of affairs".[57] However, I suggest that, even if particular original philosophical frameworks have been abandoned, it is not a further option to drop altogether the linguistic constraints that are imposed upon us. Indeed we might even be led into thinking that this is more obvious in the case of an emotivist morality. For if all that our linguistic moral utterances report are our urges or feelings as expressions, then such language, even if fragmented and separated from its original conceptual contexts, still exists as a social practice. If we take the idea of linguistic communication as a constraint seriously then it is very difficult to conceive of ourselves as individual, entirely original, pre-social selves. Taken to the extreme I am not my language. On the other hand, nor in any meaningful sense could I be outwith it. Thus, and if we follow Wittgenstein's argument against the possibility of a private language, we must concede that so long as our language is to a greater or lesser extent the taking part in a shared enterprise then we must allow for the possibility of agreement, for the "testability" of meaning. This does not mean that we need ever agree, say, on some contentious moral or social issue,

[57] MacIntyre, n. 2 above, 31.

but that at the bare minimum, in order to understand even that we are disagreeing requires a level of agreement.[58]

Now it may be that contemporary moral disagreement is carried out in such a way that debate is often ultimately unfruitful, unyielding of substantive consensus. But is it not to give too much credence to (the definition of) emotivism to suggest, as MacIntyre does, that this lack of consensus is because the sole function of language in that particular debate is to report preferences or urges? There are two possible reasons why such a suggestion might test the bounds of even our most generous sympathies. First the assertion that my (or anyone's) shared language would be able to report something which was so pre-social, pre-linguistic and uniquely personal to me is one that we might think extremely difficult to take on board. How would any communication concerning these personal feelings take place if they were indeed so original to us as individuals? Besides, even if we could communicate them, why would we need or want to? Secondly, if we accepted that such communication was indeed possible, then we could not escape the notion that once—and even because—expressed in that language, any subsequent debate about that which had been expressed would be somehow inauthentic. But to pin any moral disagreement purely on the role of language would not be correct since language would itself be a part of the very process of communication, shared in a way that the emotivist self could not escape. No matter how much we dislike the idea, and no matter how little genuine consensus it may produce, we cannot discount the fact that the linguistic parameters within which we operate, though they are not the only ones, necessarily constrain us in way that is *irreducibly social.* As such, the language in which we debate moral questions cannot be merely another "contingent state of affairs" which the self can evade. The option of evading language, save for becoming mute, is simply not available.

Whilst MacIntyre finds mileage in the description of contemporary moral debate as essentially emotivist, this can be properly sustained only if extended beyond the arena of the "merely" linguistic. What these points do not yet address, however, is the argument that such language

[58] This is arguably similar to a part of Habermas' argument concerning the possibility of and justification for communicative ethics and discourse theory, but I will not go into these arguments here. I will keep to the level of Wittgenstein's point. See Ludwig Wittgenstein, *Philosophical Investigations* (2nd edn., 1958, Oxford, Basil Blackwell, 1989); also Saul A. Kripke, *Wittgenstein on Rules and Private Language: An Elementary Exposition* (Oxford, Basil Blackwell, 1985). Cf. Jürgen Habermas, *The Theory of Communicative Action* (Boston, Beacon Press, 1984).

as we do use remains a series of fragmented survivals whose original context has been lost. But it does suggest that there is a difference between shared meaning—expressable only through language (and to this extent Rorty is correct)—and shared values or shared patterns of normative justification. What MacIntyre's argument about "fragmented survivals" draws our attention to, however, is the dire need for a sensitivity toward the construction of meaning in and through language, as well as the idea that whatever meaning one person or group ascribes to a particular usage may or may not be expressable or understood in a quite different framework. If one person's or group's sense of "ought" is tied to and informed by a different set of meanings as to the context, authority or specificity of that "ought", then MacIntyre is correct to point out the requirement of understanding the historical genesis and particular present locating meaning of that "ought" (the importance of recognising the difference, say, between an Aristotelian and Kantian "ought"). Moreover, he is also correct in pointing out that where we fail to pay such attention, there exists the danger of, at the least, confusion and, at the worst, corruption and mistranslation of the other(s)' meaning.

But all this is different from his argument that all contingent states of affairs—including language—can be evaded. What, then, of Rorty, who brings moral theory (like everything else) within the domain of language? Why can he still fall prey to the charge of emotivism when he appears to deny the accusation of de-contextualisation through his argument about the contingency of language? The answer here goes back to MacIntyre's more searching insight about moral disagreement. Whether or not language merely reports or gives expression to "preference, attitude, or feeling", Rorty remains firmly attached to the idea of judgments being made without reference to rational, perhaps indeed any, criteria. His emphasis on redescription is quite at one with MacIntyre's argument that for the emotivist self's view of morality there can be "disagreements but no contradictions". But if Rorty's awareness of the contingency of language improves on the above criticisms made of MacIntyre, he too fails sufficiently to draw attention to the difference between shared meaning and the possibility of shared justification which lies outwith the purely private realm of the "strong poet". Though I do not want to suggest that these two ideas—understanding and justification—are entirely separate, drawing attention to the difference between them may prove important.

Think back to Sartre's student. What is significant about this—and *contra* MacIntyre's understanding—is that we (and he, the student) *understand* that he faces a dilemma. And to understand that he faces a choice between, say, familial loyalty and commitment to his country is to understand that he has a *moral* dilemma. Of course this does not mean that we can objectively read off an answer to that dilemma, and to this extent Sartre is correct. There is a jump between understanding someone's meaning when they express their choice as a dilemma and saying that there is a pre-existing solution to that dilemma. All the same, that we do understand it as a moral dilemma suggests both that its construction is in some sense not entirely original to him (it is a problem that has been encountered before and is communicable as such), and, therefore, that it cannot be a purely "private" problem. To avoid potential confusion these points require fuller explanation.

Simply at the level of understanding it is possible to recognise the student's choice as one important enough to be termed a moral dilemma. It is not, in other words, simply a trivial issue, a decision about which pair of shoes to wear, say. (Though of course one could imagine a context where such a choice might indeed be non-trivial, but this is partly my point.) To recognise it as such requires a level of communicative ability that would seem to be more than the emotivist self is capable of. It is not thus a purely private matter because it can be (and indeed has been) articulated in a language in which it is understood. As argued above in the reference to Wittgenstein, there is sufficient shared meaning available to recognise a choice—why otherwise would it work as an example even of Sartre's argument? In this limited sense of private and public, then, the fact of its expressability brings it into the public realm of shared meaning. (In fact, "brings it" might seem to suggest that it existed elsewhere before, in some "truly" private realm, beyond even language, before language. Even this, excepting the most solipsistic egos, is unlikely.)

But it is also public in a more expansive sense. The two options the student faces are brought about in both cases by circumstances beyond his control. On the one hand, he did not cause the war to begin and, on the other, he did not choose to have a mother. To say that the ontological construction of the dilemma is his own is therefore incorrect. (Of course, he could avoid constructing it as a dilemma at all. Indeed, this would fit Neil MacCormick's suggestion that "the only true existentialists are psychopaths—and vice versa"![59]) And here we might differentiate between Sartre's position in the *actual* scenario and his (or our own)

[59] See his *Legal Reasoning and Legal Theory* (Oxford, Clarendon Press, 1978), 274.

in understanding it as a moral problem. Sartre as listener and Sartre as teller of a story years later is in two quite different positions. This further reinforces the conceptual distinction between understanding the dilemma and seeking to act according to some criteria. Indeed, we might even rebuke Sartre the listener for making an irresponsible response to the initial question. If my brother comes to me and asks, "should I go to the war or stay to look after our sick mother?", if we have grown up together and we are close, my response, "You are free, therefore choose", would seem a singularly inappropriate one. In the two cases (as immediate listener and as listener to a hypothetical) I can understand the problem, but between the two there is a difference. So, for example, it would not be correct to say that we fully understand yet the student's dilemma even though we understand that the one he faces is a real and a moral one. Certainly, this does not yet mean that there are readily available criteria according to which one can justify the decision; a choice remains and an option may have to be taken. But this is not a purely private choice. It is a public matter in the sense that the construction of the dilemma, factually—the war, a sick relative—and normatively—loyalty versus patriotism—constitute a feature that the individual could not construct alone. In this sense it is incorrect to say, even of the emotivist self, that it can "choose the composition of its moral world". To say with Sartre that the individual is "the source of all values" is therefore to miscontrue the nature of the situation.

And here is the crux of the matter: a choice there may be, but it *cannot* be an unconstrained choice. The reason for this is that for it to be an unconstrained choice there would have to be no dilemma in the first place. One who was truly the source of all his or her values, one who was truly free, would not, could not, be faced by such a dilemma.

Harry Frankfurt, in a response to MacIntyre's essay "How Moral Agents became Ghosts",[60] makes out a case that would seem to argue against both MacIntyre's conception of the emotivist self and Rorty's privatised self on precisely this issue. If we start, says Frankfurt, with the presumption that "[t]o identify something, or even to characterize it, is essentially a matter of distinguishing it from what it is not", then "in order for the nature or uses of a thing to be understood, the limits of the thing must be known". Consequently:

[60] See Harry Frankfurt's "Comments on MacIntyre" *Synthese* 53 (1982) 319–21; responding to Alasdair MacIntyre, "How Moral Agents Became Ghosts, or, Why the History of Ethics Diverged from that of the Philosophy of Mind", in *ibid.*, 295–312.

> . . . anything which enjoys altogether unlimited freedom must be unintelligible, even to itself. It can remain limitlessly free only if it continuously faces the option of recreating itself, since otherwise its freedom is impaired by dependence on its own past; and the way in which it deals with this option must be entirely arbitrary, for it cannot be wholly free if it acknowledges or submits to the authority or the superiority of any constraint whatever. Hence it is doomed to proceed blindly, with no basis at all for the commitments it must unendingly make.[61]

I believe that this criticism strikes at both MacIntyre's and Rorty's versions of the self. Even minimally, as I have suggested, MacIntyre's emotivist self cannot escape linguistic constraints. What Frankfurt now adds is that the idea of acting without any constraints makes even the notion of identity incoherent. In fact, Frankfurt cannot even present the argument for a self acting with unrestrained choice without lapsing into error; presenting such a self in the way he does (the option that "it" continuously faces, that "it" acknowledges the commitments "it" must make) founders on the original assumption that a thing without limits has no identity—"it" does not exist. The radical freedom ascribed to the emotivist self—that "it" "can choose the composition of its moral world", or, *per* Rorty, that "it" can, indeed should, constantly redescribe itself—is then erroneous in two senses: one, the very existence of such a "self" is highly questionable and, two, as such, so is the very existence of a "moral world" at all where morality includes any hint of constraint.

Where does this leave us? I suggest MacIntyre's version of the emotivist self is too unconstrained to be coherent. A self which acts without constraints could not even recognise Sartre's example of a dilemma. Therefore it certainly could not recognise it as a moral dilemma. Moreover, if this is correct, then even MacIntyre's initial insight about the nature of contemporary moral disagreement would become meaningless; moral debate would not just be interminable, it would be non-existent. In his darker moments—who knows?—MacIntyre might believe this to be true. Yet given the need for his argument to start with the "state of contemporary moral disagreement", I cannot think he could seriously hold this position. As such the difference between shared meaning and shared normative understandings becomes vital.

On the other hand Rorty's recognition of linguistic contraints is insufficient to counter the point that for the notion of a constantly redescribing, "privatised" self to be coherent, his theory must recognise the one

[61] Frankfurt, n. 60 above, 319.

contingency that it does not deal with, for all its talk of contingency. That is, that the relation between the public and the private is itself contingent. Rorty continually jumps between the level of the "self-creating self" and the level of "one's fellow citizens". What he fails to grasp is the conceptual and practical connection between the "private self" and the public realm. In one of the clearest cases of this, he chastises Foucault for failing to "separate his two roles . . . his moral identity as a citizen from his search for autonomy".[62] But to accept this, as Nancy Fraser rightly points out by reference to Marxist, feminist, and indeed Foucauldian critiques, "is to turn our back on the last hundred years of social history".[63] It is to neglect their insights that, *contra* Rorty's liberalism, the economic, the personal and the cultural may well be political. At the very least it fails properly to recognise that there is no *a priori* way of deciding what is to be private and what public; that this distinction is as contingent and contestable as any other. Yet Rorty's defence of an intolerably crude, harm-principle liberalism—a defence without argument remember—seems stubbornly to reject this contingent relation.

The effect of this—as MacIntyre would predict for an emotivist culture—is to squeeze the meaning of morality until it becomes meaningless. There is nothing left between the self and the citizen that might recognisably be called the realm of shared and conflicting values. "Public morality" becomes a misnomer and an oxymoron where it is defined by reference solely to aspects of a legally-defined citizen whose only means of debate and deliberation are the "institutions of procedural justice"[64] and whose outcomes are "codifiable in statutes and maxims".[65] Determined, in the face of decades of critique, to maintain the separation of public and private, "private morality" becomes equally anomalous. "Rorty's 'private morality'", note Guignon and Hiley,[66] "is morality in name only." If as they suggest, it is the case that "[p]eople generally stand 'unflinchingly' for their convictions because they see these convictions as pointing to a good life", once again Rorty's refusal to hold private redescription and the good life in community in the one vision effectively reduces to nothing the idea or even point of talking

[62] See Rorty's "Moral Identity and Private Autonomy: The Case of Foucault", *Philosophical Papers: Volume II* (Cambridge, CUP, 1991), 196.

[63] Fraser, n. 55 above, 313.

[64] See Rorty's "On Ethnocentrism", n. 51 above, 210.

[65] Rorty, "Freud and Moral Reflection", n. 62 above, 153.

[66] In "Biting the Bullet: Rorty on Private and Public Morality", in Malachowski (ed.), n. 55 above, 358–9.

about morality in the private sphere. The failure to recognise the contingency and mutuality of the public and private thus signals the incoherence of the self in Rorty's vision; a self which is at once radically contingent, yet hopelessly unattached, committed to itself in a way that precludes any reasons why it should be committed to anything at all. For as Bernstein argues:

> When we turn to Rorty's attempt to privatize irony, to encourage the playing out of private fantasies, it is difficult to understand why anyone who becomes as narcissistic as Rorty advocates would be motivated to assume public responsibilities.[67]

But, I would suggest, not just "public responsibilities" become problematic, but the very coherence of such a self. As indeed the myth of Narcissus suggests, the youth who is so obsessed with his own self-image turns into a flower, not a human being at all. Rorty's self veers dangerously to the same conclusion.

So where MacIntyre's version of the emotivist self failed to account for the irreducibly social nature of language, both MacIntyre and Rorty fail to give a coherent account of the social reflexivity of the self and the intimate relation between that reflexivity and the idea of meaningful normative constraint, points I will seek to address in a later chapter. Yet while I have argued that their conception of the self is untenable, their arguments concerning the ultimate irresolvability of questions of value in contemporary society remains a live one. To turn now to these brings us into two more recognisably public domains, the domains of politics and of law.

[67] Bernstein, n. 29 above, 287.

2: The Politics of the Emotivist Compromise

A Four-Level Analysis

I have argued that both MacIntyre's and Rorty's conceptions of the self are flawed. Nevertheless, their arguments have a further dimension that needs to be engaged with, a dimension that has been hinted at in the previous sections but will now be brought properly to the fore. It concerns the understanding of liberalism and the liberal legal order that is taken to be consequent upon and supportive of the self and its moral understandings in the modern world. While I have used Rorty's work to identify the construction and function of the emotivist compromise, given that his political analysis is underdeveloped and consists largely—as I have just noted—in an uncritical endorsement of American procedural justice and institutions, I will return to MacIntyre's writings to draw a fuller picture of the argument. Once again it should be noted that to lump together MacIntyre and Rorty here may seem to overlook the discrepancies between the two. But as I have tried to show, the premises for the latter's optimism are essentially the same as those for the former's pessimism. As such, it is the issue of the compromise deemed to occur in liberal institutions rather than the authors' evaluative reactions to it that are of importance.

The institutions and procedures of the emotivist compromise—of liberalism for MacIntyre—go hand in hand with the conception of the emotivist self. We will recall that the defining characteristic of such a self was its expression in language of nothing but "preferences, feelings or attitudes". Such preferences will, he says, usually take the form "I want it to be the case that such and such".[1] As each self (or group) will have its own preferences or ranking of preferences there will inevitably be conflict. Hence the necessity for compromise. But *that* there must be compromise does not yet deal with the question of how compromise is to be reached. MacIntyre's breakdown of this issue into four levels of "activity and debate" is instructive and raises serious questions for liberal theory, and for liberal legalism.

[1] Alasdair MacIntyre, *Whose Justice? Which Rationality?* (London, Duckworth, 1988), 338. Note that page references, in brackets, in the text of this section are to this book.

The charges they raise will be discussed both here and later on, for if MacIntyre is correct the consequences are broad and far-reaching. The underlying ideas in what follows have been canvassed already, but consideration of their institutional aspect will now push the debate further.

The first level of MacIntyre's four-level analysis "is that at which different individuals and groups express their attitudes in their own terms, whatever these may be" (at 342). As we have seen however, since these expressions are deemed to have been set loose from the contexts of teleology or from justification through universalisation, debate at this level, says MacIntyre:

> is necessarily barren; rival appeals to accounts of the human good or of justice necessarily assume a rhetorical form such that it is as assertion and counterassertion, rather than as argument and counterargument, that rival standpoints confront one another [at 343].

The resultant interminable nature of debate—if "debate" is the right term—at this level we have already discussed, and do not need to go into again here. However, the response to this impasse raises us to the second level.

Here "preferences are tallied and weighed", but in order to carry this out there is a presumption that:

> the procedures which govern such tallying and weighing are themselves the outcome of rational debate of quite another kind, that at which the principles of shared rationality have been identified by philosophical enquiry [*ibid.*].

Here we are dealing with what MacIntyre terms the production of the "principles of justice" (rather than the more precise discourse conditions exemplified in the work of, say, Habermas and Robert Alexy, though as attempts to clarify the presuppositions and justifications for the procedures that may be identified at this level, these might be closely related to the "principles of justice"). However it will come as no surprise that MacIntyre rejects the unending search for such procedures as necessarily elusive on grounds with which we are again familiar. That is, *no* "principles of shared rationality" have been nor will be identified, for the reason that both the starting point (the self and its preferences) and the lack of contexts (such as a teleological common good) have deprived practical reasoning of any sense of what it would mean successfully to find such a shared rationality. In other words, the very reason there has to be a move to the second level effectively precludes the possibility that resolution will occur at this level. Nevertheless, says MacIntyre, this does not mean that pragmatic or "socially effective" rules do not operate. What they lack, for him, is conclusiveness at the level of philosophical enquiry.

Such principles as do come into operation for the weighing and tallying of preferences at the second level must then be seen to be able to justify how individuals are treated as individuals according to these principles. The third level—which might be thought to constitute in essence the particularisation of principles to preferences—therefore works as a "certain kind of sanction for the rules and procedures functioning at the second level" (at 344). Here, to use MacIntyre's example, what "equality" as a principle of justice at the second level means in its application to certain individuals, groups or interests has to be justified. So if absolute equality is unattainable, the third level operates to show how certain inequalities (economic, say) are nevertheless justified according to principles of justice. Initial preferences will therefore be upheld or not, and rules at this third level will ideally be used to show why the application of second level principles occurs as it does.

But once again we find that third level questions such as "does the principle of equality sanction positive discrimination?", or, "on what occasions and for what groups is economic freedom curtailable?" are as contested and irresolvable as debate at the previous two levels. The reasons for this are again familiar and the inability of liberal theorists to agree, moreover, attests as much as anything does to "the necessary inconclusiveness of modern academic philosophy" (*ibid.*). Yet decisions are and indeed must be made. How they are achieved brings us to the fourth level and to the crux of MacIntyre's argument.

The fourth is that level "at which appeals to justice may be heard in a liberal individualist order, that of the rules and procedures of the formal legal system" (*ibid.*). It is important to remember that although MacIntyre has argued that the inconclusiveness of debate in liberal societies is clearly evident at the first three levels of debate, and has sought to explain this in terms of the lack of "scales" on which arguments can rationally be weighed, he cannot of course deny that argument about and resolution of social conflict does occur. But what is significant now is the way in which he sees such resolution taking place, and the reasons behind it. Ostensibly unable to produce rationally-based criteria of morality or justice at lower levels, he argues that at the fourth level:

> The function of the [legal] system is to enforce an order in which conflict resolution takes place without invoking any overall theory of the human good. To achieve this end almost any position taken in the philosophical debates of liberal jurisprudence may on occasion be invoked [*ibid.*].

It is in this last point that the real tragedy of modernity is to be discovered. For the consequence of this is that:

> the mark of a liberal order is to refer its conflicts for their resolution, not to those debates, but to the verdicts of its legal system [*ibid.*].

The progression through the emotivist self, its preferences, and their compromise finds their institutional vesting in the legal system, not because of the wisdom or justness of law, but because of the failure of contemporary philosophy to provide any other means for rational resolution. The difference between the terms "resolution" and "verdict" is telling: the force of argument and rational debate has been usurped by the force of law to decide. But such usurpation is not a contingent victory for an imperialistic legal system—though the latter is the consequence: it is a necessary result of the failure of all other levels of debate to produce sufficient standards of rational justification. As MacIntyre concludes somewhat disdainfully, "[t]he lawyers, not the philosophers, are the clergy of liberalism" (*ibid.*).

Some points come out of this analysis that are worth taking up. First there is the assumption that liberalism's basic unit is the individual, who expresses preferences in the "I want . . ." form. While I have already touched on problems with such an atomistic view of the self, the combination now with preferences in this form is a strong—though in fact commonplace—argument against liberal theory. Marx gives one of the clearer expositions of it when discussing the consequences of the way in which rights, and in particular property rights, were delineated after the French Revolution. Looking at the 1793 "Declaration of the Rights of Man and of the Citizen" he sees the contradiction between "man as a communal being" and "man as a private individual" in civil society as existing in the definitional opposition of the two, the result of which is to disallow anything but a thin meaning of community. The language and substance are all but identical to MacIntyre's:

> not one of the so-called rights of man goes beyond egoistic man, man as a member of civil society, namely an individual withdrawn into himself, his private interest and his private desires and separated from the community . . . society appears as a framework extraneous to individuals, as a limitation on their original independence.[2]

[2] Karl Marx, "On the Jewish Question", in *Karl Marx: Early Writings* (ed. Lucio Colletti, transl. R. Livingstone and G. Benton, Harmondsworth, Penguin Books, 1975), 230.

While Marx goes on to examine the role of private property and its relation to interests, in moral theory MacIntyre treats the issue of preference as integral to the construction of his argument about the inability of rational debate to take place at the first level (which is in turn essential to his critique of debate at the other three levels). Given the form of preferences ("I want . . ."), MacIntyre suggests that, as no impersonal criteria can be brought in to evaluate between competing preferences, what we are witnessing is the "obliteration of the distinction between manipulative and non-manipulative social relations".[3] That is, when debate occurs, any ensuing compromise takes the form—in Marx's terms—of coincidence of interests rather than genuine communal resolution; and where such preferences can only be aligned, not argued out, it becomes perfectly feasible to "treat others as means not ends". The distinction between self and society is then premised on the inability to do anything communally or in terms of philosophical enquiry that could do any more than line up and arbitrarily decide between any number of "I wants".

In line with my point earlier about the questionable originality of such "desires, feelings, or preferences" I want to suggest here that the ahistorical, abstract or atomistic version of the self this picture presupposes is also unrealistic. Though it appears on the surface to be a telling point against liberal theory, and though some writers are more susceptible to this criticism than others—Rawls's "original position" argument has, for example, come under continued critique from many sides on this point—it is not however a conclusive rebuttal of liberalism. One reason why not (which is, I believe, more telling against MacIntyre than Marx) is analogously presented by Alan Hunt in his criticism of the use made of the "fundamental contradiction" (that between self and others) by the Critical Legal Studies movement. He argues that while their critique is directed at liberal *philosophy*, it:

> slides over into using the same conceptual categories in the critique of liberal capitalist societies. What occurs in this process is that the conceptual categories through which liberalism seeks to understand the world become converted into real relations; it comes to appear as if the dualities of liberal thought are sociological categories through which we can make sense of contemporary society.[4]

[3] Alasdair MacIntyre, *After Virtue: A Study in Moral Theory* (1981, 2nd edn., London, Duckworth, 1985), 23.

[4] Alan Hunt, *Explorations in Law and Society: Towards a Constitutive Theory of Law* (New York, Routledge, 1993), 145–6.

Now such an issue raises a particularly searching point for MacIntyre who insists that "a moral philosophy characteristically presupposes a sociology"[5]: is his position sociologically valid? Is his description of the decontextualised self, seemingly capable only of aligning preferences through substantively non-justifiable procedures, accurate? One way of beginning to answer these questions is to turn a later part of MacIntyre's thesis back on this earlier part, as Steven Lukes has done.[6] In part of MacIntyre's work I have not dealt with, he suggests that we need to resurrect Aristotelian theory and argument as a means of clawing our way out of the "New Dark Ages". But, as Lukes has cogently argued, if one of the defining features of contemporary society is, for MacIntyre, that we lack the means to conduct rational debate, how are we to go about convincing others of the worth of Aristotelianism? If all we can do today is line up preferences, what rational means exist to persuade others to endorse the theory he supports? Surely not Aristotelian ones, since he has precisely denied their effectiveness in contemporary debate? So, says Lukes, if MacIntyre the sociologist is right, then MacIntyre the diagnosing philosopher must be wrong.

This alone is insufficient to refute MacIntyre's thesis about the isolated nature of the self. Later I will suggest that an analysis of the constitutive relation between the socially-situated self and shared and disputed values, offers a better description than that of self and preference offered by MacInytre. However for the moment I believe Lukes's criticism sets in place some doubt about the coherence of MacIntyre's philosophical project and its relation to sociological observation to make us question whether the real existence of such a self is, even for MacIntyre, acceptable. The alienated self aligning preferences in an emotivist compromise is not I think a warrantable description of moral judgement or of what compromise and disagreement are over. This picture of the self fails to pay sufficient attention to the different and subtle contexts in which values, disagreements and compromises occur; a point I will come back to in a later chapter in the discussion of Raz's theory of "constitutive incommensurabilities". It is also, I think, to fail to pick up on Hunt's argument that the arguments against liberal philosophy should not be conflated with the arguments about the reality of contemporary political and economic life. As Stephen Holmes has noted on precisely this point, "the unwillingness to examine liberal theories

[5] N. 3 above, 23.

[6] See his "Alasdair MacIntyre: The Sociologist versus the Philosopher," in Steven Lukes, *Moral Conflict and Politics* (Oxford, Clarendon Press, 1991), 248–56.

and liberal societies separately is a trademark of antiliberal thought, for some antiliberals assume that liberal societies perfectly embody liberal ideals".[7] In essence, therefore, I believe MacIntyre makes the mistake of attributing too much credence to the reasons why he thinks debate today to be interminable. While the latter aspect of interminability may well be true, there may be other—and good—reasons for this than those he puts forward in terms of the de-socialised self.

To suggest this raises another issue from MacIntyre's four-level schema which, even if his description of the self and its compromises is incorrect, nevertheless can still stand as an independent criticism. This brings us out of the realm of preferences into that of the compromises at levels two and three. Whether or not MacIntyre is correct about the *causes* of moral disagreement, it would be nearly impossible to argue that it did not all the same exist. The issue here is the way in which that disagreement is constructed and the possible consequences of how it is constructed. To understand the significance of this let us consider an apparent anomaly.

On the one hand MacIntyre argues that, contrary to its own premises about the plurality of goods and the desire to promote no one in particular, liberalism does indeed subscribe to one such theory. The principles of justice at level two, he says:

> are not neutral with respect to rival and conflicting theories of the human good . . . they impose a particular conception of the good life, of practical reasoning, and of justice upon those who willingly or unwillingly accept the liberal procedures and the liberal terms of debate [at 345].

And what is that conception? It is "no more and no less than the continued sustenance of the liberal social and political order."(*ibid.*). But if this is the case, where does that leave his earlier arguments that contemporary society lacks consensus on any shared goods; surely here is an idea of the good which, albeit different from an Aristotelian theory, is nonetheless a shared standard against which we can judge the rightness of individuals' moral actions? Where does this leave his argument that our society is so conflict-ridden that rational debate cannot even occur? Is, then, the radical inconclusiveness of conflict more apparent than real?

To answer this we must begin to enquire into the characteristics of the way in which disagreement occurs in liberal societies. The argument

[7] Stephen Holmes, *The Anatomy of Antiliberalism* (Cambridge, Mass., Harvard UP, 1993), p. xiv.

MacIntyre makes is that the effect of the anomaly is that conflict is made to be *both* real and unreal. Thus he writes:

> It is not just that we live too much by a variety and multiplicity of fragmented concepts; it is that these are used at one and the same time to express rival and incompatible social ideals and policies *and* to furnish us with a pluralist political rhetoric whose function is to conceal the depth of our conflicts.[8]

Conflict is real in this scenario in the following sense: in line with his argument about "fragmented survivals", contemporary moral theory's interminable debates do not allow for rational resolution; individuals and groups genuinely do hold conflicting opinions which an emotivist culture is philosophically at a loss to do anything about. However, conflict is *made to be unreal* because of the rhetorical and institutional channelling that it receives. What tends to occur is that, where the common good of liberalism may be expressed ultimately as "the continued sustenance of the liberal social and political order", challenges to this order are dealt with in one of two ways: either conflict is brought within the rhetorical structures of liberal debate and is thus made amenable to debate on liberalism's terms, or it is denied a hearing in debate at all. In the former case what appears as genuine conflict turns out to be in fact no more than debate within already-defined liberal parameters. As MacIntyre notes, "the contemporary debates within modern political systems are almost exclusively between conservative liberals, liberal liberals, and radical liberals" (at 392). And the effect of this, he concludes, gives evidence for the second technique, that of exclusion: "[t]here is little place in such political systems for the criticism of the system itself, that is, for putting liberalism in question" (*ibid.*). So, even when MacIntyre says that at level one "different groups or individuals express their attitudes *in their own terms*, whatever they may be", we must treat this with more caution than he himself sometimes appears to do. This way of putting it may be to underestimate the power of rhetorical structures at the least to distort the manifold possibilities of individuals' expression of meaning "in their own terms". For here is precisely another way in which genuine or radical conflict can be masked or "concealed".

This is a particularly important facet of debate at level four, the legal system, which we will come to in a moment. But at the level of debate on principles of justice and their particularisation, MacIntyre must undoubtedly be correct to point out that the effect of this is to dimin-

[8] N. 3 above, 253.

ish the reality of *meaningful dissensus*. Where the effects of rhetorical and institutional restraints tend towards some variation on the position "adapt your aspirations to our ends, or else", or reduces choice simply to a series of pre-given arguments, this appears to put in jeopardy the flourishing of radical disagreement at all. What may be put forward as a moral issue or issue of justice may or may not register within liberal debate as conflict at all, depending on the ability of the arguments to attract liberal stakes. Moreover, in some important sense the unreality of (allowable) conflict works to devalue even liberalism's own premise that there is no one justifiable overarching good for human beings.

The significant theoretical questions, then, are not just, what moral conflicts are there and what should we do about them?, but how does disagreement take place and how is it structured? And here we come to the final issue I want to take from MacIntyre's four-level analysis. For it will be recalled that what MacIntyre perceives to be the failure of modern philosophical debate to produce justifiable resolution at the first three levels leads to the way in which the legal system is drawn in for its ability to produce "verdicts". What this use of the legal system, the most important part of the overall "structure" of dealing with contemporary disagreement, signifies is essentially the *capitulation* rather than the embodiment of philosophical debate. This is potentially his most damning argument against liberal institutions and jurisprudence, for it attacks not just the rationality or reasonableness of legal decision-making and justification, but its very rationale. It is an external critique of the function and role of the legal system within liberal societies rather than one aimed at its internal justificatory arguments and substantive conclusions. For my purposes I want to extrapolate three related strands of this argument.

First, it is indicative of liberal orders, as MacIntyre has noted, that because of their inability to provide for rational, consensus-based resolution of moral conflicts at lower levels, courts, and particularly supreme courts, play the role of ultimate arbiter on issues of serious contention, such as abortion, the extent of free speech, or the legitimate interest of the state in people's private lives. Now few liberal legal theorists would deny this. So, for example, Neil MacCormick makes precisely the same point:

> Issues of [this] kind . . . are not the subject of moral consensus among contemporary citizens of contemporary states. Yet for the purposes of social life in complex societies they are issues upon which it seems necessary to to have some determinate norm of public action.[9]

[9] Neil MacCormick, "The Relative Heteronomy of Law", *European Journal of Philosophy* 3: 1 1995, 69–85, at 76.

The production of such "determinate norms" by the legal system seems to attest to MacIntyre's placing of level four as the supreme feature of resolution in his schema. But what MacIntyre emphasises in his reading of this, is the *nature* of the public, legal, compromise that is made; that is, the issue is to problematise how and why such compromise occurs, not simply that it does. In criticising Dworkin's thesis, which sees the Supreme Court "invoking a set of consistent principles, most and perhaps all if them of moral import", the problem is that which MacIntyre has pointed out all along (and is the same one acknowledged by MacCormick): that the court cannot invoke "our shared moral first principles. For our society as a whole has none."[10] If it did, so the argument goes, the role of courts would not be that which it presently is.

What MacIntyre does, then, is to transfer his arguments about the unresolvability of moral debate into the fourth level. This, I will argue, opens the possibility for radicalising both the question (and its consequences) that liberal legal theorists often refuse to draw: how from the morass of disagreement can rational or consensual norms be invoked by courts when the premises of liberal society preclude this possibility at the previous three levels? In contradistinction to most liberal legal theories that from this point go back to try to retrieve some such coherent principles—which may find their expression in integrity, coherence, rational argumentation or whatever; the invocation, in other words, as I have noted already, of "almost any position in the philosophical debates of liberal jurisprudence"—MacIntyre refuses to get into this debate. The point he wants to make instead is that the form, structure and relative positioning of legal resolution in contemporary debate work to devalue pretty much *any* attempts of liberal jurisprudence to justify its decisions on coherent and shared principles of justice. For if such did not exist at levels one, two or three, they will not magically appear at level four. It is no wonder, then, that lawyers, to take a liberty with a well-known phrase, postulate an "artificial reason and judgement of law"; given the nature of contemporary disagreement they could not find a "real", "natural" reason in the realms of morality, determinative of solutions in the realm of the legal.

Yet for MacIntyre, the fact of the real and inconclusive nature of moral disagreement should not be elided. This brings us to the second consequence that can be taken from MacIntyre's analysis. Using the same type of argument he makes against the way in which liberal argu-

[10] N. 3 above, 253.

mentation may work to produce collaboration or exclusion, so too, he says, can genuine disagreement be distorted or masked at the fourth level. In making this point he is essentially emphasising what Robert Cover has called the jurispathic function of judges in the legal system. That is, on a broad definition of law as the diverse and varied sources and meanings of social norms, Cover argues that the problem the legal system encounters in resolving any particular issue is not that the law is unclear, but that "there is too much law" emanating from these sources. The court exists not because it embodies any community morality, not, in other words, because law is *needed to express* such morality, but "to suppress law, to choose between two or more laws, to impose upon law a hierarchy".[11] Judges must therefore "kill off law"—hence their jurispathic function—in order to produce what MacCormick above termed "determinate norms of public action". So, as MacIntyre puts it:

> The nature of any society is not to be deciphered from its laws alone, but from those understood as an index of its conflicts. What our laws show is the extent and degree to which conflict has to be suppressed.[12]

In saying this he links the existence of interminable conflict at levels one to three directly to the function and extent to which law in liberal societies must act, in Cover's terms, to "kill off law".

The way in which conflict is suppressed is something we will come to in a moment, but the thrust of MacIntyre's argument here can be taken as being directed toward the role he assigns to law. While liberal jurisprudence does acknowledge the need to produce a single coherent and authoritative system of law, it tends to downplay the meaning of this in relation to moral and legal argumentation by, as I have pointed out, returning quickly back to debates internal to liberal jurisprudence. So, rather than bringing the argument about the philosophical origins and nature of disagreement, as MacIntyre suggests, completely and consistently from the first three levels into the fourth, the tendency is to announce that, while there is indeed a problem about moral conflict, it is essentially a practical one with which law must deal, rather than a philosophical one which may in fact work to undermine the very validity of the law's response. Then to work in principles of justice—as, say, Dworkin does—to give substance to that response tends to neglect the utilitarian function and requirement of using law in the first place. It is

[11] Robert M. Cover, "The Supreme Court 1982, Foreword: *Nomos* and Narrative," 97 *Harvard Law Review* 4–68 (1983–4) at 40.

[12] N. 3 above, 254.

to downplay—because, for MacIntyre, of the failure of contemporary moral philosophy—the purely instrumental role of law at the fourth level as an expedient coordinating and peace-keeping force whose self-reproducing tactic is to suppress the conflicts which would threaten the liberal order. In fact, the contrast with Dworkin could not be clearer: even though Dworkin's theory of adjudication will note the existence of conflict over any particularly contested issue (as he says, "if we wish to use the concept of a community morality in political theory, we must acknowledge conflicts within that morality as well"[13]), he is still prepared to assume, and sees no problem in asserting, that how his super-judge Hercules decides the case will be to enforce the "institutional right, as defined by the community's constitutional morality"[14]; that is, for Dworkin, a right answer *will* somehow magically appear at level four. Yet for MacIntyre, quite to the contrary, such sophistry in legal reasoning as produces such a Herculean result will be merely indicative of, like liberal government itself, "a set of institutional arrangements for imposing a bureaucratised unity on a society which lacks genuine moral consensus".[15]

Though MacIntyre does not acknowledge it, his argument clearly has overtones of Hobbes. However, perhaps only positivist theories have fully developed this point. Again, taking MacCormick as our exemplar, he notes that "[w]hat the law's institutions can do is that which moral deliberation cannot itself achieve. They can lay down a common [authoritative] rule in relatively determinate terms".[16] Moreover for the positivist this fact constitutes the:

> clear conceptual distinction between the moral and the legal . . . Law is heteronomous [externally binding on the will] as well as authoritative and institutional; it thus stands in clear conceptual contrast to morality, which is autonomous, discursive and controversial.[17]

Yet it is not the conceptual separation of law and morality that particularly interests MacIntyre, but the limited, though highly prominent, role that law comes to play in a liberal order, given the nature and meaning of moral conflict as he has described it. While MacCormick rightly acknowledges that there is "a moral price to be paid for the utility of

[13] Ronald Dworkin, *Taking Rights Seriously* (1977) (London, Duckworth, third impression 1981), 126.

[14] *Ibid.*

[15] N. 3 above, 254.

[16] MacCormick, n. 9 above, 76.

[17] *Ibid.*, 78.

law as an institutional establishment of common norms for conduct in society",[18] MacIntyre might extend this in two ways: first, by suggesting that a moral price has already been paid *before* enforced resort to the fourth level is made and, secondly—to push the metaphor one last step—that the legal system creates a further, unpayable, debt by imposing for reasons of pragmatic utility what cannot be justified at the level of coherent principle.

MacIntyre, it seems to me, is then prepared to question further the implications of the authoritative nature of law *given* its relative positioning in the schema of debate in contemporary liberal society. By approaching the role of law in this way and by problematising the meaning of morality as he does, he arguably goes further than most positivists would in emphasising the brute power of law in a society where there are "no shared moral principles". But in doing so he also offers a glimpse of a problem that needs to be taken seriously. That is, if at levels one to three contemporary liberal society, because of its emotivist underpinnings, fails to produce rational resolution to moral conflict, then the likelihood is that "the contrast between power and authority . . . is effectively obliterated as a special instance of the disappearance of the contrast between manipulative and non-manipulative social relations".[19] In other words, regardless of the issue about the conceptual separation of law and morality, if—even positivist—liberal jurisprudence neglects to account for the state and meaning of moral conflict as it impinges on the role of law *and* how this role in turn impinges on the moral realm, it risks becoming merely an endorsement of the non-rational use of power and one that is, moreover, blinded to the fact that this is all it is doing. To acknowledge this transcends the positivist's question of legal validity at a formal level and raises the far more serious question of the *legitimacy* of the modern liberal legal order.[20]

I will return to aspects of this argument later but want now to turn to a third implication raised by MacIntyre's four-level classification. This also concerns the question of power, but not this time in terms of the authoritative positioning of law, but as something more akin to a sociological critique, one that concentrates on the locating of various levels of power as they are manifested in different constituencies within the state. As this brings together arguments about conflict, law and the liberal state that have already been touched on, it can be dealt with briefly

[18] *Ibid.*

[19] N. 3 above, 26 (discussing Weber).

[20] See *ibid.*, 254.

here, though it will be raised again, specifically in relation to law, in a later chapter.

I pointed out earlier that, whether or not MacIntyre is correct about the sources of moral disagreement in the emotivist conception of the self, it is nevertheless the case that conflict does occur and that it may have to be dealt with institutionally. One dimension of how such resolution is attempted has been covered, namely the philosophical and legal attempts to construct rational debate at all four levels. But the other dimension to this concerns *who* participates in these processes. What Rorty had seen as the benefits of the separation of public and private, MacIntyre translates into the nightmare of modern life, the separation between the atomistic self and the iron cage of bureaucracy. "Modern societies", he writes, "oscillate between a freedom which is nothing but a lack of regulation of individual behaviour and forms of collectivist control designed only to limit the anarchy of self-interest."[21] Bleak if nothing else, what still lacks from this picture is the shading in of the personnel who dominate the agenda-setting of this "collectivist control". Given the link between the self and the expression of the preferences it brings into the public domain, it matters who controls the "weighing and tallying" of these preferences. And here MacIntyre follows other sociological critiques by attending to the significance of elites in these processes. Thus:

> . . . in a liberal order power lies with those who are able to determine what the alternatives are to be between which choices will be available. The consumer, the voter, and the individual in general are accorded the right of expressing their preferences for one or more out of the alternatives which are offered, but the range of possible alternatives is controlled by an elite, and how they are presented is also so controlled [at 345].

This is again in line with his points about the way in which liberalism may distort debate and meaning so that even the extreme of the oscillation which is the freedom from a lack of regulation is a freedom tempered by constraints of which the individual may or may not be aware. While this might suggest a reading tending toward the kind of dispersal of power advocated by Foucault,[22] MacIntyre is ultimately more concerned with the philosophical—and, one could add by extrapolation from the above arguments, legal—smokescreens that are set off to mask

[21] N. 3 above, 35.

[22] See for example his "Two Lectures", reprinted as "The Juridical Apparatus," in William Connolly (ed.), *Legitimacy and the State* (Oxford, Basil Blackwell, 1984).

and control the kind of argumentative strategies that would challenge liberalism itself. As he says (with a characteristic lack of charity), "[t]he ruling elites within liberalism are thus bound to value highly competence in the persuasive presentation of alternatives, that is, the cosmetic arts" (at 345).

The appearance of preferences as genuine choices, as well as how they come to be channelled at the various levels, is thus an essential part of the way in which liberalism manages both to exult in and to stifle genuine moral disagreement. The elites MacIntyre has in mind presumably range from the politician and the lawyer to the liberal (of whatever persuasion) philosopher. Though he does not go on to explore this at the fourth level, I will argue later that the combination of these arguments presents an opening for a critique of liberal legalism, though one that will diverge in its underpinnings from MacIntyre's own. But for the moment it is sufficient to flag the connexion between this kind of power—as opposed to the power of state law already discussed—and the chanelling of conflict and debate in the contemporary liberal order, a point we will return to later. As such it is time to draw together the strands of these arguments.

Conclusion

We have travelled a long way from Aristotle and the good life, and the more technical arguments of moral philosophy. But the significance of these arguments should be clear for my approach. To end up in debates about the construction of moral conflict is—as my interpretation of MacIntyre has sought to show—integral to an understanding of several features of liberalism and of the legal system within a contemporary liberal order. Let me summarise what I take to be the most prominent.

First, that the way in which the conception of the self is understood is integrally related to questions that liberalism seeks to address. However, what my criticisms of both MacIntyre and Rorty have attempted to show is that that relation is a contested one. That is, it is possible for MacIntyre to be wrong about the existence of the barely articulate "emotivist self", and Rorty to be wrong about the limits of its freedom, yet for the idea of the self still to be relevant to an understanding of liberalism. Conversely, both writers could still be wrong about their understanding of the self, yet still (MacIntyre especially) have important things to say about the meaning of moral disagreement in contemporary liberal societies. Considered in this way the possibility exists for an alternative, historically-based picture of the self to be drawn that is neither complicit with the perceived failures of contemporary liberal structures, nor as inarticulate and as self-ish as the emotivist self.

Secondly, that the existence and significance of moral conflict is necessarily related to an understanding of the role of law in liberal societies. Furthermore, it matters *how* liberal legal institutions respond and relate to, construct and deal with, questions of moral conflict. It is thus vital to recognise that the dynamic between law and morality—or more precisely, between liberal legalism and moral conflict—must be explored in a way that pays attention to constitutive and destructive dimensions of that relation in a way that many liberal theorists, or their detractors, may not fully pursue.

And thirdly, that if the construction of self and its relation to moral values espoused by liberalism is a contingent one, but that the role of law in contemporary liberal societies may presently mask and distort these values or their expression as conflictual, then there may be a discrepancy between the values of liberalism and the role of law—that is, between liberalism and liberal legalism. The influence of what I have termed "rhetorical and institutional restraints" as well as the power of elites within such liberal orders may therefore have to be addressed in a way that sees them as potentially antithetical to the values and insights they are supposed to uphold. To explore this requires presenting a critique of the institution of law in light of the significance of moral conflict.

PART TWO

3: A Liberal Response

Time and again MacIntyre has complained that there are no shared standards of rationality to which contemporary societies can have recourse to solve their moral, and hence legal, conflicts. I have hinted that despite this point of view it might be possible to defend an alternative reading of liberalism, but that this is only feasible where the role and techniques of law in liberal societies are seriously put into question. Is such a version of liberalism available? Before coming to the institutional dimension I want to recover some elements of the meaning of moral conflict in liberal society that may allow for two things: first, the radicalisation of conflict in a way that releases it from MacIntyre's criticism that liberalism tends to stifle conflict by taking debate into the liberal paradigm, whether consciously or not. While some liberal theories do tend to do this I will look now at one which arguably does not. This is the version put forward by Isaiah Berlin in his "Two Concepts of Liberty".[1] It is possible, I will argue, that it is not liberal theory as such that stifles conflict in the way MacIntyre suggests, though the institutional vesting it takes in contemporary liberal societies does do so. On the contrary, the insights of a certain understanding of liberalism, when they challenge current institutional settings and attitudes, do allow for conflict to be made explicit, and, possibly, do so in a way that other theoretical visions for society do not allow. The strength of such a liberal theory is to put moral conflict over *values* rather than preferences at the heart of its concerns. If the logic of such conflict is pushed through to a greater extent than many contemporary liberal theorists are willing to do, this version of liberalism is defensible against the charges that either liberalism stifles debate into certain pre-ordained forms, or that such debate as does exist amounts to no more an inorganic alignment of preferences. But of course this is only feasible where the institutional dimension is rethought, and I will come to this aspect once I have considered the alternative reading.

The second aspect to retrieving worthwhile dimensions of moral conflict relates to the first, but adds a rigorously socialised version of the

[1] Isaiah Berlin, "Two Concepts of Liberty" in his *Four Essays on Liberty* (1969; Oxford, OUP, 1991 reprint). Note that page references, in brackets in these sections are to the text of this edition.

moral self and moral understanding which challenges the picture of the emotivist self that MacIntyre saw as the embodiment of the failure of liberal morality. It opens up the possibility of meaningful dissensus while at the same time challenging the atomism ascribed to liberalism by Rorty and MacIntyre above. While I have already hinted at problems with the feasibility of the concept of the emotivist self, I now want to suggest that the reflexive dynamic between the socialised self and moral values undercuts the picture of the isolated self MacIntyre describes. The meaning of moral conflict one can find in the work of Berlin can be upheld only when the constitutive relation between values and self is fully delineated. As I point out there exists an antecedent to this in the historical trace that has largely been ignored in liberal theorising (and in most contemporary blanket critiques of the Enlightenment), but which provided understanding of the embeddedness of moral judgement without primary reliance on reason or moral rules to secure its validity. In some respects the version of the socialised self relevant to Berlin's liberalism was preceded by the moral theory of Adam Smith in the way that it sought to analyse moral judgement as deeply contextual, though concerned still with the ability critically to reflect on social practices.[2] While I touch on this in what follows I will however use Berlin's theory to examine how this version of the self can be seen in a way that allows disagreement to flourish without reducing that disagreement to the type MacIntyre has suggested is prevalent in contemporary liberal societies.

Once again, however, to follow this insight through involves a questioning of the role of the legal order that many liberals would not endorse. But to treat moral values and the possibility of their conflict in liberal societies seriously, this further step needs to be taken. In drawing out these two strands of thought I have just outlined I hope to show that a certain understanding of liberalism is defensible, but only when it forces conclusions many liberals would themselves fail to draw. As I suggested at the end of the last chapter, MacIntyre might be correct about the role law plays in liberal societies, but he may be wrong about

[2] A point noted in Michael Ignatieff's recent biography. See his *Isaiah Berlin: A Life* (London, Chatto & Windus, 1998), 257. It is also worth pointing out here that in the reading of liberalism I offer I concentrate largely on Berlin's thought throughout, rather than presenting a history of liberalism as such or of the influences on Berlin himself, in good part since these have been done elsewhere, and because, as John Gray has put it, Berlin's unique work "does not share the hopes (or illusions) of the dominant liberalisms, of our own day and in the past", including even that of John Stuart Mill: John Gray, *Isaiah Berlin* (London, HarperCollins, 1995), 1, and 59 where Gray notes that Berlin's "pluralism distinguishes his liberalism starkly from that of John Stuart Mill".

this being a failure of liberalism as such. By looking at Berlin I want to consider a different understanding of liberalism through the relation between values and the self, but one that has important implications for the role of law. To the extent that MacIntyre correctly captures that role, the ultimate destination of my arguments here is to show that law cannot be part of a solution to the understanding of the meaningfulness of moral conflict espoused by liberalism, precisely for the reason that it is part of the problem.

Berlin's Liberalism

Some 40 years since it was written Isaiah Berlin's "Two Concepts", despite the critical battering it has taken, is still a remarkably profound piece of work. Its central distinction, between positive and negative concepts of liberty, has been interpreted, reinterpreted, challenged, reworked and generally been subject to the full gamut of academic treatments that befall an important philosophical argument. But, rather than concentrating on that distinction, I want here to explore the intellectual framework within which, for Berlin, the significance of the distinction made sense. So in what follows the differences between positive and negative liberty will only be relevant to the extent that they might exemplify the broader issues they raise. They will not be the main focus of this reading.

Instead I want to concentrate on the presuppositions that underpin his version of liberalism. There is, curiously enough, some affinity between his position and that of those theorists who have endorsed certain aspects of postmodern thinking about conflict and difference. There is a strong sense in which Berlin's attack on the kind of thinking that justifies totalitarian regimes—and in whose service the concept of positive liberty is usually employed—resembles critiques made of the "grand narratives" of modernity by Jean-François Lyotard and others. Berlin's distrust of those who believe in, postulate and act upon insights into "all-embracing final solutions" and the ultimate compatibility of human ends and aspirations—an "ancient and almost universal belief", he says—mirrors more recent onslaughts onto the perceived consequences of these self-same goals as they are deemed to be expressed in the mindset of a modernity identified largely with the spirit of the Enlightenment. And Berlin himself, like many postmodernists, does not spare, for example, consequences of theories such as those of Kant and

Rousseau from his critique of the dangers which pertain to belief in an aspirational unity of either morality, peoples or ideas. In this sense, then, there is something about his defence of liberalism that should make us wary about seeing it simply as another version easily amenable to the often undiscriminating attacks of postmodernists who too readily link modernity and liberalism as copartners in the denial of difference or the creation of oppression. That said, however, the nuances of Berlin's analysis should be brought out in order that such distinctive features as there are in his defence of liberalism are seen precisely as that; an argument in support of liberalism. Where appropriate I will draw attention to similarities and differences with certain postmodern writers, though my aim, as stated above, is to look at the meaning and supports for conflict in Berlin's work. To begin then, we must consider some of the key elements of Berlin's thinking.

(i) Conflict

Politics thrives on conflict. Even more basically, conflict is the condition for politics; without conflict, politics is neither possible nor necessary. Such is Berlin's opening gambit in "Two Concepts":

> Where ends are agreed, the only questions left are those of means, and these are not political but technical. . . . That is why those who put their faith in some immense, world-transforming phenomenon, like the triumph of reason or the proletarian revolution, must believe that all political and moral problems can thereby be turned into technological ones [at 118].

The end of conflict is thus the end of politics; and the "all-embracing" solutions proposed for how humans should act signals this end. Moreover—it hardly requires saying—with the end of politics comes the end of political theory, with the end of moral conflict, the end of moral theory.

The shadow of totalitarianism spreads over Berlin's writing, yet his is not an attitude that can be relegated to a Cold War past. The main reason for this is that he does not spare Western democracy from his critique either, though politically there is no doubt of his absolute rejection of recent totalitarian regimes and of his (qualified) support of certain aspects of Western democracies. His position takes a long view of the political developments culminating in the twentieth century's broader political landscape which has, in hugely varying degrees in totalitarian and democratic regimes, resulted in an increased homogenisation of perspectives and intolerance of dissent. Such homogenisation, he argues, sees the shift from conflict over political theories and ideas to the increasing side-stepping of politics in favour of the finding of technical solutions. The general tenor of Berlin's argument can be found in the following passages:

> We are often told that the present is an age of cynicism and despair, of crumbling values and the dissolution of the fixed standards and landmarks of Western civilisation. But this is neither true nor even plausible. So far from showing the loose texture of a collapsing order, the world today is stiff with rigid rules and codes . . . it treats heterodoxy as the supreme danger. Whether in East or West . . . conformities are called for much more eagerly today than yesterday; loyalties are tested far more severely . . . [The individual's] area of choice has grown smaller not in the name of some opposing principle but in order to create a situation in which the very possibility of opposed principles, with all their unlimited capacity to cause mental stress and danger and destructive collisions, is eliminated in favour of a simpler and better regulated life, a robust faith in an efficient working order, untroubled by agonizing moral conflict.[3]

We might read this situation—where the "possibility of opposed principles" is denied—as at one with MacIntyre's criticism of liberalism's ability to stifle debate. But Berlin's conclusion is precisely the opposite. It is the anti-liberal tendencies of the contemporary political landscape that close off debate; liberalism, as Berlin understands it, allows for the flourishing of conflict, and this—and hence the possibility of politics at all—is reduced as societies move toward programmatic solutions to unchallengeable ends already given or imposed. The range of Berlin's attack can be seen, then, as remarkably broad. For it criticises not only communitarian and communist versions of political organisation, but also a range of liberal theories. And it will do so on exactly the same grounds for all of these, namely, their willingness to homogenise, to diminish the possibility for conflict, whether that is carried out in the name of the proletariat, the "community", or a rationalist-based liberalism. As he says:

> Today the tendency to circumscribe and confine and limit, to determine the range of what may be asked and what may not, is no longer a distinguishing mark of the old "reactionaries". On the contrary, it comes as powerfully from the heirs of the radicals, rationalists, "progressives" of the nineteenth century as from the descendants of their enemies.[4]

[3] "Political Ideas in the Twentieth Century", in *Four Essays*, n. 1 above, 37–8.
[4] Ibid., n. 1 above, 37.

To understand where this broad critique comes from, and hence to understand the distinctiveness of Berlin's version of liberalism, we need to explore further what he envisages by the notion of conflict.

If the "general pattern" of socio-political organisation in the twentieth century has been toward increased homogenisation, what does Berlin mean by conflict? In what does conflict consist? One way to introduce the idea is to think about one of the best known lines from his "Two Concepts". That is, "[e]verything is as it is: liberty is liberty, not equality or fairness or justice or culture, or human happiness or a quiet conscience" (at 125). This claim is both a call for analytical clarity and an insight into the grounding of Berlin's observations on conflict. Conflict lies in the incommensurability of the values we may hold most dearly: liberty conflicts with our desire to do justice; it conflicts with claims to equality. Most significantly, it conflicts with alternative understandings of itself; liberty might well be liberty and not justice or equality, but what liberty is is itself contested. Negative liberty—the lack of obstacles in one's path, a "free area for action" (at 131)—competes with its "twin brother", positive liberty—"self-mastery, the elimination of obstacles to my will" (at 146). Concepts of liberty—freedom from, and freedom to—may be related; they may both be profoundly important to how we live our lives, but they are not the same; they are certainly not identical. Just as human "twin brothers" might look the same but cannot be exactly the same being, the values inherent in the two concepts contain elements that cannot be reduced to a single proposition. The two concepts conflict in such a way that to make them identical or to make either concept of liberty identical with another value (liberty with equality, liberty with justice) denies what is distinctive about the value of the other. To move toward the endorsement of one may impinge detrimentally on one's ability to uphold the other.

What pushes Berlin to this conclusion? For him conflict is intimately linked to the notion of the incommensurability of values. It is negative liberty as a value that clashes with positive liberty as a value; at other times it will be equality as a value that conflicts with liberty as a value. And such clashes of value are not finally resolvable. Everything is as it is, and two values in conflict are two values in conflict, not one value mistakenly masquerading as two. "If the claims of two (or more than two) types of liberty [or of any other values] prove incompatible in a particular case, and this is an instance of the clash of values at once absolute and incommensurable, it is better to face this intellectually uncomfortable fact than to ignore it."[5] Moreover, as we shall see shortly, the most profound danger lies in assuming that all values are or can be made commensurable.

If incommensurability is sometimes equated with or charged with relativism, how Berlin recognises incommensurablity must go some way to avoiding that charge. His response, then, to the question of how he knows that values are incommensurable—and thus also to the issue of why the existence of conflict is so important for politics—is an empirical one. It is based on observation. That values—of liberty, justice, equality or whatever—conflict, seems to be an:

> irremovable element in human life . . . [I]f we are not armed with an *a priori* guarantee of the proposition that a total harmony of true values is somewhere to be found—perhaps in some ideal realm the characteristics of which we can, in our finite state, not so much as conceive—we must fall back on the ordinary resources of empirical observation and ordinary human knowledge. And these certainly give us no warrant for supposing (or even understanding what would be meant by saying) that all good things, or all bad things for that matter, are reconcilable with each other. The world that we encounter in ordinary experience is one in which we are faced with choices between ends equally ultimate, and claims equally absolute, the realization of some of which must inevitably involve the sacrifice of others [at 170–1].

The incommensurability of values may or may not be desirable, but it is a fact of life. "Ordinary experience" tells us so. Of course someone like MacIntyre reads this same feature of contemporary life as one of conceptual breakdown. What is interesting and significant about Berlin's analysis, however, is the particular way in which he reads this observation and the different conclusions he draws. In "Two Concepts" the immediate example of a clash of irreconcilable values is that between positive and negative concepts of liberty. These two concepts evidence what was called above "an instance of the clash of values at once absolute and incommensurable". The conflict, put in its most concise form is, he says, precisely this: those who seek to promote the value of negative liberty "want to curb authority as such"; those who cherish positive liberty "want it [authority] placed in their own hands" (at 166). "These", he says, "are not two different interpretations of a single concept, but two profoundly divergent and irreconcilable attitudes to the ends of life

[5] "Introduction" to *Four Essays*, n. 1 above, l.

. . . each of them makes absolute claims. These claims cannot both be fully satisfied" (*ibid.*). That such attitudes conflict is not for Berlin a failure of contemporary moral philosophy; it is not a sign that modern societies are facing a new dark ages. On the contrary it is the *demise* of such conflict that signals a loss.

But is incommensurability nevertheless the end of reason, the end of the hope that the human intellect through rational discourse rather than irrational violence, say, might provide a way of resolving disagreement over differences? Does not incommensurability result in the endorsement of an essentially emotivist self whose commitments (*à la* Rorty) cannot be grounded in anything other than contingency and the uncommitted hope for common survival? Berlin's response to these issues is, in one sense, both ambiguous and determinedly clear. It is ambiguous in the way in which he treats the issue of rationality, but clear in the way in which it finds commitment unproblematic. And both can be brought together only when we see how incommensurability and the value of conflict come to focus on the relation between values and the self. Let us begin with the ambiguity.

(ii) *Rationality*

What Berlin rejects for the notion of rationality is the possibility that it can direct humans in resolving the fundamental conflicts they have over the ends of life and the values they differently adhere to. He argues variously that when values conflict, the conflict "is not to be solved by any hard-and-fast-rule"[6]; that "clear-cut solutions cannot, in principle, be found"[7]; that there can be no "correct, conclusive solution [which] must always in principle be discoverable".[8] As noted earlier, this line is directed as much against rationalist liberal theories as anything else, for it is the uniformity that claims to reason engender that Berlin is reacting against. If we consider his interpretation of Kant on this point, he writes that:

> the limits of liberty are determined by applying the rules of "reason", which is much more than the mere generality of rules as such, and is the faculty that creates or reveals a purpose identical in, and for, all men. . . . The authority of reason and the duties it lays upon men is identified with indi-

[6] "Introduction" to *Four Essays*, n. 1 above, pp. xlviii–xlvix.
[7] *Ibid.*, l.
[8] *Ibid.*

> vidual freedom, on the assumption that only rational ends can be the "true" objects of a "free" man's "real" nature [at 153–4].

But why should Berlin find the notion of reason or rationality in this sense problematic?

The answer lies in two directions. One concerns the assumptions that have to be made in order to support such a role for reason. The second deals with practical consequences of making such assumptions. In the former, the assumptions made require the belief in the idea that "man has a 'true' self, a 'real' nature". Only where such a belief is held, can reason be applied to discover true ends or purposes "identical in, and for, all men". To be rational requires uniformity—and here we might think back to what makes an action moral in Kant's theory, the categorical imperative: "[m]y action is moral if and only if I can will that my maxim should become a universal law"—and as such a morality based on this uniformity assumes that where differences appear in ends sought or standards formulated such differences pertain to an improper grasp of what it is rational for the "real" moral self to do. In Berlin's words, "[reason's] laws will be the rules which reason prescribes: they will only seem irksome to those whose reason is dormant, who do not understand the true 'needs' of their own 'real' selves" (at 147). Hence, if reason is uniform, and if its dictates are to have authority in the moral realm, the assumption must be made that it is possible to discover what the true moral self is or requires; if there is no true self then claims to reason cannot attain an authoritative objectivity, morality cannot be the "correct use of a universal human faculty". Thus, "[t]he rational ends of our 'true' natures must coincide, or be made to coincide, however violently our poor, ignorant, desire-ridden, passionate empirical selves may cry out against this process" (at 148). In this picture no-one has rights against reason he says, quoting Fichte. Reason, otherwise, would become fragmented, useless; in Hume's phrase, inert.

The belief in the existence of a "true nature" for all humans is intimately linked, Berlin says, to the conception that all ends are, finally, commensurable, that there can be harmony and not permanent discord in human lives and goals, either now or at some point in history yet to come. Yet for that harmony to exist, it must be possible to rank values, to weigh them up against each other in a way that denies that they can each be equally ultimate, that denies they can clash incommensurably. This draws us toward the second problem he has with such a notion of reason. He argues that where "no-one has rights against reason" it is up to those who *do* accurately perceive the dictates of reason to make sure that those "poor, ignorant, desire-ridden" others who do not properly grasp such dictates, are shown the path to enlightened, rational, behaviour. Moreover, to act in this way will not be autocratic since it merely requires the "defective" others to live up to the rational requirements of their own "true selves"; and being told to do what is rational according to one's true nature can hardly be an imposition. But it is this assumption that Berlin finds problematic. Where the authority of reason assumes that two ends or values or duties cannot conflict if reason is properly applied—for reason could not require one to act in two contradictory ways—then any conflict "is due solely to the clash of reason with the irrational or the insufficiently rational" (at 154). To make such an assumption consequently allows for the practical conclusion that some individual or group can direct others to act in the way they prescribe because such direction is authorised by reason.

It thus clears the way for an imposition of value-ranking based on the commensurability of all values. Just how far this is carried out in practice may well vary, but the logic of any such enforcement will be the same:

> In the name of reason anything that is non-rational may be condemned, so that the various personal aims which their individual imagination and idiosyncrasies lead men to pursue . . . may, at least in theory, be ruthlessly suppressed to make way for the demands of reason [at 153].

The conjunction of such ideas is why Berlin rejects reason or rationality when given this form. The tendency to impose the single, "all-embracing solution" based on claims to reason and the ultimately harmonious nature of the world when "properly understood", are clearly implicated in tendencies toward a homogenised view of human being. Based as it is in the treatment of fundamental conflict as essentially rooted in mistake or an inability to grasp the true nature of things or beings, its logic drives it, seemingly inexorably, toward the suppression of conflict itself. And the end of conflict, as we already know, is the end of morality and politics as such; once the ends are fully grasped, whether by everyone or in fact only those who have seen the light (of reason, revolution, or true justice), the only issues left are those of means.

Now we must appreciate the ambiguity in Berlin's analysis of rationality. If Berlin is prepared to disavow the techniques and consequences of reason as just described, he is not however prepared to abandon the idea of rationality entirely. What is left though, one might ask? We should recall first that a part of what makes Berlin reject the "all-embracing solutions", the possibilities for harmonious resolution of conflicting views on the ends of life to which a uniform reason grounded in beliefs in the true self aspires is that, empirically, these beliefs do not square with our observations of the world as it is. True it is that there is a tendency toward homogenisation, observable in a range of twentieth-century political doctrines. Yet conflicting attitudes to the ends of life continue to appear in moral and political beliefs. In this sense, aspired-for unities which would resolve such conflicts seem to fly in the face of experience. Of course, this experience cannot be empirical in some "pure" sense; our understandings of conflict (and not just our observation of the fact of disagreement) must be mediated through conceptual categories which themselves may be incommensurable. This is most significant in Berlin's reading. As he says, "since some values may conflict intrinsically, the very notion that a pattern must in principle be discoverable in which they are all rendered harmonious is founded on a false *a priori* view of what the world is like".[9] Simultaneously, then, the empirical observation that our understandings of certain values do conflict incommensurably justifies the argument that, as such, claims to the ultimate harmony of values go against what the world as we know it is actually like, and, it also acts to support an argument that the existence of incommensurable conflict over values *ought* to be maintained rather than suppressed.

For Berlin, to act as if the conflict over values was merely the result of an error that could be corrected by the proper application of reason or understanding or whatever does damage to the very real existence of conflicting attitudes to the ends of life. In the example used above, to reduce the notion that one seeks to curb authority to the notion that one seeks to put authority in one's own hands (or vice versa) fails to take account of the clash of these values or ends as "at once absolute and incommensurable". There is an (empirically observable) conceptual clash which is informed by radically differing attitudes toward what is valuable. To collapse them, and hence to assume that that (or any other similar) clash can be resolved in some harmonious schema, neglects, or more usually unjustifiably suppresses, that difference in the name of some higher or greater good or goal.

Here we see in part an unholy alliance of ideas between MacIntyre and Berlin. Conflict between values is ineradicable, though such conflict

[9] "Introduction" to *Four Essays*, n. 1 above, p. li.

may well be distorted in practice by acting as if it were not. Such is Berlin's bottom line, and it is here that his understanding of rationality becomes significant. For if appeals to reason are potentially dangerous in the way just described, what is it rational to do in any situation of incommensurable conflict? Berlin cannot answer this question in the abstract. To do so would be to provide a prescriptive framework of the type he shuns, where all values or ends could be brought together and made commensurable. Where the ends of life conflict, where concepts (such as positive and negative liberty, or of equality or justice) clash, one can only act rationally *in the concrete situation*, not rationally in the abstract. "The concrete situation", Berlin writes, "is almost everything."[10] And here we have his distinctive view of rationality: where a choice must be made in such circumstances then the ability of that choice to be made by individuals or groups *themselves* "is part of being rational or capable of moral judgment".[11] Being reasonable may include aspects of following rules or principles, "but when these rules or principles conflict in concrete cases, to be rational is to follow the course of conduct which least obstructs the general pattern of life in which we believe".[12]

Here we re-encounter the ambiguity I have suggested exists in Berlin's approach. If, as he says, the "capacity for choosing is intrinsic to rationality", then he must acknowledge (as he does) that harm is done to individuals or groups "in an instrinsic, Kantian, not merely utilitarian, sense" when the capacity for choosing is curtailed.[13] And yet he cannot support any Kantian or other version of reason that would allow such individuals or groups to resolve such conflict in a conceptually harmonious way. The reasons for this wariness we have touched upon and will deal with again more fully shortly, but what compels this conclusion is his vision of the essentially tragic quality of human life. "That we cannot have everything", he says, "is a necessary and not a contingent truth" (at 170); "[t]he need to choose, to sacrifice some ultimate values to others turns out to be a permanent characteristic of the human predicament".[14] Hence choice, rationality, and the meaningfulness of conflict, are rooted in the fact "that ends collide", "that one cannot have

[10] Isaiah Berlin, "The Pursuit of the Ideal" in his *The Crooked Timber of Humanity* (London, Fontana Press, 1991), 18.

[11] "Introduction" to *Four Essays*, n. 1 above, p. li.

[12] *Ibid.*, p. lv.

[13] *Ibid.*, p. lii.

[14] *Ibid.*, p. li.

everything".[15] Still, even though hard choices must be made, this does not mean that such choices are or must be arbitrary.

To be rational, then, must involve the ability to choose between values or concepts where that choice cannot be determined *a priori* by reference to abstract principles of rationality. Berlin treats reason or rationality thus in a reduced sense, and one in which the fact that we cannot rationally ground our arguments once and for all is not problematic. Yet his argument is different from Rorty's here. The ambiguity in Berlin's treatment of rationality can only be properly understood when we consider the situation-specific location in which rational judgements are made, and involves consideration of the relation between self and commitment in which the above arguments about rationality make sense. While Berlin does have important things to say about self and commitment (which we will come to in a moment) he does not, to my mind, sufficiently delineate the ambiguous nature of rationality itself. To understand it, we need to turn to a more rigorous approach to this same problem. Such is available in part of the work of Joseph Raz.

In a consideration of the issues that arise over questions of incommensurability in moral theory, Raz writes that (and the full significance of this will only emerge in the following section) "[i]ncommensurability speaks not of what does escape reason but of what must elude it".[16] One of the criticisms made of the belief that ultimate values are incommensurable is that, where a conflict occurs, the conflict may well be over competing values, but this does not mean they are incommensurable in the absolute sense in which Berlin uses the term. To assume incomensurability, the critic argues, assumes that the ends are *equally* valuable, so that there is no way in which a point of view can be found to resolve the conflict. But this, so the argument runs, fails to recognise two things: one, that all ends are not equally valuable and, two, the fact that decisions *are* made in cases of conflict between values and that such decisions are not made arbitrarily, but made according to some standards. The critic's point is therefore that incommensurability may be more apparent than real.

To concretise this dispute let us use an example of the type Raz himself uses. Is it possible to put a monetary value on friendship? Assuming we live, as we do, in a society where having money plays to some degree an important part in our lives, could we weigh up the choice between having a large sum of money against having a particular friendship? The

[15] *Ibid.*

[16] Joseph Raz, *The Morality of Freedom* (Oxford, Clarendon Press, 1986), 334.

critic of the incommensurability thesis argues that if we decide that friendship wins out against having the money, we thereby *do* make the two values commensurable in the very act of comparing the two. Even though we choose friendship we do so on the ground that friends are more important than money. And in this way, when a decision is reached it will not be arbitrary but come with reasons why one option is preferred over the other. In other words, we compare the two options, rank them and decide. This could not be an example of incommensurability, therefore, since the values are not equal, they can be ranked on a scale which treats them as comparable, and a decision can be reached on the basis of such a ranking.

Raz's response to this is, however, instructive. In the first instance, he says, two values do not have to be of exactly equal weight in order to be described as incommensurable. They may, in Berlin's phrase, be equally ultimate in the demands they make on someone, but the idea that one is neither better nor worse than the other does not amount to saying they are therefore of equal weight.[17] In the second instance, Raz notes, it is often the case that people asked such a question in the abstract, in the example we are using, say, to compare friendship and monetary value, will refuse to compare the two. But this refusal alone does not yet answer the critic's argument; the fact that someone refuses in the abstract to engage in comparison does not signal on its own the incommensurability of two values. What of the case when, as a matter of practical reasoning in a concrete situation, a response is sought regarding the two values and a decision is in fact given? In that case, says Raz, we should pay close attention to certain features.

First, "[t]he ability and willingness to choose does not depend on valuing the chosen option more than the rejected one. One is able to choose when the two are of exactly the same value, as well as when they are incommensurate." It might well be significant therefore that "[t]he fact of the choice does not reveal why it was made".[18] But when such a choice is made, does not this still amount to a comparison at some level being made between the two? To suggest otherwise, so the critic would argue, is to suggest the choice is made without criteria. Again, Raz would argue no. The second feature of a choice made in such circumstances would thus be as follows: the fact that a reason *can* be given still does not assume that a ranking between the two options has been made.

[17] As Berlin has suggested elsewhere, "in concrete situations not every claim is of equal force". See "The Pursuit of the Ideal", n. 10 above, 17.

[18] Raz, n. 16 above, 338.

As Raz says, "[t]hough the reason [given] is incommensurate with the reason for the alternative it shows the value of *that* option and when that option is chosen it is chosen because of *its* value".[19] In the example we are using, the choice to value friendship over money may be made in a particular case not because a comparison has been made, but because of the (again to use Berlin's phrase) ultimate value of friendship itself. One might, when pushed, say that one prefers the option of friendship over money, but that is because of what friendship is—what it means—in itself, not because it is better or worse than having a large sum of money. To suggest otherwise is to fail to pay attention to a third, temporal, feature. The fact that a choice has been made and a rationalisation given which appears to have ranked the two options does not mean that the way in which the decision was reached corresponds precisely with any reason that can be given after the event. As Raz puts it, "[i]f one takes seriously the early sincere refusal to compare the value of the different options then one must conclude that the test [for assigning judgments of comparative value] *changed* these people's valuations *rather than revealed them*".[20] This would seem to be an important, if not decisive, point. For to suggest that original valuations were revealed requires a specific mind-set in the first place. That is, it is only making the "*a priori* methodological commitment to commensurability"[21] that could preclude us from seeing this final feature.

Here we come to the crux of the argument, and a better way of understanding the ambiguity in Berlin's work as described above. The fact that a choice must be made does not assume that all values are commensurable. But neither does this mean that choices are arbitrary. There is still a role for reasoned conclusions in such cases. That there are, in Berlin's terms, no hard-and-fast rules according to which a decision must be made does not preclude the possibility that in the particular case a rational decision can be made. There is a difference between giving good reasons for deciding one way, and giving poor (or seemingly arbitrary) reasons. Coin-tossing may provide a reason for doing something, but while it may be a good one for deciding who kicks off a game of football it is not a good one for deciding between money and friendship, and there may be good reasons for this difference. But there is also a difference between producing good reasons in a particular case and suggesting that it is the application of reason that compares and decides

[19] *Ibid.*, emphasis added.
[20] *Ibid.*, 339, emphasis added.
[21] *Ibid.*

between two options when a choice is required. As Raz puts it, "[r]ational action is action for (what the agent takes to be) an undefeated reason. It is not necessarily action for a reason that defeats all others".[22] Berlin's concern with the use of the kind of reason he ascribes to those who endorse the "single all-embracing" power of reason is thus precisely directed against those who would query this statement. To defeat all other claims assumes the possibility of a ranking; but, as Raz suggests, in the kind of example we are considering, "[r]efusals to evaluate must be significant".[23] That is, rationality in this sense does not require the commensurability of all claims necessary in the production of a ranking. Indeed, as we shall see in the next section, rationality might require the *denial* of such ranking.

But for Berlin not only is the overriding of such a point dangerous, it is unfeasible; it treats incommensurability as a mistake, an error to be corrected, rather than (as Raz's example tends to show) a coherent possibility inherent in a genuine clash of values. Where refusals to rank are treated as insignificant or are overridden, such treatment acts as if incommensurability was not a reality on exactly the same grounds for both Berlin and Raz: the "*a priori* methodological commitment to commensurability". Berlin denies the soundness of this commitment and it is vital to understand why. In order to do so, we need to go further into his analysis of the relation between values and commitment. Only then will we find that his reduced notion of rationality becomes fully coherent.

(iii) *Values, Commitment and Identity*

A question MacIntyre raised might come back to haunt Berlin. Does Berlin's thesis about conflict and rationality mean that we have no shared standards of rationality to which we can appeal; no scales, in MacIntyre's image, on which we can weigh competing claims or conflicting ends or values? Moreover, if there are no such standards, and incommensurability of values is indeed the case, does this not reduce the self to a mere chooser of preferences, a self for whom the ultimate directive in making choices takes the form of "I want such-and-such to be the case"? Is his version of rationality no more than a smokescreen hiding what is in essence merely the will to power of an emotivist self? My reading of Berlin's version of liberalism will argue that such criticism is

[22] Raz, n. 16 above, 338.
[23] *Ibid.*, 336.

made ineffective, given the setting in which both rational judgement (in the sense I have begun to outline) and the incommensurability of values makes sense. To justify this reading I will again complement Berlin's analysis with some insights from the work of Raz.

Everything is as it is, but we cannot have everything. The need to choose is therefore, as noted above, an inalienable part of being human. Attempts can be made to deny that need, to ameliorate it by proposing harmonious systems where ends do not conflict. But, as ends do conflict—an empirical observation—curtailments of the ability to choose them for ourselves curtail a part of our humanity. Hence, for Berlin, the importance of negative liberty as a value, though not one that itself is to be upheld at all costs. Conflicts with other values must be addressed, though we have no clear-cut means of resolving *a priori* such conflicts. We seek, says Berlin, in a phrase that might be at home in many post-modern arguments, "to adjust the unadjustable".[24] But in doing so, in order to retain a semblance of the rationality that constitutes our being human as opposed to being automatons, we must maintain the possibility for our participation in such adjustment by allowing for the emergence of conflict as part of that ever-changing process of adjustment. Even if this "freedom to choose ends" is, as Berlin suggests, historically contingent, this makes it no less significant a part of our lives, and certainly no less valuable to us.

Why not? The reasons for Berlin lie in the reciprocal relations between the ability to choose between values, commitment to these values and the understanding of our identity. In fact the notion of reciprocity does not fully embrace the meaning and significance of these relations; they may be reciprocally related, but they are also, in a most important sense, constitutive relations. Choosing between values that conflict incommensurably, whilst essential to our rationality, is also a constitutive part of what it means to be human. In the most totalitarian regimes of the century, we find, Berlin argues, that when denial of incommensurability of values (in the name of a race, a nation, a greater good, or whatever) occurs, the price to be paid will include not just curtailment of certain liberties, but the very denial of humanity, of human identity, to individuals or groups. The reason for this is that the relations between values, choice, and commitment, are constitutive relations. As Berlin says:

[24] "Introduction" to *Four Essays*, n. 1 above, p. lv.

> In the end, men choose between ultimate values; they choose as they do, because their life and their thought are determined by fundamental categories and concepts that are, at any rate over large stretches of time and space, a part of their being and thought and sense of their own identity; part of what makes them human [at 172].

Thus the commitment to the values we hold, the meaning of these values to us, make us what we are as much as we make them what they are. This awareness of the constitutive relation of values and the self has important consequences. For one, it recognises the social construction of the self as a starting point for any further talk of morality and moral conflict. As he says, "[m]y individual self is *not* something which I can detach from my relationship with others, or from those attributes of myself which consist in their attitude towards me" (at 156, emphasis added). What this entails is thus the realisation of the inseparability of identity and its social embeddedness. Moreover it also collapses the possibility of maintaining the distinction between public and private in the way that we have seen Rorty trying to do. For, as Berlin argues:

> Even Mill's strenuous effort to mark the distinction between the spheres of private and social life breaks down under examination . . . some, perhaps all, of my ideas about myself, in particular my sense of my own moral and social identity, are intelligible only in terms of the social network in which I am an element [at 155–6].

With these words, Berlin gives the lie to the critique of liberalism based on the "fundamental contradiction" between self and society. How could this be a *contradiction* when the very relation between self and society is a constitutive one? There may well be political debate about what is to be defined as a private realm free from state intrusion, say, but this is different from saying that conflict begins when the self enters an arena in which it encounters multiple other selves that necessarily impinge upon its domain. As Gray writes (of Berlin's theory), "the particular selves which engage in self-creation by choice-making are themselves deposits of common forms of life".[25] Indeed, for Berlin himself, "I am in my own eyes as others see me . . . I feel myself to be somebody or nobody in terms of my position and function in the social whole; this is the most 'heteronomous' condition imaginable" (at 156).

There is, as I have suggested, a remarkable similarity here with Adam Smith's moral theory. David Hume's challenge to conventional epistemological enquiry had focussed in part on the fragmentary or protean

[25] Gray, n. 2 above, 159.

nature of identity.[26] "We may observe", Hume wrote for example, "that what we call a *mind*, is nothing but a heap or collection of different perceptions, united together by certain relations, and suppos'd, tho' falsely, to be endow'd with a perfect simplicity and identity".[27] The problem that his theory worked within saw its solution in the notion that, as George Davie has put it, "self-consciousness is inseparable from mutual consciousness".[28] At the level of perception it is also quite clear that Smith adopted this approach, as the following passage shows:

> Were it possible that a human creature could grow up to manhood in some solitary place, without any communication with his own species, he could no more think of his own character, of the propriety or demerit of his own sentiments and conduct, of the beauty or deformity of his own mind, than of the beauty or deformity of his own face. All these are objects which he cannot easily see, which naturally he does not look at, and with regard to which he is provided with no mirror which can present them to his view. Bring him into society, and he is immediately provided with the mirror which he wanted before.[29]

This is indeed strikingly similar to the "heteronomous condition" Berlin has just noted. Moreover, the problem transferred from Humean epistemology became evident in moral theory too, and became this: how on the one hand to accept that moral judgement is not based on reason and is always to some extent subjective, but on the other to explain actually existing shared moral standards and show that individual judgement is not simply a direct reflection of these standards.

To answer this Smith too argued that moral judgement and, indeed, like Hume, the self's identity itself, was inescapably rooted in its social context. As such his view of identity is replicated in terms of moral judgement. Again, for Smith:

> We begin, upon this account, to examine our own passions and conduct, and consider how these must appear to [others], by considering how they would appear to us if in their situation. We suppose ourselves the spectators of our own behaviour, and endeavour to imagine what effect it would, in this light, produce upon us. This is the only looking-glass by which we can, in some

[26] For an interesting overview of this issue in Scottish literature broadly at the time, see Kenneth Simpson's *The Protean Scot: The Crisis of Identity in Eighteenth Century Scottish Literature* (Aberdeen, AUP, 1988).

[27] David Hume, *A Treatise of Human Nature* (2nd edn., ed. L. A. Selby-Bigge, Oxford, Clarendon, 1978).

[28] George Davie, *The Crisis of the Democratic Intellect* (Edinburgh, Polygon, 1986), 136.

[29] Adam Smith, *The Theory of Moral Sentiments*, (6th edn., 1790, eds. D. D. Raphael and A. L. Macfie, Oxford, OUP, 1976), III.1.3.

measure, with the eyes of other people, scrutinize the propriety of our own conduct.[30]

Smith's was a highly sophisticated account of the development of morality from these social and spectatorial roots, and one, as MacIntyre noted, that was fundamentally at odds with the other Enlightenment tradition that stemmed from Reid and Kant. For Hume and Smith, morality could never be legitimised *a priori* by abstract rules of reason. On the contrary, moral evaluation lay in the realm of the interactive relations between real and imaginary spectators. Moral understanding was thus a process of mutual perception and adjustment amongst spectators, and, where the particular details of each case were of paramount importance, judgement could not be abstract nor found to be based on *a priori* criteria. In such a theory, and again in a way similar to Berlin's, the particular contexts of judging were of the utmost importance: as Smith says, sympathy, the human faculty for relating to others, "does not arise so much from the view of the passion, as from that of the situation which excites it".[31] Smith (and Hume before him) saw that questions of morality always came back to the sympathetic reactions of spectators, real or imaginary. Again, as Davie puts it, man:

> cannot know the limits and possibilities of his own personality until he is in a position to compare what he knows about himself by direct observation of his behaviour with other aspects of his behaviour, which are directly observable, not by himself, but by those living in day-to-day contact with him, and which he learns about from them, and could know nothing about apart from them.[32]

The concept of the impartial spectator was the highpoint of Smith's moral theory because it showed how, even though moral judgement was rooted in social practice rather than in the dictates of reason or of moral rules, an individual's judgement could transcend and critically reflect upon that social practice. But any such transcendence was always an outgrowth of such practice, and could never be separated from it. As Haakonssen points out:

[30] Adam Smith, *The Theory of Moral Sentiments*, (6th edn., 1790, eds. D. D. Raphael and A. L. Macfie, Oxford, OUP, 1976), III.i.5.

[31] *Ibid.*, I.i.1.10.

[32] Davie, n. 28 above, 116 (discussing C. M. Grieve's *A Drunk Man Looks at Thistle*). Robert Burns, conversant with Smith's work, succinctly summed up this position in his poem "To a Louse" as, "to see ourselves as others see us".

> just as with Hume, we must remember that in Smith's view men can never start morally from scratch: they are always living in a society and thus in a context of aims, values, and ideals. Moral evaluation is therefore only relevant in such a context. It is never a matter of goodness or badness, justice or injustice, *per se*; but of goodness or badness, etc., against the background of a number of other values.[33]

Significantly, and as a consequence of this approach, Smith in turn reinforced the limited role that reason played in moral judgement. Following Hume's lead, he wrote that "reason cannot render any particular object either agreeable or disagreeable to the mind for its own sake"[34]—tracing it to his teacher Hutcheson—and argued—with uncharacteristic derision—that "if any controversy is still kept up about this subject [that morality is not derived from reason], I can impute it to nothing, but either to inattention to what that gentleman [Hutcheson] has written, or to a superstitious attachment to certain forms of expression, a weakness not very uncommon amongst the learned".[35]

But if reason was, as Hume put it, "wholly inactive" as a source of morality, it was not completely redundant. For Smith the production of moral rules was an inductive process, and here reasoning from observation was valid. However, it is a mistake to presume, he says, that such rules as are produced can themselves be the original source of moral judgement. The rules of morality, he argues, "are ultimately founded upon experience of what, in particular instances, our moral faculties, our natural sense of merit and propriety, approve or disapprove of. We do not originally approve or condemn particular actions because, upon examination, they appear to be agreeable or inconsistent with a certain general rule."[36] So here we see quite clearly the sensitivity to the particular instance, yet, as with Berlin, the refusal to endorse the collapse of moral judgement when the role of reason is seen to be reduced.

Two other features of Smith's work are worthy of note in this context. First, Smith had an antipathy to what he called the "man of system" in much the same way as does Berlin. The problem with the "man of system", says Smith, is that he "erect[s] his own judgment into the supreme standard of right and wrong"; he thus fails to see that, "in the great chess-board of human society, every single piece has a principle of

[33] Knud Haakonssen, *The Science of a Legislator: The Natural Jurisprudence of David Hume and Adam Smith* (Cambridge, CUP, 1981), 62.

[34] Smith, *The Theory of Moral Sentiments*, n. 29 above, VII.3.2.7.

[35] *Ibid.*, VII.iii.2.9.

[36] *Ibid.*, III.4.8. Too-unsubtle critics of "the" Enlightenment would do well to keep such points in mind.

motion of its own, altogether different from what the legislature might chuse to impress upon it".[37] Within a theory of natural liberty, and though this was taken to be of greater import when applied to his writings on economics, it can be treated as a response to the kind of moral theory that would seek externally to impose standards and which neglected to account for the social contexts of moral judgement, the attention to particular circumstances which this required, and who was best placed to have and deal with such knowledge. As with Berlin, the "man of system" (and here it has been argued that Smith had in mind the recent revolution in France when revising his book in 1790) was to be treated with concern for precisely the reason that he tended to overlook the variability of contexts and reasonings that constituted the very existence of moral judgement.

Secondly, it is worth noting merely in passing, for we will return to this in more detail when we compare Berlin's thesis to MacIntyre's, that morality for Smith could never be seen as merely a way of (in MacIntyre's terms) satisfying preferences. Smith opened his *Theory of Moral Sentiments* by arguing that "[h]ow selfish soever man be supposed, there are evidently some principles in his nature, which interest him in the fortune of others, and render their happiness necessary to him, though he derives nothing from it except the pleasure of seeing it".[38] While Berlin's theory may question the use of human nature in Smith's sense, it seems nevertheless at one in seeing that morality is concerned with real relations with others and, in the processes of mutual adjustment that comprise moral understanding, that these processes can neither be divorced from their constitutive settings nor be treated as a way of simply lining up preferences. For Smith and, I would say Berlin, processes of adjustment, conflict and compromise are organic in a way that MacIntyre's conception of the emotivist self fails to grasp. Indeed it was precisely a failure to grasp this element of Smith's work that led to much intellectual effort being spent on trying to figure out "*das* Adam Smith *Problem*"; that is, how Smith's moral and economic theory could be thought of as compatible. Of course, this was not *Smith*'s problem, but one created by an ironic turn of intellectual events that saw his economic theory being divorced from the moral contexts within which he himself saw economic progress – and its attendant problems—occurring. Smith was arguably the last great thinker who, in these terms, tried to hold the two strands together in a conceptual unity, and it is a further,

[37] Smith, *The Theory of Moral Sentiments*, n. 29 above, VI.ii.2.17–18.
[38] *Ibid.*, I.i.1.

sad, irony that it was the power of his own economic thought, or rather the way in which it was utilised, that perhaps led him to be the last one who *could* do so.

Leaving Smith and returning to Berlin, it is for him impossible to separate self-identity (including moral identity) from its constitutive setting in social norms. As such, moral conflict cannot be simplistically treated as individual selves (and/or their wishes or preferences) colliding with others (and/or their wishes or preferences). Furthermore, nor can moral debate merely be treated as a way of, in the phrase used earlier, lining up those wishes or preferences that individuals express. For what collides in Berlin's analysis of moral conflict is not individuals or their preferences, but the values that they hold and which are constituted in and by them only as part of a "social pattern" in which those values and the individuals themselves exist. It is values that conflict incommensurably, not individuals or their preferences. Commitment to a particular set of values may well come from individuals themselves (it may come from groups too), but what those values themselves mean cannot be severed from their social and intellectual location: the "concepts and categories that dominate life and thought . . . are difficult, and practice impossible to think away".[39] They could certainly not be thought away by individuals for precisely the reason that they constitute the very ability to think—and even exist—as an individual. Of course, and just as Smith had shown in his notion of the impartial spectator, this did not mean that individuals were *simply* a reflection of external norms. It was possible, and indeed desirable, for the individual to transcend and reflect upon such norms; but it was not possible to escape them entirely. To realise this is finally to begin to answer MacIntyre's question about how shared or objective (or intersubjective) values are possible in a society where values conflict in a way that allows of no ultimate resolution. To see why, let us once again turn to the work of Raz to amplify Berlin's argument here.

In *The Morality of Freedom*, Raz argues for the existence of what he calls "constitutive incommensurabilities". These exist, he says, when in circumstances where two options are presented—A and B—one of three general features is observable. First, "[i]f A and B are incomparable options of this kind then if an agent is in a situation in which option A is his and B can be obtained by forgoing A he will normally refuse to do so". Secondly, such incommensurabilities "obtain between options

[39] Isaiah Berlin, "Introduction" to *Four Essays*, n. 1 above, p. liii.

which have special significance for people's ability successfully to engage in certain pursuits or relationships: the refusal to trade one option for the other is a condition of the agent's ability successfully to pursue one of his goals". Thirdly, "it is typical, where options of this kind are involved, for agents to regard the very thought that they may be comparable in value as abhorrent".[40]

In relation to the first and third features, we are already familiar with the significance that a refusal to evaluate might have on our understanding of the juxtaposition of two values as incommensurable. In the example that was used we saw that a refusal to compare friendship and monetary value did not necessarily mean that a ranking—based on the commitment to commensurability—had occurred, and that this was so even when a decision between the two was required of someone. We now turn to a further aspect of this scenario raised in particular by the second feature of constitutive incommensurability just introduced. For simplicity we will use the same example.

Two related aspects of the second feature are of paramount importance. They concern (from the quotation above) the "special significance for people's ability", and the idea of the refusal to trade options as a "condition". In Raz's analysis—which again I take to be a better developed though essentially similar one to Berlin's—the implications of a refusal to compare options depends upon the constitutive nature of the values involved. This in turn, as was seen, is a function of a practice that can only be understood as a social practice in which the meaning to the individual only makes sense as part of a wider "social pattern". Raz breaks these features down into two closely related parts: the "convention-dependency" of values, and their "symbolic significance".[41] Consider again our example: Can one compare friendship with monetary value?

Take friendship: the idea and existence of such an "institution" depends on certain socially-grounded conventions. This would seem to be uncontroversial. At its most basic level, one cannot be or have a friend without at least some other person with whom such a convention could be instituted. (One could, colloquially, be a "friend to oneself", but this still requires the existence of such an institution beyond oneself to make such a claim undertandable in the first place.) Such a convention will, in Raz's phrase, be most likely one of many "social forms which delineate the basic shape of the projects and relationships which

[40] Raz, n. 16 above, 346.
[41] *Ibid.*, 350.

constitute human well-being",[42] and one which, as the case of friendship makes quite clear, could not be reduced to a purely "atomistic" level. The institution is thus convention-dependent and is, therefore, irreducibly social.

But such conventions also have a symbolic dimension. By this Raz means, in brief terms, that "actions which are otherwise similar may differ in their meaning".[43] Consider the following example given by Raz. Imagine a situation in which it is proposed that someone leave their spouse for a specific time because they were offered a sum of money. Regardless of what one would do, the *symbolic* significance of one's act would differ (especially if one went away) in the situation where the money was to be gained by going away to carry out one's job, as compared to the situation in which the money was to be gained merely because it was a bribe to get one away from one's spouse. Where, in this example, one refused to go away in the second situation, the "crucial fact", says Raz is that "what has symbolic significance is the very judgment that companionship is incommensurable with money".[44]

And here we reach the general claim that he makes for constitutive incommensurabilities, namely, that "incommensurability is itself a qualification for having certain relations".[45] That is (and as it was expressed above in the second feature), the "special significance" of one of two proposed options leads to a refusal to trade options, and this refusal is itself "a *condition* of the agent's ability successfully to pursue one of his goals". So, for example, that one refuses to compare the value of friendship to the value of money is a condition for being capable of friendship at all; when asked how much friendship is worth—£10, £1,000, whatever—if the friendship is "worth" anything at all, one will reject the comparison out of hand. One refuses to put a (comparative) monetary value on friendship because a part of what constitutes the very meaning of friendship depends precisely on such a refusal: "[o]nly those who hold the view that friendship is neither better nor worse than money, but is simply not comparable to money or other commodities are *capable* of having friends".[46] To return to the language of commensurability, in such instances "failure of commensurability is a success".[47] For if one does otherwise, namely to put a monetary price on friendship,

[42] *Ibid.*, 348.
[43] *Ibid.*, 349.
[44] *Ibid.*, 350.
[45] *Ibid.*, 351.
[46] *Ibid.*, 352, original emphasis.
[47] *Ibid.*, 353.

then, says Raz, one is simply not capable of having friends. And it is the existence (or not) of this "capability" that shows the constitutive nature (to the individual) of commitment to certain values as they are expressed through the dimensions of convention and symbolic significance.

One more point needs to be added to this, and it ties in with something mentioned in the previous section. For Raz adds that just because one chooses money instead of friendship—it must be expressed this way since one could not successfully bring the two comparatively together without losing the capability for friendship—does not mean that one acts (in words reminiscent of Berlin's) "mistakenly, wrongly, or against reason". One simply becomes incapable of having friends. Similarly, were one to refuse to value money over friendship, it is equally possible to reason to that position. But in this latter instance such reasoning is *internal* to the convention and cannot be used to make commensurable two conflicting values. To repeat what was said above, "[t]hough the reason [given] is incommensurate with the reason for the alternative it shows the value of *that* option and when that option is chosen it is chosen because of *its* value".[48] Reasoning is internal to the practice in which the value of friendship, say, is found and cannot emerge across or transcend the two options given; thus "incommensurability forms the foundation of duties"[49] such as friendship.

To come up with reasons that could compare friendship and monetary value could only be done, so to speak, at a price; in this case, the loss of the ability to participate in the institution of friendship. Hence the full significance of the line also quoted in the previous section: "[i]ncommensurability speaks not of what does escape reason but of what must elude it". That is, what must elude it if the conventions and "social forms which delineate the basic shape of the projects and relationships which constitute human well-being"(supra) are not to be devalued or collapsed out of existence. It is clearly possible that they could be—as the case of choosing to compare money and friendship shows—but, as Raz rightly points out, "then life according to commensurate principles will be radically different from our own".[50] But if this is so, then the application of reason must have its limitations.

It is in this sense that I talk of ambiguity in Berlin's use of the idea of reason. For if reason's capability is not reduced, then success will mean failure: in making commensurable certain values, one is in serious

[48] Raz, n. 16 above, 338, emphasis added.
[49] *Ibid.*, 356.
[50] *Ibid.*, 357.

danger of losing the distinctive institutions with which we are familiar because the institutions which we value, and which in turn constitute our own sense of identity, depend for their very existence on retaining their incommensurability with other institutions. As Tolstoy put it, "[o]nce say that human life can be controlled by reason, and all possibility of life in annihilated". Not quite, we might say, but it would certainly be unrecognisably different.

But "not quite" in an important sense. For again as Raz's argument shows, not all reason is lost once one accepts incommensurability. Reasoning—and evalution and commitment—internal to an institution (such as friendship) is still required once one has accepted rather than rejected the possibility of that institution. And here again the dual aspects of convention and symbolic significance have to be constantly negotiated and weighed up. One can be a good friend or a poor friend. One can be a good lawyer (or parent or spouse or whatever), or a poor one. And being that "good" whatever is not something that any individual alone can define or seek simply as a preference. These are standards that cannot emanate from the individual; as Wittgenstein said of the practice of rule-following, there is a difference between *thinking* one is following a rule and following a rule.[51] In other words, within such conventions of the type we are discussing, there exist standards, the extent to which one's own input of definition will vary, but for which one will never be the sole source of definition so long as they remain rooted in social practices and in "concepts and categories" that as individuals we cannot choose, for the very reason that they choose us—they constitute our own sense of self—as much as we choose them.

Berlin is adamant that his version of value-incommensurability does not equate to relativism. This latter doctrine rests, he says, on the belief that all judgement is "the expression or statement of a taste, or emotional attitude or outlook . . . with no objective correlate which determines its truth or falsehood".[52] In the context of Raz's argument, it should be quite clear that although certain things must "elude reason" if we are to maintain them as they are, this does not mean that all standards of behaviour have no rational or intersubjective basis. Moreover, because of the constitutive nature of values and practices it would be difficult to shed such standards without losing (at least a part of) who we are. And this has been Berlin's point all along. The conflict

[51] Ludwig Wittgenstein, *Philosophical Investigations* (Oxford, Basil Blackwell, 1989), s. 202.

[52] "Alleged Relativism in Eighteenth-Century Thought", in n. 10 above, 80.

of incommensurable values plays a vital role in being able to hold on to certain institutions and ultimately a certain understanding of who we are or might want to be. When that conflict is thought to be eradicable—when "all values can be graded on one scale . . . to represent moral decision as an operation which a slide rule in principle could perform" (at 171)—we are in danger not just of suppressing contradictions, but in so far as these contradictions are constitutive, suppressing parts of who we are.

Incommensurabilities can therefore be seen as constitutive of institutions in and through which we commit and define ourselves. That we refuse to put a monetary value on friendship, say, makes us capable of participating in that institution. And commitment to the value of friendship helps—among a variety of other constitutive commitments—define who we are as persons at all. Moreover, admitting incommensurability does not, as we have seen, deny the possibility of rational behaviour—we are not mistaken, or deluded, because a greater reason or goal or value should not be allowed to overcome incommensurability. Reason, in the sense used by Raz and Berlin, is capable of directing our actions, but we should be aware that to maintain certain institutions it must be confined *within* these institutions. That reason can be circumscribed within limits does not lead to reason's complete demise since "it is not a requirement of reason that there should be one value which in all cases prevails over the other".[53] Just when such limits must be placed on reason must always remain open; they cannot be foreclosed by appeal to a higher standard that comes with the "*a priori* commitment to commensurability". Openness to conflict requires a commitment to conflict, and to incommensurability as a value itself. But, as we have seen, this is not a sign of some emotivist anomie for the very reason that it is a commitment to standards that are inescapable in large part because of their constitutive role.

When values are emaciated to become mere interests or preferences, they lose one of their most vital features. That is, interests or preferences (say as MacIntyre defines them) can indeed be tallied according to some ranking scheme. In MacIntyre's critique of liberalism such ranking usually takes the form of merely "lining up" or counting preferences; an inorganic *process* in other words. But Berlin's incommensurability thesis is equally critical of any such attempt to treat moral conflict as resolvable through any "operation which a slide rule in prin-

[53] Isaiah Berlin and Bernard Williams, "Pluralism and Liberalism: A Reply" (1994) *Political Studies* 306–9 at 307.

ciple could perform". Openness to conflict clearly has a price, in that it is messy conceptually and demanding politically. But for Berlin, unlike MacIntyre, that there are no "rational standards" which could resolve deep-seated conflicts is the—all too precarious—success of, and reason for commitment to, his version of liberalism.

(iv) *Authority and Expertise*

It is a notable feature of Berlin's liberalism that he is just as wary of the use of authority and expertise as is MacIntyre. His—Berlin's—antagonism towards experts stems from, as we have seen partly already, his fear that politics turn into merely an exercise in technical skill, into operations that, in his words, a slide-rule might perform. In decrying the state of affairs in which the possibility of conflict is subverted, his language is, if not redolent with scorn, then at least reminscent of Foucault:

> human behaviour can be manipulated with relative ease by technically qualified specialists—adjusters of conflicts and promoters of peace both of body and of mind, engineers and other scientific experts in the service of the ruling group, psychologists, sociologists, economic and social planners, and so on.[54]

What I want to explore in this section is the relation between expertise and authority, and to do so in order to draw out conclusions for the role of law within the picture of liberalism Berlin has portrayed. I will also, where appropriate, draw in part on a comparison with Foucault himself.

(a) Adjusting Conflict

In an earlier section we considered Berlin's analysis of Kant as an example of just how it might be possible for well-intentioned rationalist theories to be used to stifle conflict when they employed a singular use of reason allied to the notion of "man's true self". It will be recalled that where the latter idea was proposed it became possible for some to speak in the name of others where those others were taken to be defective in their use of the universal faculty of reason, and to do so without necessarily appearing to constrict either their freedom or their rationality. "Even Kant", Berlin writes, "when he came to deal with political issues, conceded that no law, provided that it was such that I should, if I were

[54] Isaiah Berlin, "Political Ideas in the Twentieth Century" in *Four Essays*, n. 1 above, 29.

asked, approve it as a rational being, could possibly deprive me of any portion of my rational freedom" (at 152). While Berlin is prepared to admit that the argumentative steps traceable from a rationalist theory such as Kant's to practices of "an authoritarian state" are "not logically valid"—they indeed constitute a "strange reversal"—they remain, however, "historically and psychologically intelligible" (*ibid.*). Why this is so was hinted at earlier, but needs now to be brought out in the present context.

Berlin's by now familiar complaint against a use of reason that sees deviance as the result of irrationality suggests that, while perhaps not faulty at a purely intellectual level, it nonetheless creates in its sociological dimension practical consequences of great magnitude. Again returning to Kant, the problem lies in the institutional vesting that occurs when considering the idea that a law would not impinge on an individual's freedom where that law was rationally grounded, and thus be approved of by all rational beings. The problem here is primarily practical, but one which is for all that highly significant. For when it comes to "political issues" one "*cannot* consult all men about all enactments all the time" (at 152, emphasis added). Theories such as Kant's (and, as we will see, Rawls too) lose much in translation to practice. For there is a gap here – to say the least—between democracy and rationality, and in this space, says Berlin, "the door was opened wide to the rule of experts" (*ibid.*).

The philosophical argument here should be reasonably familiar. Since "the pronouncements of reason must be the same in all minds" (at 153), those who do not act according to reason must be treated as having an incomplete grasp of what reason requires. Beyond reason in this scenario lies unreason, irrationality. But, when it comes to practical or political matters or the creation of laws, the gap exposed—that "one cannot consult all men about all enactments all the time"—becomes even more important. Berlin, in the following passage, assumes the voice of the benign rationalist legislator to explain the consequences:

> I issue my orders, and if you resist, take it upon myself to repress the irrational element in you which opposes reason. My task would be easier if you repressed it in yourself; I try to educate you to do so. But I am responsible for public welfare, I cannot wait until all men are wholly rational. Kant may protest that the essence of the subject's freedom is that he, and he alone, has given himself the order to obey. But that is a counsel of perfection. If you fail to discipline yourself I must do so for you; and you cannot complain of lack of freedom, for the fact that Kant's rational judge has sent you to prison

> is evidence that you have not listened to your own inner [objective] reason, that, like a child, a savage, an idiot, you are not ripe for self-direction or permanently incapable of it [*ibid.*].

The link between expertise and authority is made when one substitutes in that last sentence the word "judge" for any other expert in a given field. The institutional vesting, as I have called it, of expertise can and does occur in a broad range of activities, and the assumption of authority that it adopts follows the logic of "reason versus unreason" in its justification for directing behaviour. Here we find entering the "psychologists, sociologists, economic and social planners"—all the "adjusters of conflict"—that were mentioned at the start of this section. But there is more to Berlin's critique here than a rehashing (or in fact prehashing) of ideas with which we are familiar since at least the work of Foucault. As far as Berlin is concerned, again with his eye on the totalitarian regimes of Europe in the earlier part of the century (though once again he says his observation applies to "all stable societies"[55]), the use of experts is intimately linked with the notion of system-maintenance. Here the "adusters of conflict", in whatever guise they may appear, are "harnessed to producing the maximum of unclouded social contentment compatible with opposition to all experiment outside the bounds of the system".[56] The tendency to reduce conflict, through a calculus of utility and albeit for the contentment of the many, thus requires the ability to suppress dissent in the name of a system which seeks stabilisation through the ability to neutralise attacks on itself. The most effective means of doing so is of course to attempt to place beyond the bounds of conflict those matters that appear to challenge the system; in other words to turn the sources of *political* challenge and conflict into disagreement merely about the means to ends already assumed. Moreover, once this stabilisation is seen to be protective of the interests of a significant "many", the desire to curtail conflict, to curtail meaningful politics, becomes potentially overwhelming. This is how Berlin puts it, and his observation now applies equally he says to "western" societies:

> Growing numbers of human beings are prepared to purchase this sense of security even at the cost of allowing vast tracts of life to be controlled by persons who, whether consciously or not, act sytematically to narrow the horizon of human activity to manageable proportions, to train human beings into

[55] "Political Ideas in the Twentieth Century", in n. 1 above, 29.
[56] *Ibid.*

> more easily combinable parts of a total pattern . . . to stabilize, if need be, at the lowest level.[57]

Clearly in these circumstances the role of experts becomes crucial. In the "end of politics" scenario with which Berlin is centrally concerned, experts both play the stabilising role within the system and provide opportunities for removing or "adjusting" conflictual debate to the realm of disagreement over fact. When this neutralisation occurs, authority ceases to be challengeable on political terms, since it tends to assume a form in which that authority appears as simply the application of expert technique, as unproblematic, and therefore incontestible. Here, in other words, Berlin sees the danger of (quoting St-Simon's phrase) the government of man being replaced by the administration of things; the instability and inefficiency of critical pursuits being subjected to the "approbation of the official auditor".[58]

Once again the issue of commensurability raises its head, though this time we find its exemplification in more expressly sociological rather than philosophical terms. For the tendency Berlin identifies, which sees the reduction of political conflict to debate over means to pregiven ends, has as its adjunct the rhetoric and authority of experts to define or "canalise" dispute in a particular way, to reduce what may or may not be genuine value conflict over "ends equally ultimate" to the homogenising language of the expert. In contemporary settings, says Berlin, that language is most often one associated with therapy. Today, he says:

> interests are all conceived almost entirely in therapeutic terms: tensions that need to be released, wounds, conflicts, fixations, "phobias" and fears, psychical and psycho-physical abnormalities of all sorts which require the aid of specialised healers—doctors, economists, social workers, teams of diagnosticians or engineers or other masters of the craft of helping the sick and the perplexed.[59]

It is interesting to note here that in one respect Berlin is openly ambivalent about such developments. He is quite clear that progress has been and is being made in certain areas often associated with the power of experts. Indeed, he gladly endorses many such developments. As he says, "to the degree to which such suffering exists and can be treated by the applied sciences . . . such policies are, of course, entirely beneficent and their organized support is a great moral asset to an age and a coun-

[57] "Political Ideas in the Twentieth Century", in n. 1 above, 30.
[58] *Ibid.*, 40.
[59] *Ibid.*, 34–5.

try".[60] He writes elsewhere of such institutions as public education and public health services that would easily fit this mould. But what he does not problematise is the apparently relaxed claim that "where such suffering exists and can be treated" then it is worthwhile; that is, he does not go into the particular realms of therapeutic practices to pursue in detail issues of the construction of knowledge and its effects within them. Moreover he does not dwell on the interrelations between bodies of expertise to any great extent. Instead his ambivalence comes to rest on the assumption that there is *always* a flip-side to advances in the use of expertise as a justification for state or professional intervention. There is always, in other words, a danger, a "tendency", an incipient threat, that exists when the exercise of authority becomes clouded in the language of the expert. This danger takes the form of a tendency "to assimilate all men's primary needs to those that are capable of being met by these methods: the reduction of all questions and aspirations to dislocations which the expert can set right".[61]

The use of the term "dislocations" signals the return of an idea we explored earlier, namely Berlin's treatment of techniques which work to rectify a disjuncture between reason and unreason, which act upon the assumption of correcting mistakes in the name of a single authoritative reason (or indeed of any overarching theme—the victory of the proletariat, the destiny of a race, whatever). But just as Berlin argued against the desirability of such a notion of reason because of its dependency on an (invalid) "*a priori* commitment to commensurability", so once again he runs empirical and evaluative claims together when he comes to deal with the sociological realm of the expert. For the problem with attempts to set right, to "heal", wounds, phobias, etc. as part of an overall therapeutic approach is that it tends to assume that very same logic of commensurability that reduces conflict to irrationality, deviance to error, and values to interests. And this, he says, is the ever-present danger:

> Some believe in coercion, others in gentler methods; but the conception of human needs in their entirety as those of the inmates of a prison or a reformatory or a school or a hospital, however sincerely it may be held, is a gloomy, false, and ultimately degraded view, resting on the denial of the rational and productive nature of all, or even the majority of, men.[62]

Once again the bottom line for Berlin is the empirical evidence that people will disagree about the ultimate values of life, and where the

60 *Ibid.*, 35.
61 *Ibid.*
62 *Ibid.*

existence of this disagreement is threatened by the "adjustment" of conflicts by experts as if it did not exist, then Berlin sees the potential for the occurrence of the denial of that which makes us human. Two of the trends Berlin identifies with the collapsing of values into interests and the denial of the "rational and productive nature of all" are "American 'materialism'" and "communist or nationalist fanaticism",[63] and it is easy to see that his antipathy exists towards both, to the extent that they deny conflict through the endorsement of a therapeutic commensurability instituted by experts of the market, the party, or any other promoters and stabilisers of the "system". Thus we discover his wariness of expertise, and, in his ambivalence, his fear that any "remedy grows to be worse than the disease".[64]

But still the ambivalence remains, and indeed, for Berlin, so it must. The main reason is that Berlin's approach is not an emancipatory one. As we saw earlier, for Berlin we cannot escape the "concepts and categories" through which we live, because these, and the values that coexist in and through them, constitute our sense of understanding in the first place, constitute in fact our very sense of being. The problem he associates with the power of experts is that where there must be compromise between ends equally ultimate, those tendencies to think conflict away that he sees being a part of even the best-intentioned therapeutic institutions and discourses are always in danger of overriding the potential for conflict between those disparate and equally ultimate ends. It is not that there can ever be an undistorted compromise, but instead that the institutional and rhetorical power of experts usually tends to obscure the nature of fundamental disagreement and treat it in the same way as it treats an illness in need of a cure.

The issue here is as much definitional as anything else. That is, it concerns the power to define: "what this age needs", argues Berlin:

> is not more faith, or stronger leadership, or more scientific organisation. Rather it is the opposite—less Messianic ardour, more enlightened scepticism, more toleration of personal idiosyncrasies . . . more room for the attainment of personal ends by individuals and minorities whose tastes and beliefs find (whether rightly or wrongly must not matter) little response among the majority.[65]

The power to define, or define away, idiosyncrasies or values or goals, given that such power is linked inextricably to the very possibility of

63 "Political Ideas in the Twentieth Century", in n. 1 above, 35.

64 *Ibid.*, 39.

65 *Ibid.*, 39–40.

identity, must be treated cautiously, suspiciously. And, when its effect is to reduce identity to merely following a programme or treatment diagnosed by the experts, thereby reducing identity and politics to the patient or schoolchild in need of correction, to create or maintain avenues of challenge.

We come back then full circle to the requirement for politics as an argument about identity. And the threat of expertise must always be treated as precisely that for Berlin; namely, a threat, a danger that would lead to the cutting off or wishing away of the very conceptual tensions and conflicts that make us what we are. The struggle against this danger is ongoing, for the threats come not only from the power of experts to define discrepant identity as in need of therapy, but also from the very tendency of ideas themselves to harden into constricting presences: "the history of thought and culture is", he says, "a changing pattern of great liberating ideas which inevitably turn into suffocating straight-jackets, and so stimulate their own destruction by new, emancipating, and at the same time, enslaving concepts".[66] Where this history is overlooked, ignored or, at the very worst denied by the power of experts to dominate agendas on what ideas are permissible at all, then the danger exists and should be noted and, if necessary, acted upon. The problem Berlin sees with the illiberal tendencies of contemporary society is precisely that as expertise and authority coalesce within the stabilising requirements of the system, it potentially becomes harder and harder not just to act on this danger, but even to note it in the first place.

(b) Openness and Closure

Though Berlin does not make the distinction Foucault does between juridical and disciplinary power, nor does he attempt anything like the in-depth analysis of the dispersion and techniques of power that one finds in the work of Foucault, there are in the current context at least some similarities in their central preoccupations. At the level of Berlin's "concepts and categories", Foucault sees in the notion of "subjugated knowledges" which form the focus of his genealogical studies, the same concerns as those identified by Berlin. By subjugated knowledges Foucault means:

> the historical contents that have been buried and disguised in a functionalist coherence or formal systemization . . . [and which draw attention to] the

[66] Isaiah Berlin, "Does Political Theory Still Exist?" in P. Laslett and W. G. Runciman (eds.), *Philosophy, Politics and Society* (Second Series) (Oxford, Basil Blackwell, 1969), 19.

> ruptural effects of conflict and struggle that the order imposed by functionalist or systematizing thought is designed to mask.[67]

What the "genealogical project" seeks to do, then, is:

> to entertain the claims to attention of local, discontinuous, disqualified, illegitimate knowledges against the claims of a unitary body of theory which would filter, hierarchize and order them in the name of some true knowledge and some arbitrary idea of what constitutes a science and its objects.[68]

The ambiguity in Foucault's use of the term illegitmate here is precisely that which Berlin draws attention to in his plea for greater tolerance toward "idiosyncracy"; it is not that some knowledge or identity is illegitimate or idiosyncratic as such, but that it has been made so and becomes threatened by the "unitary body of theory" that seeks to define it as such for specific purposes. Foucault's subjugated knowledges then must seek to "wage their struggle" against "the coercion of a theoretical, unitary, formal and scientific discourse",[69] much in the same way as Berlin's "idiosyncrats" must fight against the power of the homogenising tendencies of the single all-embracing system in whatever form that may take.

While in Berlin's version of liberalism the very existence of the individual is not problematised as it is in Foucault's work, it does however see the power to define as crucially implicated in the struggle to maintain and subvert identities. For Berlin, the link between authority and expertise is paralleled in Foucault's reading of the complex relation between power and knowledge in disciplinary discourses. As Foucault says, "[w]e are concerned with the insurrection of knowledges that are opposed primarily not to the contents, methods or concepts of a science, but to the effects of the centralising powers which are linked to the institution and functioning of an organised scientific discourse within a society such as ours".[70] Moreover, the problem of the "hardening" of new, potentially liberating, knowledges, that Berlin identified in the history of ideas, is the same for Foucault when he asks of the status of subjugated knowledges, "if we want to protect these only lately liberated fragments are we not in danger of ourselves constructing, with our hands, that unitary discourse to which we are invited . . . ?"[71] For both writ-

[67] Michel Foucault, "Two Lectures" in W. Connolly (ed.), *Legitimacy and the State* (Oxford, Basil Blackwell, 1984), 202.

[68] *Ibid.*, 204.

[69] *Ibid.*, 205.

[70] *Ibid.*, 204.

[71] *Ibid.*, 206.

ers there appears to be an undeconstructible tension between subjugating and subjugated knowledges, combined, again in both, with the need for a theoretical and public vigilance in regard to what exactly it is that is being masked.

Finally, where Berlin sees threats of control coming to be located in the power of the "therapeutic", Foucault, as is well-known, identifies the "global functioning of . . . a *society of normalisation*"[72] as one of the defining features of disciplinary discourses. Yet what I take to be significant about Berlin's liberalism in this context is, as I have noted, his sweeping indictment of the possibility of a liberatory discourse. For him, as we have seen, there may be positive, even moral, advances, in the institutionalised use of therapy (though there is always potentially a price attached). Yet the idea that it would be possible to escape aspects of normalisation, in the sense of escaping from normative influence at all, is as ridiculous for him as saying (as we saw earlier) that when reason cannot be used to make all values commensurable all choices therefore become arbitrary. Significantly, the effect of this realisation is also to disallow the kind of liberalism Rorty espouses that would see the possibility of a private realm of self-redescription as existing quite separately from the broader political realm. In drawing attention to the link between expertise and identity, Berlin cannot be so naïve as to assume, as Rorty appears to, that a private realm can ever be cut off from the public realm of politics. Any private realm for Berlin will be existent only as it is contested within the larger normative and political framework of which it is a part, and exist as such in a state of reflexive and partly constitutive tension. This is why politics as conflict is so central to Berlin's liberalism, and hence also why, like Foucault, he is so keen to view the role of experts as integrally bound up with the exercise of authority.

The liberty with which Berlin is so concerned in his "Two Concepts" is thus construed as a contested but significant value in the ability constantly to be alert to the processes of homogenisation and normalisation that he sees in contemporary society. Where these processes are instituted or augmented by the dominant dicourses of therapeutic expertise, then they ought to be opened to challenge. The irony is, of course, that, as these processes themselves become more effective, the possibility for a politics that would maintain the openness to conflict itself recedes. Hence again, for Berlin, the importance of the value of being able to

[72] *Ibid.*, 220, original emphasis.

challenge authority as such, and the difference he sees between this and the desire to have authority in one's own hands. Clearly related—"twin brothers" even—these two values play out quite differently in cases when it is either not possible to consult everyone all the time or when the paternalism of expertise assumes that it is neither necessary nor desirable to do so. Expertise and authority, twin brothers themselves we might say, must then be constantly opened to critique in Berlin's liberalism in order that, for him, politics and identity do not become something that either a slide-rule or a headache tablet might adequately deal with.

It now remains in this chapter to turn our attention to that aspect of authority that we have not yet explored, in order to complete, for present purposes, the picture of liberalism Berlin has drawn.

Law and Politics

Roger Hausheer, in whose praise Berlin could drown, suggests that Berlin has provided "one of the most complete, cogent, formidable and satisfying accounts of the radical liberal humanist conception of man and his predicament that has ever been formulated".[73] If this is so, then Berlin does not seem to have thought that distinct attention to law was required for such an account. There is, scattered through Berlin's writings, mention of law, but little systematic treatment of it. Rather than try to build up a coherent picture from what does exist I intend in this section to outline first a duality appreciable in Berlin's work regarding the relation between law and conflict and, secondly, to draw out some tentative conclusions for the use of law in the "radical liberal" theory Berlin does offer us. To do this I will build on the features of his liberalism that have already been discussed, and add a few more where they seem necessary. Let us turn first to the duality.

(i) *A Duality*

Hausheer is correct to say that Berlin's is a humanist approach. What might distinguish it from many recent postmodern writings with which I have said it has some affinity is Berlin's strong belief in certain empir-

[73] Roger Hausheer, "Introduction" to Isaiah Berlin, *Against the Current: Essays in the History of Ideas* (ed. H. Hardy, Oxford, Clarendon Press, 1981), p. liii.

ically observable features of human beings against which the "all-embracing systems" and the powers of therapeutic experts may do damage. We have seen earlier how the ability to choose, to behave rationally according to one's or one's group's appreciation of what is valuable, is central to Berlin's conception of human identity. Implicit, then, in Berlin's work is, so to speak, a consensual norm which should not be breached if the very idea of humanity as we know it is minimally to stay intact. In an essay entitled "European Unity and its Vicissitudes", Berlin makes clearer what this is:

> if we meet someone who cannot see why (to take the famous example) he should not destroy the world in order to relieve a pain in his little finger, or someone who genuinely sees no harm in condemning innocent men, or betraying friends, or torturing children . . . they are as much outside the frontiers of humanity as creatures who lack some of the minimal physical characteristics that constitute human beings. We lean on the fact that the laws and principles to which we appeal, when we make moral and political decisions of a fundamental kind, have, unlike legal enactments, been accepted by the majority of men, during, at any rate, most of recorded history . . . we cannot conceive of getting these universal principles or rules repealed or altered . . . [because they are] presuppositions of being human at all, of living in a common world with others, of recognising them, and being ourselves recognised, as persons.[74]

This is what I will call the first part of the duality. If it sounds like a minimalist natural law position, Berlin openly agrees. The main difference between his and traditional and many modern natural law theorists is, however, that Berlin refuses to treat such fundamental principles as he thinks do exist as having "theological or metaphysical foundations".[75] They find their origin instead in the empirical observation of rules of behaviour and their universality in their acceptance by a majority of people over time. They constitute what I have called a consensual norm, which, when rejected, disallows us from living in the common world of humanity.

The examples Berlin gives above of what constitutes this norm are, I imagine, quite unproblematic, yet his expression finds him perhaps unguarded. For there is here a curious mixture between the normative and the descriptive which he seems unwilling to problematise. It is instructive that he should use a physical comparison in the above extract to make his point. Thus he says that universality is a feature of

[74] "European Unity and its Vicissitudes," in n. 10 above, 204.
[75] *Ibid.*

observation: just as we might say that most cows over time have tails and most humans do not, an animal with a tail, while not necessarily a cow, is probably not a human; it is barred from being called human because of the classification of what a human is (an animal without a tail). Likewise, the argument runs, a person who sees no problem in torturing innocent children is "inhuman", since one of the requirements of being human is to treat torturing innocent children as wrong. Yet, we do not have to stretch our minds too far to notice a difference between physical classification and the normative power that attaches to moral principles. Moreover, just what features count as so essential that to override them makes us inhuman would seem to be clearly a matter of degree, of political debate. Is work such a feature—or play? In other words, though Berlin does not produce a list of what these universal features are, once we imagine starting to go beyond the ones he does list, we come up against clear definitional difficulties. Nevertheless it does seem that Berlin believes some such features can be identified, and the reason he sees identification in at least certain instances as unproblematic is that their identification depends not upon *a priori* criteria, but upon observation over time.

There thus exists a second part to the duality, and this is where contestation about moral and political principles takes place in a far more conflictual manner. Here the degree of universality is rightly seen as problematic and the force of principles opened to debate. Here now we see a different approach to the nature of conflict. As he writes:

> When such canons seem less universal, less profound, less crucial, we call them, in descending order of importance, customs, conventions, manners, taste, etiquette, and concerning these we not only permit but actively expect wide differences. Indeed we do not look upon variety as being itself disruptive of our basic unity; it is uniformity that we consider to be the product of a lack of imagination, or of philistinism, and in extreme cases, a form of slavery.[76]

Here we return to the familiar terrain of Berlin's dislike of uniformity. But what this duality draws attention to is the minimal consensual level that such conflictual debate requires in order to take place in the first place. This is not of course to suggest that all would-be first principles are not themselves debatable; presumably Berlin would think that they may well be, but that there are at least some which no-one who called themselves human would deny, and that this can be confirmed by obser-

[76] "European Unity and its Vicissitudes," in n. 10 above, 205.

vation. But it is upon this minimalist edifice—which "constitutes our basic unity"—that all further politics takes place. Anything beyond those most basic principles not only is, but should be, opened to the broadest range of dissent: as he says, "we not only permit but actively expect wide differences". Here then we find the equally ultimate values, the incommensurably varied ends which different people pursue and which the "all-embracing systems or solutions" would hamper. But these conflicts should not be seen as "disruptive of our basic unity"; indeed, they are, in a final ambiguity, required to combat the possibilities of extending that basic unity too far.

We thus end up with another tension in Berlin's work: a minimal requirement of unity and an expression of fear that too much be done in the name of unity. But this tension is again constitutive; "temperaments differ", he says at one point, "and too much enthusiasm for common norms can lead to intolerance".[77] Hence the vigilance he espouses to keep channels of conflict open, to sustain that discord that does not disrupt the basic unity, to stem the curtailment of politics that would take place in the name of those who know what the true self, or proletarian, or nationalist, requires. And, finally, his belief that, historically, attention to negative liberty has been less destructive of this meaning of politics than that which has been carried out in the name of positive liberty.

If this minimalist, empirically-grounded, natural law is like other forms of natural law, it will exist even though it is not recognised in particular legal systems at particular times. And indeed this is the case as far as Berlin is concerned; basic principles have been, and no doubt continue to be, breached. But to the extent that such principles are not given legal backing, there would be clearly a moral imperative to try to institute them. But what of the "principles of dissent"? How should legal institutions deal with that second aspect of the duality, that part where conflict does and should take place? To answer this we need to extrapolate from Berlin's "radical liberalism" and make the best of the small insights on law we get from his work.

(ii) *Challenging Liberalism*

John Gray has recently drawn attention to what he sees as the distinctive radicalism of Berlin's "agonistic liberalism" as it compares with traditional and even most modern liberal theories. Where these latter, he

[77] "Introduction" to *Four Essays*, n. 1 above, pp. lvii–lviii.

says, attempt to draw a distinction between the right and the good they tend to see the institutionalisation of liberalism as a way of setting in place a framework of rights within which the pursuit of disparate goods can occur. In his words:

> in this standard liberal view, principles of justice or liberty are not substantive goods to be traded off against other goods, but regulative principles, principles of right which set the terms on which competing goods and conceptions of the good can be pursued. Liberal principles of justice and liberty are deontic principles which specify constraints on the pursuit of goods; they are in a different category from the goods themselves.[78]

What is intriguing about Berlin's thesis, however, is that it refuses to accept this distinction. While it does, as we have just seen, adopt a stance towards certain criteria as being essential to human beings as such—at least as perceived as such by most people over time—it rejects the possibility that when it comes to conflict it should be possible to set in place neutral laws of right within which that conflict should occur. The reason for this goes back to the incommensurability thesis discussed earlier; and, if it is correct, the consequences are indeed radical. Again in Gray's words, "[t]he central flaw in this common [standard liberal] reasoning is in the assumption that principles of liberty or justice can be insulated from the force of value-incommensurability. If Berlin is on the right track, this is an illusion, since there are conflicting liberties, rival equalities, and incompatible demands of justice".[79] We will come shortly to look at how this compares with MacIntyre's critique of liberalism, but first let us look a little further at the reasoning here.

We will remember from earlier Berlin's line that everything is as it is, that a clash of values may not be a mistaken interpretation of one genuine or overarching value, but instead be a real and incommensurable clash of values equally ultimate. The value of justice might clash with the value of liberty, and concepts of liberty may themselves clash with other concepts of liberty. What Gray is getting at is that, given this argument, it becomes unfeasible to suggest that there are existent principles of justice or liberty on which we all agree, perhaps even minimally, which could either direct the rational resolution of a genuine clash of values, or, for that matter, act as a framework within which the pursuit of disparate goods could take place. In refusing to draw the distinction between the right and the good, Berlin takes the notion of

[78] Gray, n. 2 above, 146–7.
[79] *Ibid.*, 147.

value-incommensurability to the point where there are not or, at least, there should not be, uncontested singular principles which, when applied, allow us to produce criteria of right. As Gray pointed out, to do otherwise is to insulate any such principles from the incommensurability thesis itself; that is, it is to fail to realise the absolute conflicts amongst values themselves, and thus would put principles of right beyond the pale of politics.

But why is it also the case that there "should not be" such principles? The answer can be found in Raz's analysis of incommensurability: "incommensurability speaks not of what does escape reason, but of what must elude it". That is, it means that reason, as we saw earlier, should play a limited role in attempts at resolving clashes between values. To insulate certain principles from contestation, in the form of instituting them as right say, may work to override and mask the genuine clash of values taking place. Furthermore, and this again was the significant point we saw earlier, there are good reasons why reason—or any putative overarching principle—should be limited in this way: there are "social forms" (Raz) that would be in danger of disappearing otherwise. This will be the case not just for the example of friendship we considered, but by extension also for conflicting values "embedded in different cultural traditions".[80] As Gray notes:

> The standard view that liberal principles are regulative principles which can be insulated in their content and their application from deep conflicts of values suppresses the fact that the liberties and equalities these principles specify derive all their content and weight from their contribution to forms and aspects of human flourishing which themselves generate such conflicts.[81]

What I think Gray is suggesting here can be traced through aspects of Berlin's thesis with which we are already familiar.

Primarily, it means that what I called earlier the reciprocal or constitutive relation between values, commitment and identity, and the importance of conflict to that relation, becomes integral itself to the critique of a rationalist liberalism that would seek to set in place a theory of rights incontestible both at the level of content and at the level of interpretation. That is, Berlin's thesis attacks the very core notion of traditional liberalism that would see general regulatory principles being put in place to allow for the flourishing of disparate views of the good. Moreover, it would deny that such principles as were put in place were

[80] *Ibid.*
[81] *Ibid.*, 148.

in fact neutral as to competing values or views of the good. What Gray thus suggests merely confirms our earlier analysis of Berlin's liberalism, yet it points to some remarkable conclusions.

The inability rationally to resolve certain clashes of values lies in the very heart of Berlin's thesis about both incommensurability and the limited role of reason as they relate to the constitutive relations between values and identity. But if it is the case that resolution of conflict cannot, and in certain instances—in those cases where we have a clash of values equally ultimate—should not, be finally resolvable, then this has clear implications for the meaning of such compromises that are reached. What Berlin's argument brings out is that the reaching of compromises in cases of incommensurable clashes always involves the potential for harming identities since the genesis of the clash is rooted in the commitment to values that are themselves integral in defining identities and the social forms and institutions within which they exist and make sense. Berlin refuses to acknowledge that a neutral framework can be set up within which clashes can take place for precisely this reason. Thus the *terms* of such frameworks as do exist are no less susceptible to claims of incommensurability than the forms of good they are supposed to allow to flourish. Moreover, they no less embody a claim to a view of the good than do the other goods they would seek to adjudicate between. Berlin cannot therefore be committed to a proceduralist version of liberalism since any procedures will themselves be, and indeed ought to be, just as open to conflict as any other claims that are made, as they are just as supportive of any particular values they embody.

In order to hold to this insight, it would seem necessary to set certain bounds on the exercise of authority, a point I will return to later. As we have seen already, Berlin is wary of the use of expertise because of the effects it may have on the way in which conflict is channelled or diverted. Yet if this is true, then the authority of law and the expertise of lawyers must similarly be questioned. The *problem* Berlin perceived with the use of expertise has been outlined already, and is worth repeating here:

> It consists [he says], not in developing the logical implications and elucidating the meaning, the context, or the relevance and origin of a specific problem—in seeing what it "amounts to"—but in altering the outlook which gave rise to it in the first place . . . The worried questioner of political institutions is thereby relieved of his burden and freed to pursue socially useful tasks, unhampered by disturbing and distracting reflections which have been eliminated by the eradication of their cause.[82]

[82] Berlin, n. 3 above, 23.

In a later chapter I will develop more fully the argument about how contemporary law and legal reasoning tend to "eradicate" the causes and original contexts of "specific problems", but already within the confines of Berlin's theory we can see how the reluctance to accept any overarching formula to resolve political problems must have consequences for the role of law as an authoritative resolver of social problems. This is due not merely to the fact that even liberal theories of law must fail to produce neutral standards of adjudication, but because of the deeper claim that the exercise of legal authority is itself susceptible to the very claims made against other disciplines of expertise. For it too comes with the same tendencies and dangers to mask and distort conflict, and hence to treat individuals or groups as in need of treatment, as does any other exercise of expert authority. Berlin's argument must therefore acknowledge that, in Foucault's terms, "law's power is also, and most importantly, disciplinary".[83] If this is so, then presumably law's exercise of authority, as well as its techniques for resolving conflict must be opened to the same kind of political critique as other expert disciplines.

(iii) *Trade-offs*

I want to suggest both that this follows from Berlin's work and that it constitutes in its radicalism a departure from other liberal legal theories. However, there is an instructive objection that can be brought in at this point, and it is one suggested by Perry Anderson. While Anderson also draws attention to Berlin's lack of treatment of law in his theory of liberalism, he nevertheless reads Berlin's version of value-pluralism as one that ultimately suffers a failure of nerve, a failure to live up to its potentially radical premises. He suggests that "beneath the surface radicalism of Berlin's assertion of irreducibly discrepant norms lies a tacit ecumenicism willing to compound them".[84] One reason he sees this is because he takes the "minimalist natural law" position which I identified earlier in Berlin's work as such a pervasive and significant bedrock for his theory that it actually shifts the balance away from radicalism and towards a universalist moral position. But more than this, it also shifts the focus, he argues, away from conflict over values to one that rests on a theory of choice. As he says, "[a]lthough [Berlin's philosophy] appeals to our intuitive sense of the rewards of human difference for much of

[83] Sheila Duncan, "Law's Sexual Discipline: Visibility, Violence, and Consent" (1995) 22(3) *Journal of Law and Society* 326–52 at 327.

[84] Perry Anderson, "England's Isaiah", *Times Literary Supplement* 20 Dec. 1990, 6.

its persuasive force, it is actually not a theory of individual identity at all, but of social choice".[85] In other words, Anderson takes the connection between values, incommensurability and identity that I have discussed as one that becomes undone, when Berlin is prepared to hold out the minimalist position of "what it means to be a human being at all" as a relatively fixed point in human affairs and history. For Anderson, "even on the plane where value-conflicts look most intractable, the doctrine seems on its inspection to lose its sting, as the challenge of cultural diversity is neutralised by the insurance clauses of human identity".[86] In saying this Anderson concludes that conflicts over values do not come down to serious questions about identity, but instead remain simply at the level of choice between available options for people whose identities are largely the same.

This seems to me a point open to interpretation, and one that, in line with my earlier examination, would not necessarily put a hole in Berlin's theory. There is, as I have argued, a dualism evident in Berlin's work, and one that is productive of a constant tension between those empirically observable norms of general concurrence, and those norms that are always contestable as a function of their origin in social, conflictual settings. That Berlin certainly does believe there are some features that are constant as part of human being, does not in itself mean that what they are, or what their limits may be cannot be debated. It seems to me to some extent to be a matter of degree, and the limited argument Berlin puts forward in terms of where to draw lines, prohibits a conclusive interpretation. I believe, as I have tried to show, that his work cannot rest simply on an "insurance clause" of human identity, given his insistently strong reaction against those whose theories seek to put in place any version of what the "true self" is or requires. It seems to me, then, that Berlin's antipathy toward homogenisation does come down to an argument about the contestability of identity. That said, Anderson has another reason to object here, and it is in the current context more pressing, since it goes to the issues of procedures with which we are presently concerned.

Anderson argues that when it comes to reaching decisions in cases where there appears to be an incommensurable clash of values, the nature of such decisions as are reached—that "adjusting the unadjustable"—is one which further reduces the potential radicalism of Berlin's ideas. Once again, he says, we see a failure of nerve on Berlin's part. Anderson, quoting Berlin, notes that:

[85] Perry Anderson, "England's Isaiah", *Times Literary Supplement* 20 Dec. 1990, 6.
[86] *Ibid.*, 7.

> he writes that "claims can be balanced, compromises can be reached . . . priorities, never final and absolute, must be established"—"we must engage in what are called trade-offs." In other words, the major goods *are* commensurable after all: how else can claims between them be weighed?[87]

Given this, Berlin's value-pluralism, according to Anderson, "is not ultimately agonistic".[88]

I think there is a clearer case here to dispute Anderson's interpretation. As I have tried to show using the examples taken from Raz, the fact that compromises can be reached does not mean that we must therefore treat values as commensurable. "Claims can be weighed" without invoking a ranking dependent upon the *a priori* assumption of commensurability. The real issue instead, it seems to me, is just what Berlin means by "trade-offs". And this leads us directly to a consideration of the institutional settings and frameworks within which such trade-offs are reached. Now it appears that on this point the general tenor of Berlin's argument is one that endorses an openness to the occurrence of conflict within particular situations. We saw earlier how great sensitivity was required in analysing just what was meant when we talked about "trading off" friendship and monetary value, and such sensitivity would have to be very carefully deployed when moving from analysis to institutionalising trade-offs in cases of similar conflicts. Thus Berlin's pluralism works here, as ever, as a tension between strongly-held values and the need for particularisation of conflict in any given context. Most of all the tension acts in such a way as to forego any programmatic resolution of conflicts by requiring that attention be paid to the causes of the conflict and the reasons for its emergence in the first place.

"Trade-offs" may thus occur without a commitment to commensurability, but with a commitment to an openness that demands that no necessary ranking between values be given from the outset. What seems weak about this scenario is either the feeling that it masks some underlying values that determine outcomes to which value-pluralists such as Berlin deny they are committed, or that there would be no reason to be committed to any values whatsoever. Yet Berlin sees that commitment to certain values on behalf of a group or individual is unproblematic; it is the assertion that those values or any others ought to trump any or all others that is the problem. The apparent weakness—a genuine openness to conflict—is in fact its greatest strength, yet because of the

[87] *Ibid.*, 6, original emphasis.
[88] *Ibid.*

position it adopts it cannot but seem to hold its fire in the abstract, and it is this that may dismay those who *do* want to hold on to an *a priori* commitment to commensurability and all that, for Berlin, comes with it.

The problem with trade-offs lies not in the theory, but in the institutional vesting which they normally receive. This becomes extremely clear when Anderson takes his final shot at Berlin's liberalism. For Anderson:

> the classical charge against pluralism as a theory of competing interests was always that it was less plural than met the eye, since political power was exercised within structural constraints set by one ultimate interest. However unlike it in many ways, pluralism as a theory of values is open to a similar kind of objection: in effect, that it is rather more discreetly monist than it suggests.[89]

Anderson here has neatly drawn attention to the problem; that the issue of trade-offs is dependent for its meaning on the "structural restraints" set by political and institutional power. Where such power does act with a commitment to one "ultimate interest" or ultimate value, then Anderson is correct in saying that it will treat trade-offs in a way that sees them as ultimately commensurable. Yet, in the reading of Berlin I have offered here, this position is as untenable and as dangerous for Berlin as any other that treats values as ultimately commensurable. As a result, when it comes to the matter and exercise of legal or institutional power or reasoning, to be consistent with his overall approach, Berlin's liberalism must eschew any such attempts that would reduce conflicts of value to a pregiven pattern within which they could be ameliorated. If Berlin does seem to have an ultimate value to which he is committed, it is one that seeks to allow the flourishing of identities and social forms that do not admit of resolution according to values that supersede or override those conflicts. His reluctance openly to endorse authority is thus premised on the fact that Anderson is indeed correct in one respect, namely, that institutional power usually *will* tend to assume a commensurability at odds with a radical pluralism. As Berlin says:

> The doctrine that accumulations of power can never be too great, provided that they are rationally controlled and used, ignores the central reason for pursuing liberty in the first place—that all paternalist governments, however benevolent, cautious, disinterested, and rational, have tended, in the end, to

[89] Perry Anderson, "England's Isaiah", *Times Literary Supplement* 20 Dec. 1990, 7.

> treat the majority of men as minors, or as being too often incurably foolish or irresponsible.[90]

But this tends to confirm the radical reading of Berlin when it comes to the issue of whether his theory is ultimately monist or not. It remains legitimate for Berlin to argue for the value of liberty in its negative sense, say, while at the same time realising (and in fact supporting) the fact that this clashes with other equally ultimate values such as equality. And that, as we have seen, Berlin is so adamant that the concrete circumstances of each occasion of a clash be given prominence, further argues against a hidden monism in operation. His point is neither to argue that negative liberty should triumph in specific instances of a clash, nor to suggest that liberty can thereby always be reduced to some other value such as equality. It is instead to acknowledge that such clashes do occur, and that to relocate them away from their original contexts and treat them as an instance of an improperly grasped application of some overarching principle is precisely to fail to acknowledge the genuinness of the values and identities at stake. And the consequent tensions that this leaves in place work to disavow the monist accusations that Anderson levels.

We took this detour through Anderson's criticisms as a way of beginning to address Berlin's approach to liberalism as one that breaks down any attempt to institute a distinction between the right and the good, any attempt, that is, to institute a neutral procedural framework within which disparate views of the good can be pursued. In outlining a response to Anderson's criticism, we can now see that in reading the notion of trade-offs as highly dependent on the institutional setting in which they occur, then Berlin's insights into the incommensurability of values can only be made concrete and meaningful where that setting is itself attentive to the particular origins of conflict, and tends to assume no *a priori* substantive or procedural values that are not themselves seen as integrally bound up with the way in which a trade-off is reached. Now this does seem to be a radical thesis, since it opens up any norms of decision-making to critique in a way that goes beyond the regulative "framework" liberalism of norms within which goods can be pursued. It does so because of its insistence that such norms themselves will be located in a particularity that ought not to be masked as they themselves interact with the clash of values that they seek to redress.

[90] "Introduction" to *Four Essays*, n. 1 above, p. lxii.

In this sense Berlin's is a radical liberalism more attuned to contemporary critiques which seek from various perspectives to query the "way that is not a way"[91] of liberal legal structures. Of course often liberal theorists would not deny at least some of these charges. Indeed they will defend the political values that these structures set in place.[92] But I would argue (and I will develop this point subsequently) that when it comes to the legal realm of decision-making, Berlin's thesis constitutes a greater challenge. For Berlin is seriously questioning the *terms* on which authority (and thus legal authority) is exercised, and whether it ought to be exercised at all, rather than that when it is it has to be done in a way that reflects as much as possible what, for example, Dworkin calls the "best constructive interpretation of the political structure and the legal doctrine of [the] community".[93] Berlin is always going to ask of such a line, best according to whom, or according to what? That there could be a single, "best" interpretation is something Berlin is always going to be wary of when he glorifies the "very right to disregard the forces of order and convention, even the publicly accepted 'optimum' goals of action",[94] that such uniformity may impose.

(iv) *Questioning Authority*

As I have noted already, there is some similarity here between Berlin's thesis and the ideas of those who would seek to find new challenges to liberalism in the realm of postmodern theory. One example indicative of the latter will suffice to show this similarity and how at least one postmodern theory has painted in too broad strokes the notion that liberalism can be condemned across the board when it comes to the relation between law and conflict.

Thus in a critique of Dworkin's liberalism Anne Barron writes that:

> The living person becomes an abstract legal subject, characterised by an autonomous responsible will, and as such becomes bound to obey rules of which s/he is notionally both author and addressee. Liberal theory thus posits freedom as a universal human essence, but only in order to legitimate the imposition of limitations upon that freedom. Our sameness as human beings is said to enable the *expression* of diversity, but also to require its *suppression*;

[91] Ngaire Naffine, *Law and the Sexes: Explorations in Feminist Jurisprudence* (Sydney, Allen and Unwin, 1990), 123.

[92] See for example Neil MacCormick, "Reconstruction after Deconstruction: A Response to CLS" (1990) 10 *Oxford Journal of Legal Studies* 539–58.

[93] Ronald Dworkin, *Law's Empire* (London, Fontana Press, 1986), 255.

[94] "Political Ideas in the Twentieth Century" in *Four Essays*, n. 1 above, 28.

> we are free to choose to be different, but "choices" that conflict with the law are proscribed.[95]

While this criticism may well be levelled at Dworkin, it seems out of place when directed at Berlin's theory. First, it would seem to be entirely in agreement with Berlin's critique of Kant's rational legislator which we saw in the section on expertise. Moreover, as we have seen, Berlin's theory is insistent in its demand that law and the exercise of authority *not* be put out of reach of the challenge of politics; that while law will indeed put forward a version of what is to be suppressed, this has no precedence of allegiance just because it is the law. Indeed, to the extent that law tends to put in place freedom (or equality, or whatever) as a "universal human essence", Berlin's liberalism would seek to question the uniformity that this would impose where it neglects to take into account the "meaning, the context, or the relevance and origin of a specific problem"(supra). Because Berlin refuses to endorse the notion that there are principles which, in Gray's terms, can be insulated from the incommensurability thesis itself, it does not fall prey to the notion that certain principles of right or law remain above the fray of conflict. "Choices that conflict with the law" are thus not proscribed in Berlin's theory for the very reason that the values embodied in law spring from sources that make the notion of an "abstract legal subject" meaningless; the subject is abstract only in the sense that it is abstracted from a specific social form, but one that, once instituted, is always in danger of supervening multiple identities and value-clashes in the particular contexts which it, perhaps inevitably, fails to acknowledge.

To some extent Barron's criticism is the same as Anderson's, namely that liberalism tends to assume a monism it claims to shun. But, again as I have shown, when we read Berlin's argument as one that relates value incommensurability and identity, then the diversity at issue is not just one that deals with "expression", but one that treats expression as intimately bound up with identity itself. In fact when Barron outlines the postmodern position as she takes it from Lyotard, both the language and ideas she associates with postmodernism are stunningly similar to Berlin's (and, arguably, Hume's):

> That which precedes and makes possible individual consciousness is itself a fractured, highly differentiated and always unstable reality: it yields a

[95] Anne Barron, "Ronald Dworkin and the Challenge of Postmodernism" in Alan Hunt (ed.), *Reading Dworkin Critically* (New York, Berg Publishers, 1992), 154–5, original emphasis.

> plurality of incommensurable identities, both within and between persons. In opposing the Enlightenment vision of a society as an ordered totality, unified by reference to an essential subjectivity, postmodernism insists upon the irreducible heterogeneity and multiplicity of human experience . . . Postmodernity demands that "dissensus" be given a voice where otherwise it would be repressed in the production of coherence and truth.[96]

Hear, hear, one might imagine Berlin saying. Still, he would insist that there remains the consensual norm identified earlier, and it is an interesting question whether or not postmodern theorists would deny this. But it should be clear that Berlin's theory, while similar to such postmodern thinking in relation to dissent and conflict, nevertheless as a theory of liberalism still stands in opposition to the kind of non-radical liberalism Barron is criticising. In its agonistic dimension it is prepared to put the issue of authority to questions of politics in much the same way as all along it has demanded the openness to conflict as a way of allowing the flourishing of social forms a space that is constantly in danger of being closed off by a dominant narrative, whatever that might be. And since it is the claim to totality and uniformity that it rejects, be that in the form of reason or the nation or a class, then where law assumes the same form of claim, it too is just as susceptible to its critique.

It remains, then, to draw attention to a curious conjunction in relation to law and conflict that emerges from this analysis, which comes from a comparison of the arguments of MacIntyre and those of Berlin. For where MacIntyre criticised the role of law in liberal societies when it tried to apply something like "community standards" his argument was that it could not do so because there were no such standards available, it seems Berlin would agree. Now one reason for this agreement could be that MacIntyre is entirely correct in diagnosing the state of contemporary liberal theory as it relates to law, and that Berlin's theory simply falls foul of his criticism. But this conclusion is too hasty. The reasons for Berlin adopting the position he does are precisely that at some level there *are* shared values, identities and social forms that in fact the kind of rationally resolvable theory MacIntyre is searching for would threaten. I should say here that this still does not, for me at any rate, differentiate Berlin's theory from that of the postmodernists; the "dissenting voices" Barron talked about and which may exist as, in Foucault's terms, subjugated knowledges are, even if fragmented, still voices that are saying something, something that cannot be heard but

96 Anne Barron, "Ronald Dworkin and the Challenge of Postmodernism" in Alan Hunt (ed.), *Reading Dworkin Critically* (New York, Berg Publishers, 1992), 155.

which should be acknowledged presumably because they have some value at least to those who are trying to get them heard. (Interestingly Martha Nussbaum has suggested that feminists might also have been too hasty in rejecting liberal theory out of hand; it could well be argued, she says, that the problem is not with liberal theory itself, but that its premises have not been pushed far enough.[97] I will return to these points later.)

If values are reduced to interests then MacIntyre would be justified in criticising Berlin's version of liberalism as a failure. But Berlin, as we have seen, writes to support conflict and difference as an argument about *maintaining* both identities and choices that have their location in groups, individuals and social forms which are themselves concerned with values. That is, for Berlin, problems of conflict do not simply arise over conflicting interests, but arise over conflicting interpretations of commitment to ideas and values that constitute a meaningful life at all. To reduce such conflicts merely to conflicts over interests or preferences fails to see the embedded nature of values in Berlin's theory. That there are no mechanisms that would rationally resolve such conflicts is a precariously balanced advantage, since if there were some such mechanisms the danger is always that, in Raz's terms, "success would mean failure"; that such resolution might have a high cost for that which has to be suppressed in order to achieve it.

Here we come, then, to the curious conjunction I suggested exists between MacIntyre and Berlin, and it lies not in their acknowledgment that liberalism provides no shared standards of rationality by which its clashes can be resolved. As I have just noted, this would be too superficial a treatment of Berlin's theory. It lies instead in what both these theories have to say about the role of law in liberal societies. This will be the subject of the next chapter. As such I want to make some concluding remarks on Berlin's theory of liberalism.

Conclusion

There is inevitable oversimplification in attempting to summarise the complex ideas that I have tried to draw out in interpreting Berlin's liberalism. All I will do, then, is distil two aspects of the work that, while

[97] Martha Nussbaum, "The Feminist Critique of Liberalism", lecture at Oxford University, Feb. 1996, excerpted in the *Times Higher Education Supplement* as "The Sleep of Reason", Feb. 1996, 17–18.

not focussing on the detail, exemplify the tenor of his theory, but also hint at things beyond. The first is what I take to be the spirit of the work, the second its—related—outlook. Judith Shklar outlines what she calls the "barebones liberalism" of her own approach and it seems to me to bear the same spirit as Berlin's and is worth quoting in full:

> It is, at its simplest, a defence of social diversity . . . The assumption throughout is that social diversity *is* the prevailing condition of modern nation-states and that it *ought* to be promoted. Pluralism is thus treated as a social actuality that no contemporary political theory can ignore without losing its relevance, and also as something that any liberal should rejoice in and seek to promote, because it is in diversity alone that freedom can be realized . . . What is evident, however, is that diversity and the burden of freedom must be endured and encouraged to avoid the kinds of misery that organised repression now brings. This is a type of liberalism quite common among members of permanent social minority groups, and it surely reflects both the apprehensions and positive experiences which their situation creates.[98]

There is a lot still to be worked out within such a position, and I hope to have drawn attention to what some of these issues are and begun to delineate some of the assumptions they involve. Given this is the spirit of Berlin's liberalism, it will be necessary subsequently to work through what I have called the radicalism of this position.

The second aspect can be brought out by considering the outlook within which such a spirit operates, and by observing some ideas of particular concern to it. In *The Broken Middle*, Gillian Rose uses the notion of diremption as a way of understanding philosophical relations in the treatment of morality and law. Diremption for her can be understood in the way that it differs from contradiction. So:

> "Contradiction" implies "resolution", whereas "diremption" may only be manifest as paradox . . . "diremption" . . . implies "torn halves of an integral freedom to which, however, they do not add up"—it formally implies the third, *tertium quid*, implicit in any opposition, *qua* sundered unity, without positing any substantial pre-existent "unity", original or final, neither finitely past or future, nor absolutely or transcendent.[99]

While Rose considers relations that do not gain explicit treatment in Berlin's theory, nor in my review of it, this is, nevertheless, a good way

[98] Judith N. Shklar, *Legalism: Law, Morals, and Political Trials* (Cambridge Mass., Harvard UP, 1986), 5–6.

[99] Gillian Rose, *The Broken Middle: Out of our Ancient Society* (Oxford, Blackwell, 1992), 236.

of understanding the kind of approach that can be found in Berlin's version of liberalism. It is one way of understanding the series of tensions one finds in his work concerning the relations between values and identity and commitment and pluralism. It is indicative, when thought of in the context of Berlin's theory, of the need constantly to be open to conflict whilst simultaneously being aware that closure is always present whether in the form of the "hardening" of once liberatory ideas, or the contrary effects of apparent progress; that sometimes success might mean failure and that though we must live in a common world that world ought never to be too common. Finally it points to notion that the very idea of "resolution", that is, what resolution means or signifies, is something to be contested and problematised when it seeks not to reconcile or mend some greater unity or one complete whole, but instead to "adjust the unadjustable" for a future as fractured as the past. As Berlin himself writes in a passage that exemplifies his thesis,

> The universe is not a jigsaw puzzle, of which we try to piece together the fragments, in the knowledge that one pattern exists, and one alone, in which they must all fit. We are faced with conflicting values; the dogma that they must somehow be reconcilable is a mere pious hope; experience shows that it is false.[100]

It is time now to see how ideas such as these work through in the context of law.

[100] Isaiah Berlin, "European Unity and its Vicissitudes" in *The Crooked Timber of Humanity*, n. 10 above, 201.

4: Liberalism and Law: MacIntyre and Berlin

The most prominent characteristic that MacIntyre's and Berlin's theories of liberalism share, for they do share some, I take to be this: it matters just how disagreement is constructed. One obvious manifestation of this is the disparaging treatment that experts receive in both theories. For MacIntyre, as we have seen, in contemporary liberal societies, "the range of possible alternatives is controlled by an elite, and how they are presented is also controlled" (supra). In the way that Berlin sees the linkage of expertise with authority, a liberal theory such as his likewise expresses disdain where choice is narrowed so far as to make it meaningless. We have seen this several times in Berlin's work: "paternalist governments . . . have tended in the end to treat the majority of men as minors", and again, "vast tracts of life [become] controlled by persons who, whether consciously or not, act systematically to narrow the horizon of human activity to manageable proportions" (supra). For Berlin however, it is a matter of degree, of something that exists as a constant threat, and this assumes, differing here from MacIntyre, that something can and perhaps should be done to check this, for it is not a definitional problem of liberal theory as such. Yet to the extent that both theories see conflict and disagreement being channelled by the techniques they identify, they equally see a loss occurring.

Berlin's expression of this was found in the way that conflict was always in danger of being treated like a disease in need of a cure; MacIntyre's was both that radical disagreement did occur because of the nature of contemporary morality being one of "fragmented survivals" from disparate traditions, and that the resultant inconclusiveness tended to be concealed within liberal debate because of the rhetorical and institutional channelling which it received. Conflict for MacIntyre could thus, as I said earlier, be made unreal, much in the same way that the therapeutic discourses for Berlin tended to do the same thing; both drew attention to the power and logic of institutions to restructure and ameliorate conflict. Of course where they differ is that, for MacIntyre, this is the condition of liberal society as inheritor to the failed Enlightnment project; for Berlin, it is the result of a prevalent illiberal tendency.

Both then point to features of contemporary societies that show how conflict can be masked. In particular MacIntyre pays attention to the positioning of law and legal structures as pivotal in understanding how conflict is dealt with. It will be instructive therefore to compare how Berlin's analysis responds to the four-level breakdown MacIntyre offered, and to see where differences and similarities emerge. This again involves some reconstructive work in relation to Berlin's thesis, but this can be done by concentrating on the central values of his liberalism that emerged in the foregoing analysis of his work.

The clearest difference between the two approaches can be witnessed at the first level in MacIntyre's breakdown. Here for MacIntyre, it will be recalled, was the root problem of liberalism. Debate at this level was interminable and this was due to the way in which rival positions were expressed; that is, as "expressions of preference". The emotivist self, freed from rational argumentative constraints in the form of teleological or universalist reasoning, could do no more than express "attitudes or feelings" which took the form "I want it to be the case that such and such". Berlin's analysis clearly takes issue, and does so, I suggest, on the following two grounds.

First, the inconclusiveness of debate at this level is non-problematic. Indeed to assume that a form of reasoning exists, grounded either in teleological terms (construed most often by Berlin in the form of arguments for the destiny of a class or a race) or universalist terms (which he associates most clearly with arguments derived though skewed from Kant), which *could* finally resolve debates, was the source of an intolerance to the empirically grounded claim that people just do disagree about what the ultimate ends of life are. Rational argument at this level—as we saw through noticing the ambiguous sense in which he treated rationality—did not fail by being inconclusive; indeed, as the argument from Raz showed, it may well be that success in the power of reason would be detrimental to social forms that require for their existence incommensurably varied commitments. The fact that debate was interminable therefore was a beneficial feature of the limits of reason; but this did not mean that, in MacIntyre's terms, "nonrational persuasion replaces rational argument".[1] Debate could still be rational without necessarily assuming that the application of reason could answer any or

[1] Alasdair MacIntyre, *Whose Justice? Which Rationality?* (London, Duckworth, 1988), 343.

all conflicts. Rational argument has not then been "replaced"; it may be possible to reason out the limitations of reason without resort to non-rational means of persuasion. Interminability may be a success. Why this is so is explained by the second ground for disagreement.

Here Berlin's theory argues that MacIntyre is mistaken about the *form* which conflicting positions take, even before they conflict. For MacIntyre that form is the "preference", the attitude or feeling. As I have interpreted it, Berlin's version of liberalism finds such a description untenable. Values cannot be expressed merely as preferences, since values require a commitment and entail a reciprocity with identity that goes beyond that which the form "I want it to be the case that such and such" would offer. It is not in itself the necessary link Berlin makes with identity that suggests this. It might be possible to have an, albeit emaciated, version of the self that was merely the constituted repository of preferences in this form. (Marx's critique of bourgeois man may perhaps be one version of this.) Instead what Berlin's version counters with is the argument that commitment to values cannot simply take this form and be validly descriptive of individuals and groups and the social forms in which they engage and which engage them. The clearest example we have of this is the one offered by Raz.

To be engaged in the institution of friendship requires a commitment to a value grounded in a social practice that is far more subtle and inescapably contextual than could be captured in the expression of a preference. We might imagine a child (a rather prosaic one, admittedly) saying, "I want it to be the case that I have a friend", and being told, "That's not just something you can choose to have like a toy; you have to be patient and giving to have a friend". What is valuable may well be something that one could say one has a preference for. But that is different from saying that how one achieves and lives in those practices that are valuable can be gained through having a preference, a manifestation of will or desire, satisfied.

So when MacIntyre's analysis suggests, in this related sense, that moral deliberation and "debate" merely takes the form of saying "I prefer" such and such, and that simply expressing this provides a bedrock of justification, it too misses the mark. For, as we have seen, preferring one value to another may be the result of reasoned interpretation of what a particular practice is and requires, and standards will exist within that practice that cannot be shrugged off. I suggested when discussing MacIntyre's conception of the emotivist self that there existed at the very least linguistic constraints. Now we could add to this the dimension that social practices require participation in and commitment to shared understandings that provide further constraints, and that to live up to and engage in what these are requires—even (perhaps especially) when one seeks to disagree with the meaning of a particular practice—a justification for which the form "I prefer" will be inadequate. Within any particular practice the question "Why do you prefer such and such?" will not be sufficiently answered by saying, "Because it is my preference". If there is a preference at work here it is in the form of a commitment to a set of social forms that are deemed worthwhile. It may not be possible in the end to produce rational criteria for all those practices which one finds valuable. In the end the requirement for justifications reaches a place where to ask for more and more reasons becomes pointless.[2]

Of course MacIntyre never pushes so far; he merely asserts the stronger argument that debate in liberal societies cannot produce even minimum criteria of justification that go beyond the form of issuing preferences. But, as we saw in the argument about the incommensurability of money and friendship, there is a subtlety to reasoning and even to understanding such debates that the notion of preference simply fails to grasp. That reason is inconclusive in determining which values ought to be ranked higher or lower than others, neither signifies the end of rational debate *as such*, nor forces one to conclude that all the liberal self can do is therefore express preferences.

It would be naïve of course to assume that ranking does not occur in forms that resemble the issuing of preferences. "I prefer" is simply a matter of will; it can only be satisfied, or it can be countered by another will. The prosaic child may have someone to tell them to be patient in the matter of friendship, and that simply willing it will not achieve it, but that does not mean that, for example, politicians in the mould of Berlusconi do not believe that enough money will buy them political power or ability, nor that there is someone to tell them that the values of politics might require more than money can buy. MacIntyre is right to point out that it matters who controls the settings in which debate occurs, and we will come to this in a moment. But Berlin is equally wary that conflict be masked by turning it into something that can produce a single standard across a range of activities, something that treating conflict as preference-alignment might well engender. And the ultimate reason he is so wary is not, *contra* MacIntyre, because he sees the mere expression of preferences as being something worth holding on to, but

[2] Cf. Ludwig Wittgenstein, *Philosophical Investigations* (Oxford, Basil Blackwell, 1989), s.217.

because the constitutive commitment to values that make for a meaningful life in diverse practices and which requires more than the expression of preferences as a will to be satisfied or not, holds out the possibility that humans be treated as reasoning human beings and not simply as automatons in a supreme system. And to seek to maintain this, for him, requires argument and commitment, not the lack of it.

MacIntyre's second level witnessed a failure to produce standards of justice because there were no rational criteria available to judge the outcome of any such debate. In this instance Berlin agrees that there are no such standards, beyond those minimally observable features existent through time that allow human interaction to occur as human interaction. But MacIntyre suggests further that such liberal debate that does occur fails in its goal since that goal *is* to produce standards of justice that can be agreed upon. Now the argument for the radicalism of Berlin's liberalism becomes important here. While someone like Rorty suggests uncritically that the "institutions of procedural justice" can be used to debate such issues, Berlin's position is different. It would be foolish to suggest that Berlin is not interested in the existence of standards of justice in liberal society. But the problem will always be the one identified by Gray's reading of Berlin, namely, that the principles of right sought in standard liberal theories (as he put it) cannot themselves be insulated from "deep conflicts of value". Again, it could be argued in relation to this point that MacIntyre simply provides a correct diagnosis of liberalism. But the point Berlin is making is that where, for example, rationalist theories of liberalism have assumed that the search for such principles may be productive of general programmatic solutions (and, in pointing out their failure to deliver MacIntyre would be correct), the radical liberal position opens up principles of right to critique in the belief that the incommensurability of values requires an openness to conflict at all times and places, and that to produce rational agreement on uncontestable "framework" procedures overlooks the fact that any such values, in Gray's terms, "derive all their content and weight from their contribution to forms and aspects of human flourishing which themselves generate such conflicts" (supra). The levels of debate model MacIntyre is using allow us to see a symmetry in argument here between the two interpretations that explains Berlin's point.

Where, for MacIntyre, the failure at level two was largely explainable by reference back to the way in which debate at level one took place, we can read the radical liberal response at level two as similarly dependent on the (different) view it took of the meaning of conflict at level one.

That is, the existence of social forms productive of and produced by incommensurably varied values at level one works as an argument to deny the feasibility of producing criteria of right that will be rationally demonstrable for all people at level two. Once again the caveat for Berlin is that there must exist some minimal standards, but these, he would argue, are not confined to debates within liberal society but are observable features across time. Failure to maintain such standards has clearly been as much evident in other societies as it has potentially in liberal ones. To be blunt, this is not a failing attributable to liberalism.

This may be correct; nevertheless the tension, as I pointed out, exists in his liberal theory both as to what these are and how far they extend. In the duality I drew attention to in Berlin's work, this remains an open issue. But in one sense, as far as MacIntyre's critique of liberalism goes, this does not matter, since the two writers are, in a significant issue at least, disagreeing about the same thing: Berlin champions inconclusiveness, MacIntyre disdains it; they simply read the same thing (inconclusiveness) differently. MacIntyre's reading suggests failure, Berlin's an ultimately precarious success.

Now if Berlin is correct in arguing for incommensurability at level one then he would seem to be, as Gray suggests, committed to incommensurability at level two. What this means is that, at least for this theory of liberalism, inconclusiveness cannot be measured as a failure, since inconclusiveness is a condition of its success. As such inconclusiveness or interminability at level two is *justified*, it is a principled response to the existence of the conflicts and social forms at level one which demand an openness to conflict that rational resolution, even in the form of settled principles of right, would always be in danger of heading off. Consequently Berlin is committed to a form of liberalism and will not endorse a return to the supposed benefits of earlier forms of political theory and organisation which might be thought, by those such as MacIntyre, to begin to provide ways of terminating debate. As he says, "[i]t is neither realistic nor morally conceivable that we should give up our social gains and meditate for an instant the possibility of a return to ancient injustice and inequality and hopeless misery".[3] Debate, then, is not, as MacIntyre suggests, simply "continued for its own sake"[4]; it is continued interminably, for good reason.

This point is an important one, and one that I will come back to in a

[3] Isaiah Berlin, "Political Ideas in the Twentieth Century" in *Four Essays on Liberty* (1969; Oxford, OUP, 1991), 39.

[4] MacIntyre, n. 1 above, 344.

later section. It will be recalled, however, that MacIntyre rightly observes that interminability does not preclude the existence of what he called "socially effective" principles that do operate in liberal societies. MacIntyre's diagnosis of failure, however, seems to be matched by a radical liberal theory that could offer up a principled response. MacIntyre rightly demands a response from a liberal theory, and, I suggest, the one that is given forces a radical approach to analysis of the role of law in liberal societies. To claim that at level two "preferences are tallied and weighed", as MacIntyre does, would seem to require the assumption either that values are reducible to preferences (which Berlin's theory denies), or that some means exist whereby decisive answers are produced which *effectively* reduce conflicts to a single scale for the purposes of ranking, whether in the form of preferences or not being unimportant. It is this second possibility that I want to explore.

(In order to develop this issue I should be clear that to call the radical liberal position I identify with Berlin "Berlin's argument" when we look at the level four debate is unacceptable. I have drawn on Berlin for what I take to be his radical liberal position, yet his limited discussions of law preclude me from putting any more words in his mouth than bear reading in his texts. At the end of the last chapter I drew some tentative conclusions about the relation to law of a theory such as Berlin's which I believe are consistent with these texts. Now however I take the presuppositions of Berlin's position regarding conflict as a radical theory of liberalism, but no longer claim that it is Berlin's liberalism, which clearly lacks a developed legal theory. I believe it to be consistent with his overall approach to political theory, and as such productive of many valuable insights, yet from now on do not claim that it would treat the conclusions I draw from it in the same way.)

I will leave aside the third level in MacIntyre's analysis which dealt with the "justification" from principles to their particular application which, though clearly important, replicates on both sides the structure of argument already outlined. The issues of interest arise again at the interpretation of level four. This is the level, says MacIntyre, "at which appeals to justice may be heard in a liberal individualist order, that of the rules and procedures of the legal system" (supra). What MacIntyre drew attention to was the question how it was possible to produce coherent principles to guide legal decisions when levels one to three had failed to come up with any; but, I noted, what he *problematised* was not the techniques whereby legal reasoning did produce such principles but instead the significance of the law's, and specifically the courts', function and position within liberal societies, given this earlier failure. I brought out several features of this point, the most important of which related first to the capitulation of rational philosophical enquiry where the pressing requirement of the legal system became the production of verdicts and, secondly, to the way in which conflict had therefore to be manipulated into a form that would allow such verdicts to be given. How would a radical liberalism respond to these issues?

First, I suggest, the extent to which law functioned to bring conflicts on to the same plane (for the purpose of, in Berlin's terms, ranking, in MacIntyre's, tallying and weighing) would clearly be a concern to a theory that saw ultimate values as incommensurable. Just how far could the legal system respond to Berlin's idea that, in such cases where "trade-offs" had to occur, it was vital to examine the "meaning, the context, or the relevance and origin of a specific problem"; or how far might it instead replicate the techniques of expert discourses by "altering the outlooks that gave rise to it in the first place" in order to bring the problem to the point where a verdict could be given? How similar is a "verdict" to a "trade-off"? When I considered Anderson's criticism of Berlin that he (Berlin) did in the end make values commensurable ("how else can claims between them be weighed?", asked Anderson), I suggested that what was of paramount importance was that attention be paid to the institutional setting within which these trade-offs occurred. Where there was a commitment to commensurability assumed in the settling of a conflict, then I argued that radical liberalism, to be true to its initial insights, must be extremely wary of, if not reject outright, such an approach. The reasons for this I discussed previously, but they also coincide now with MacIntyre's analysis that in current liberal institutional settings conflict is either made to be appear unreal and thus commensurable, or does not get picked up as a conflict at all. It will be recalled that, for MacInytre, the central institutional means of effecting these techniques was the legal system: as he said, "[t]he nature of any society is not to be deciphered from its laws alone, but from those understood as an index of its conflicts. What our laws show is the degree to which conflict has to be suppressed" (supra). If this is indeed the case then the radical liberal theory would be forced to enquire into the terms on which conflict was suppressed; it would be forced, in other words, to question the extent to which the legal system tended to become another instance of a "single, overarching principle" whose logic was to impose unity to the detriment of difference.

May it be, then, that although the radical liberal position clearly disagrees with the level-one analysis of MacIntyre, it nevertheless comes to share the suspicions offered by MacIntyre at level four? I suggest that it does, and most of what follows in the book is directed to providing an argument why. But still within MacIntyre's framework further questions can be raised. So the second issue MacIntyre drew attention to concerned the implications of the positioning of the legal system in relation to the debates at the previous three levels. MacIntyre's point, as I interpreted it, was not simply that law's role was to decide between competing claims and thus inevitably reject some (the "jurispathic function" of the courts in Cover's terms), but that, given the failure of moral debate to produce rational agreement at the other three levels, the result was the collapse of the distinction between power and authority as an instance of what he called the broader collapse of the contrast between "manipulative and non-manipulative social relations". This I took to be an open challenge to the *legitimacy* of the liberal legal order. Let me explain further why, since it demands a response from the radical liberal theory.

The problem is this: how can liberal legal reasoning invoke shared community standards when there is none? Any responses to this by liberal legal theorists might be seen to be caught in a double bind. Either they could accept that there were no such standards, in which case decisions were a matter solely of power, since they could not be grounded in consensus; or they could accept that some such standards could indeed be found in legal reasoning, in which case law potentially fails to live up to its liberal premise, that it allowed dissent and conflict to flourish. (This ostensible difference between theories within liberal legal reasoning I will come back to in more detail in the next chapter.) What MacIntyre's analysis brings out is that in either case the legal system must be opened to the question of legitimacy. And this too, I suggest, would seem to follow for the radical liberal theory. Where the first position becomes open about the use of power, that power must be questioned from a point external to itself; that is, legal reasoning cannot answer the question of its own legitimacy, since it has given up the possibility that such reasoning can be grounded in appeals to shared standards. To suggest this would be radical indeed, for it would require the conclusion that courts' decisions were not *prima facie* authoritative. Here imagined reponses might invoke a separation of powers argument.[5] But this would be unpersuasive. It could be argued either that courts are already open to democratic review, in that Parliament can indeed reverse

[5] Cf. Hugh Collins, "Democracy and Adjudication," in Neil MacCormick and Peter Birks (eds.), *The Legal Mind: Essays for Tony Honore* (Oxford, Clarendon Press, 1986).

even the final court's judgments or that all the powers courts have are delegated from another source that is itself legitimate. But such reasoning of the former type would not work in those cases of countries (such as the United States and Australia) where Parliament is not supreme and a constitutional court sits. Alternatively, where Parliament was supreme (and this was Hobbes' argument[6]), justification would depend on the derivative authority of courts from the sovereign. But this would assume (as Hobbes did) the now rather dated view that courts do not make law but only interpret it, and thus overlook the fact that serious political matters were decided by the courts. And in those cases where there was a constitution, say, what legitimacy would interpretations of a constitution have that were barred from making appeals to shared standards since it was agreed they did not exist? The distinction between power and authority clearly, then, would become problematic since legitimacy would seem not to depend on any substantive grounds but to be a matter of efficiency in imposing decisions. If this were the case then, as Niklas Luhmann has put it, "[w]hat counts is not a principle, nor a logical deduction, nor the elegant conceptual construction, but the difference a decision effectuates either in social reality or in the legal system itself . . . Logically then, the validity of a programme depends on its own execution".[7]

The second justification—that shared standards can indeed be found—would have to be questioned by the radical liberal approach for the very reasons that it has questioned such assumptions to shared standards all along. We do not need to repeat these here, except to point out that where such justifications are put forward they most often take the form of a grounding in rights, which, as we have seen, is no less problematic when the incommensurability thesis is taken seriously. Here again, though the starting points of MacIntyre and a theory such as Berlin's differ at level one, their attitude to legal structures for dispute resolution seem to come together.

Two final points should be raised from MacIntyre's analysis, and they bring us back to the opening of this section. It matters how disagreement is constructed, and the role of experts was seen to be an important feature in both theories. As I suggested in the analysis of Berlin on expertise and authority, a radical liberal theory must be attentive to the

[6] Thomas Hobbes, *Leviathan* (ed. C. B. Macpherson, Harmondsworth, Penguin, 1968), ch. XXVI.

[7] Niklas Luhmann, "The Third Question: The Creative Use of Paradoxes in Law and Legal History" (1988) 15 *Journal of Law and Society*, 153–66 at 160.

role experts play in being able to channel conflict. The suspicion here is always directed to the possibility that conflict be treated as in need of a cure for which only experts have the diagnosis. MacIntyre expressed disdain at the rhetorical powers of the "cosmetic arts" of liberal spin-doctors to distort conflict, and, albeit from different premises at level one, this suspicion is replicated in the radical liberal theory. The terms on which disagreement takes place, the nature of the "trade-off" processes, clearly require a sensitivity to the institutional settings in which these occur, and to the role of those who run such institutions. And this leads to the second point that MacIntyre drew our attention to: namely, that for both him and—I would now add, despite clear differences at level one—for the radical liberal theory, concern must be focussed on the role and position of law, and specifically the decision-making of the courts, because of the reciprocal, constitutive and dependent relations that law will have with the broader social realm. In the sense that the legal has effects back on social practices such as morality (it produces terms of debate, constructs expectations etc.), a radical liberal position concerned with a genuine commitment to values and conflict in moral and political matters, and to the contexts of these conflicts, must be attentive to precisely what impact law has on these. It is not just an issue of how liberal legal reasoning justifies its decisions, though this is important, but of the consequences of the current positioning of law and the courts within liberal societies, the point MacIntyre has raised so effectively.

Having suggested, therefore, that there are common concerns between MacIntyre and Berlin, despite their clear differences, in order to push the analysis further, it now becomes necessary to turn to look in more detail at aspects of liberal legal reasoning before the points raised here can be adequately addressed. Thus it is to these issues we now turn.

PART THREE

5: On Liberal Legalism

Legalism can be defined in a variety of ways. It can be construed more or less narrowly, in either its outlook or in its applications. Judith Shklar set the terms of her definition broadly as "the ethical attitude that holds moral conduct to be a matter of rule following, and moral relationships to consist of duties and rights determined by rules".[1] An ethical attitude then, but also a "political ideology" when it came to that subset of legalism endorsed by "those who cherish those [great] systems of law" of the "European world".[2] "Legal" legalism, so to speak, was an attitude more precisely located, the ethical perspective focussed down to the institutional setting of the formal legal system and upheld by the legal attitudes of its major proponents: "the legal profession, both bench and bar", as well as, we might add, much of the traditional legal academy. In this legal setting, "the court of law and the trial according to law are the social paradigms, the perfection, the very epitome, of legalistic morality".[3] This definition of Shklar's, with the caveat that follows in the next paragraph, is the idea of legalism I want to explore in this chapter.

The caveat is brief and need not detain us. H. L. A. Hart described law as "the union of primary and secondary rules",[4] and on the face of it this description seems compatible with Shklar's definition. Yet since Hart wrote this, the idea of law as rules has in Anglo-American jurisprudence been refined to include more carefully the sets of principles within which these rules operate, are interpreted and make sense. Most prominently publicised by Ronald Dworkin, the working of principles in law is now less contentious than it may have been 30 years ago, though what these principles are and exactly what role they play is still debated.[5] My caveat is, though, that such principles should also be thought to be

[1] Judith N. Shklar, *Legalism: Law, Morals, and Political Trials* (Cambridge, Mass., Harvard UP, 1986), 1.

[2] *Ibid.*, 1–2.

[3] *Ibid.*, 2.

[4] H. L. A. Hart, *The Concept of Law* (Oxford, Clarendon Press, 1961).

[5] Though in opposition to, for example, Dworkin, Critical Legal Studies has also concerned itself with the working of principles and counter-principles in law. See generally, Roberto Unger, "The Critical Legal Studies Movement," 96 *Harvard Law Review* 563–675 (1983); and for a particular application, Hugh Collins, *The Law of Contract* (London, Weidenfeld and Nicholson, 1986).

included within the definition of legalism I have settled on from Shklar. For as Hunt, for example, points out, "[e]ven though Dworkin insists that his move is characterised by a displacement of rules to a new focus on law as interpretation, it is apparent that this does not displace 'the model of rules,' but rather that rules remain the presupposition because it is, of course, rules that are the object of interpretive activity".[6] For my purposes, then, "legal" legalism includes both rules and legal principles.

Let there be no doubt that this "legal" legalism is also an ethical or political attitude. Even the most narrow, conservative, and, some might think, misguidedly rigid of judicial approaches to interpretation see their approach as ethically or politically inspired. As a judge in Australia has noted,[7] even though the judiciary should, according to him, "[insist] on the strict construction of all laws", the justification for this is expressly political: "[l]iberty is founded on black letter law", no less. In far more refined terms, "legal" legalism has been defined by Neil MacCormick as:

> the stance in legal politics according to which matters of legal regulation and controversy ought so far as possible to be conducted in accordance with pre-determined rules of considerable generality and clarity, in which legal relations comprise primarily rights, duties, powers and immunities reasonably clearly defined by reference to such rules, and in which acts of government however desirable teleologically must be subordinated to respect for rules and rights.[8]

This last phrase hints at what exactly the kind of ethical stance the legalism identified here is. It is, as I will call it, "liberal legalism".

Again MacCormick's theory helpfully explains:

> The moral value at issue most deeply is that of independence, or, rather, independence in interdependence, independence in community . . . Laws which themselves stifle autonomy, or warp the community to create forms of interdependence inimical to independence, attack the very values legalism prima facie sustains.[9]

I should say that the "liberalism" in this version of "liberal legalism" is, in one sense, not at all far removed from that I have ascribed to Berlin:

[6] Alan Hunt, *Explorations in Law and Society: Towards a Constitutive Theory of Law* (New York, Routledge, 1993), 302.

[7] F. C. Hutley J, "The Legal Tradition of Australia as Contrasts with Those of the United States" (1981) 55 *Australian Law Journal* 63–70 at 66.

[8] Neil MacCormick, "The Ethics of Legalism" (1989) *Ratio Juris* 184.

[9] *Ibid.*, 188, 192.

the value of autonomy in community was recognised in Berlin's theory, albeit as one element in a complex theory I drew out in the previous two chapters.[10] Autonomy, or independence within interdependence, is one of the key credos, if not the key credo, of liberal thought, and usually is of the kind Berlin mentioned when discussing its roots in Kant.

The idea of autonomy has been treated in different ways by liberal theorists. Sometimes its value is aligned more with the notion of equality, that all ought to be treated equally under law. So, for example, the "constitutive morality" of Dworkin's liberalism stresses that "human beings must be treated as equals by their government, not because there is no right and wrong in political morality, but because that is what is right".[11] In a more developed, and thus contentious, sense, it is, similarly, the key focus of John Rawls's liberalism, which draws on autonomy in terms of both liberty and equality. For him the "liberal principle of legitimacy" is that "our exercise of political power is fully proper only when it is exercised in accordance with a constitution the essentials of which all citizens as free and equal may reasonably be expected to endorse in light of their common human reason".[12] If we see a subtle shift in this description (in a manner that will be drawn out shortly), the value of autonomy in relation to law is still clearly in evidence.

Liberal legalism, then, is an ethical attitude to how humans do or ought to relate to each other when it comes to their legal relations in community. Such relations will include both citizen–citizen relations and citizen–state relations, both sets of which should be treated in the same spirit when it comes to the values of the approach to law. Commonly this form of legal organisation has been given the title "Rule of Law", though, as MacCormick has suggested, "'legalism' is not the 'Rule of Law' itself, but an attitude of commitment thereto".[13] But the fact that "legal legalism" (which I will subsequently refer to as "legalism" *simpliciter*) has an ethical justification, does not necessarily suggest that the content of laws themselves must have an ethical basis. The attitude to the doctrine of the Rule of Law deals with values which may be thought of as meta-values. As Roberto Unger has put it:

[10] MacCormick, at least when it comes to the concept of liberty, acknowledges Berlin's version of negative liberty as the one he prefers. See Neil MacCormick, *Legal Right and Social Democracy: Essays in Legal and Political Philosophy* (Oxford, Clarendon Press, 1982), 147.

[11] Ronald Dworkin, "Liberalism", in Stuart Hampshire (ed.), *Public and Private Morality* (Cambridge, CUP, 1978), 142.

[12] John Rawls, *Political Liberalism* (New York, Columbia UP, 1993), 137.

[13] Neil MacCormick, "Reconstruction after Deconstruction: A Response to CLS" (1990) 10 *Oxford Journal of Legal Studies* 539–58, at 541.

> In the broadest sense, the rule of law is defined by the interrelated notions of neutrality, uniformity, and predictability. Governmental power must be exercised within the constraints of rules that apply to ample categories of persons and acts, and these rules, whatever they may be, must be uniformly applied. Thus understood, the rule of law has nothing to do with the content of norms.[14]

Now it may be that such values as uniformity and predicability (and others, suggested by amongst others Lon Fuller[15]) do put some outside limits on the content of possible legal norms, but the general proposition remains that such meta-values will not supply in detail solutions to ethical problems any particular legal system will face on any particular issue. It would be quite possible for one legal system to outlaw marijuana use and another to decriminalise it, and in both cases to do so on ethical grounds, yet for both systems to conform to the values of the rule of law.[16]

A caveat exists here with liberal legalism however in that, as was noted above, there is a commitment to autonomy under law which may potentially act as a more prescriptive value than would, for example, the value of predictability under the Rule of Law. According to principles of liberal legalism, then, either the outlawing or decriminalising of marijuana use may be justified on ethical grounds, but only so long as individuals, most commonly through their representatives, have some say in the way the decision is reached. Only in this way could we say the legal system, in Nussbaum's terms, "[respected] the equal worth of persons as choosers".[17] If the decision was taken by one person alone, without consultation, reviewability or in accordance with established procedure, or, by some one or group outside the established political system, then it would fail to match up to the aspirations of liberal legalism. Liberal legalism therefore in some sense narrows further those "outside limits" within which law is expected to operate in liberal societies and does so on the grounds that autonomy of persons is something to be respected.

Broadly then, liberal legalism is an attitude towards how, at least in the legal realm, persons should relate to each other and to government.

[14] Roberto Mangabeira Unger, *Law in Modern Society: Toward a Criticism of Social Theory* (New York, Free Press, 1976), 176–7.

[15] See his, *The Morality of Law* (Newhaven Conn., Yale UP, revised edn. 1969), chap. 2. And for an argument for substantive constraints imposed by the rule of law in a particular context, see David Dyzenhaus, *Judging the Judges, Judging Ourselves: Truth, Reconciliation, and the Apartheid Legal Order* (Oxford, Hart Publishing, 1998).

[16] This is indeed the case among the different states in Australia.

[17] See the Introduction to this volume.

And it is, moreover, an attitude as to how decisions should be made when conflicts appear before the courts. To quote the definition again from Shklar, "the court of law and the trial according to law are the social paradigms, the perfection, the very epitome, of legalistic morality".

At this stage, let me repeat my opening hypothesis: that liberalism, in the sense I have taken from Berlin's work, and liberal legalism are incompatible. Specifically now I want to test this in the setting of courts' decisions. I have suggested that attention to the construction of moral disagreement provides the key to my hypothesis. Looking at the work of MacIntyre and Berlin I have focussed on that issue and suggested that a radical liberal theory may draw on the critique of law in liberal societies offered by MacIntyre. To begin to explore more fully why such a theory may be incompatible with liberal legalism we need now to turn to aspects of judicial decision making in more detail. As a prelude to this I will first outline two views of law taken from the work of Roger Cotterrell, and draw out the assumptions and consequences they exhibit. Though I have said previously that the main concern of my argument is with the institutional setting and dynamic of courts in liberal society, and the meaning of their position and function, rather than with justificatory arguments internal to their practice, I have also said that it is still necessary to look at that practice. Using the two models Cotterrell employs is, I suggest, a helpful way of doing so.

"Law's Images of Society"

According to Cotterrell:

> Images of law's social environment in Anglo-American legal philosophy fall into two distinct types: on the one hand, the image of a morally cohesive association of politically autonomous people (*community*) and, on the other, the image of individual subjects of a superior political authority (*imperium*).[18]

These are, he says, "*merely* images. They do not represent the complexity of actual social systems or arrangments". For example, in reality, "any actual social arrangments for community will also involve elements of imperium" (at 325, original emphasis). Nevertheless, as images of society, they are different and can be considered separately.

[18] Roger Cotterrell, *Law's Community: Legal Theory in Sociological Perspective* (Oxford, Clarendon Press, 1995), 222–3 (original emphasis). Note that page references in the text of this section are to this book; this section's title is taken from Cotterrell.

But as different images, they have in common the fact that both are, Cotterrell says, ideological, in the sense that they present "certain partial aspects of social and political life . . . as totalities" (*ibid.*). Neither image is, he admits, new, but has extensive historical antecedents. As such neither presupposes a liberal democratic theory of society or government, though it is as they play out in contemporary liberal societies that I will consider them. Let us turn in more detail to what they are.

(i) *Community*

Interestingly, Cotterrell suggests that law's image of society as community is shared by the rhetoric of the classical common lawyers of the seventeenth century and by contemporary American jurisprudence, though not by contemporary English lawyers. If we consider briefly some influential American rhetoric we see his point regarding how the American courts do or ought to view their role. So, for example, John Rawls writes that:

> The justices [of the Supreme Court] . . . must appeal to the political values they think belong to the most reasonable understanding of the public conception and its political values of justice and public reason. These are values that they believe in good faith, as the duty of civility requires, that all citizens as reasonable and rational might reasonably be expected to endorse.[19]

While Rawls does not use the term community in this passage, his notion of how law views community is nevertheless at one with Cotterrell's idea of law's image of community as "a morally cohesive collectivity linked by its members' agreement on or acquiescence in values that bind them" (at 320).

In a similar fashion Dworkin, whose insights Rawls acknowledges, writes that, "[j]udges who accept the interpretive ideal of integrity decide hard cases by trying to find, in some coherent set of principles about people's rights and duties, the best constructive interpretation of the political structure and legal doctrine of their community".[20]

[19] Rawls, n. 12 above at 236. It should be noted that "public reason" means something quite specific for Rawls: it is, he says, "characteristic of a democratic people: it is the reason of its citizens, of those sharing the status of equal citizenship. The subject of their reason is the good of the public: what the political conception of justice requires of society's basic structure of institutions, and of the purposes and ends they are to serve" (at 213).

[20] Ronald Dworkin, *Law's Empire* (London, Fontana Press, 1986), 255.

Dworkin's "community" here is not a "bare" or "rule-book" community, but a "genuine political community", a "community of principle" whose members "accept that they are governed by common principles, not just rules hammered out in political compromise".[21]

What makes Cotterrell suggest there is a coincidence between this rhetoric and that of the classical common lawyers such as Coke is, as he says, that the latter similarly:

> [invoked] communitarian images with their reference to the ancient wisdom of law, greater than any individual, and a form of reason distilled from the entire history or ancient origins of the community the judges are considered to represent and speak for [at 224].

Although for those such as Coke, Rawls's notion that all reasonable citizens ought to be able to agree to the values the court expresses would not be articulated so emphatically, the appeal to community is nonetheless paramount for both. Community, in the eyes of law, is constructable through critical insight into its present values perceived in their historical and institutional setting. The law speaks for and to that community and its decisions are legitimised only in so far as it does so.

In this sense another similarity between contemporary American and classical common law rhetoric appears. The law cannot speak with a forked tongue. It must be possible to realise in the courts' practice therefore a singular meaning both for law and for the community. So for Dworkin, for example, even when tests of, in his words, fit and substance are passed, it may be that in particularly difficult cases two reasonable but conflicting interpretations of the law are still viable. Where this is so, he says, the judge must "choose between eligible interpretations by asking which shows the community's structure of institutions and decisions—its public standards as a whole—in a better light from the standpoint of political morality".[22] The similarity Cotterrell rightly perceives here with the classical common law rhetoric relates to who exactly is best placed to work out what this community morality is. For Dworkin, there is no doubt: "[t]he courts are the capitals of law's empire, and the judges are its princes".[23] Judges then are the people who, with their special training and experience, their interpretative and reasoning skills, are those not only best placed, but indeed expected, to work out what the community, in its best light, requires.

[21] *Ibid.*, 211.
[22] *Ibid.*, 256.
[23] *Ibid.*, 407.

And, that best light is, and must ultimately be, a singular light. In Dworkin's words:

> We accept integrity as a distinct political ideal, and we accept the adjudicative principle of integrity as sovereign over law, because we want to treat ourselves as an association of principle, as a community governed by a single and coherent vision of justice and fairness and procedural due process in the right relation.[24]

Now, as Cotterrell explains, it is difficult not to see in this "a new version of Coke's famous dichotomy: while the common law is the embodiment of the community's reason and ancient wisdom, it is an 'artificial' reason which only the highly trained can master" (at 228). The community may be the inspiration for and the justification behind law's decisions, but it is for the judges, law's princes, to work out what in the end the community's values are and how they ought to be applied.

We return here to the notion of legalism introduced above. The distinctive position of the courts and their judges in the community image is one exemplification of the line I have taken from Shklar at the start of this chapter. And this line is also particularly clear in Rawls's approach. As he says, "in a constitutional regime with judicial review, public reason is the reason of the supreme court"; "the court's special role makes it the exemplar of public reason".[25] Any fears about the elitism of law's princes is allayed by their insistent justification by reference to the community. And the values of community gain specific expression, as Cotterrell puts it, through the form of law's *ratio* which provides justification not just in terms of uniformity, but at the level of substantive values.

Now while such an idea can also be present in the imperial image (and Cotterrell wisely does not push the difference on this matter), it is perhaps more prominent in that of community. The singularity of reason is ultimately more pressing for the community image than the *imperium*. For Cotterrell:

> If *ratio* is the element of unifying moral authority in law it implies social arrangments in which principles of justice are derived by elaborating a substantive rationality justified as grounded in shared moral experience. The idea of law's *ratio* suggests the image of a regulated population united by a shared rationality which makes agreement on principles of justice feasible [at 320–1].

[24] Ronald Dworkin, *Law's Empire* (London, Fontana Press, 1986), 404.

[25] Rawls, n. 12 above, 231, 216.

I will return shortly to some initial criticisms of this image, but before doing so will outline the other image Cotterrell identifies, that which he associates more clearly with the contemporary English approach.

(ii) *Imperium*

The image of law as *imperium* has its roots in an ancient lineage, but finds its more recent and direct ancestry in the influence of positivist legal theory. Though the community model without doubt employs *imperium*-type force, it differs in terms of its justificatory practices. For Cotterrell, "the typical imperium image of the regulated population in modern legal philosophy from the end of the eighteenth century onward is that of a mass of separate individuals (not a group), benefitting individually from their subjection to a rationally directed superior political authority" (at 225). Here law does not depend so much on direct community input as on a diverse populace seen as being at one remove from the main source of legal meaning, namely, that which is systemically valid. As Cotterrell suggests, even when the overly-simplistic Austinian model of "law as the command of the sovereign" is rejected, the more refined positivist theories that replace it still do not turn to the community as the "author of law". Instead, he says,

> *Law itself* is treated as ruling. Legal theory—as in Hart's concept of law—asserts that there is no need to seek legal authority outside law itself . . . Law governs society. The image is not that of society (in the form of a morally cohesive community) controlling and determining law [at 226–7, original emphasis].

So in contradistinction to the community model, as Cotterrell sees it, "law's image of imperium implies political centralisation but neither moral cohesion nor moral diversity" (at 322). Now this may seem counter-intuitive: surely the converse of a moral unity is moral diversity. In a sense this is true, and—certainly in contemporary positivist theory—moral diversity under the rule of law is indeed used as an aspirational justification for this model. But strictly speaking it is not the moral dimension that is at issue. That dimension is again at one remove from the core concern of the *imperium* model. Instead the key issue is not that individuals are morally "united or divided"; it is that, "the *political* ties that link each of them to a central authority are fundamental" (at 323, original emphasis). So when Cotterrell suggests (above) that the existence of a group is not a postulate of this image, this is only true in a moral sense. An organic moral community is not required, but a group nonetheless exists, though it takes the more precise jurisdictional sense of legal subjects of the realm.

We see a clear difference here with the first model in at least two senses. First, the *imperium* model need not articulate that strong sense of community on which the first model was so reliant. It relies instead on some model of (usually) hierarchically constituted and recognised validity. The sources of law are defined as internal to the system, not dependent for their validity on their direct link to, in Dworkin's terms, the community's constitutive morality. To repeat however, this is not to deny that there may be moral reasons underpinning an *imperium* model (though it does not necessarily confirm it either); certainly in the contemporary positivist strain liberal-democratic arguments are offered as support. But the justificatory rhetoric is quite different; the way in which arguments about a community's moral values appear in jurisprudential debate are not the same, and they do not operate in the same manner. We can see this if we turn to a second difference, namely how the courts approach questions of legal interpretation.

After a review of a series of English cases, Cotterrell concludes that the "idea of judges as custodians of popular morality in various forms is sufficiently controversial to make its explicit adoption generally counterproductive. . . . No accepted imagery of community is now available to be linked to English law. Public values are invoked but they are what political institutions declare them to be" (at 240). Now we will come to query how this might also be true of the American style in a moment, but if we turn to a recent theoretical formulation from Britain, we see the difference Cotterrell is drawing attention to. Again I will use an article by Neil MacCormick as a particularly lucid example.

Although MacCormick strenuously denies the autonomy of law in any pure sense (as for example taken from a systems-theoretical approach), the approach to legal interpretation he offers nevertheless relies on special types of legal argumentation which do not make (*contra* Dworkin) direct appeal to the community's political morality as a technique of justification. Part of the reason for this was brought out earlier and concerned the controversial nature of a community's moral values and the consequent need for (and ability of) law to produce some "relatively determinate common norms of public action". In order for law to carry this out it relies on what Robert Summers termed "authority reasons"; that is, a reason "which is supposed to hold good as a reason by virtue of the authority of its source".[26] In legal argumentation, then, the judge will focus, though not always exclusively, on providing just such reasons. As MacCormick notes, "the law is a forum of institutional argumentation to the extent that it gives, and necessarily gives, a central place to 'authority reasons' in the form of statutes, precedents, doctrinal materials, and the like".[27] Here we see quite clearly the rhetoric of authority, of a primary reliance on the valid sources of law. Of course, it is highly unlikely that those such as Dworkin who were associated with the community image would deny that these sources matter to the judge. Yet the emphasis is different, and this is especially clear when the reading of these sources themselves do not in the first instance produce a relatively clear conclusion.

Where Dworkin, say, turned to the "constitutive morality" of the community in such cases, MacCormick's approach is more cautious. The interpretative restraints are drawn primarily from "linguistic" and "systemic" sources internal to legal doctrinal argument, and in cases where these may be insufficiently determinate, the acknowledgment that "substantive" reasons are to be employed still asserts no direct reference to the "community's values".[28]

In relation to substantive arguments, two types may be employed: teleological—"what so acting or not acting will bring about"—and deontological—"appeals to principles of right and wrong, principles about what ought or ought not to be or be done".[29] However, while these are clearly general argumentative principles, that is, they are not exclusive to law, they cannot be treated in law in the same way as they would be in general practical argument. Such arguments must take a distinctive, institutional, form in legal interpretation. Thus teleological arguments are concerned with (in the example of statutory interpretation) the "end or purpose imputed to a piece of legislation on the assumption of its having been enacted by a rational legislature in a given historical setting",[30] and not the telos of an independently conceived common good. Likewise deontological arguments focus on the "terms and principles of

[26] Neil MacCormick, "Argumentation and Interpretation in Law" (1993) 6 *Ratio Juris* 18. Cf. Joseph Raz on "exclusionary reasons" in his *The Authority of Law* (Oxford, Clarendon Press, 1979).

[27] MacCormick, above n. 26 at 19.

[28] It should be noted that MacCormick points out that linguistic, systemic and substantive arguments, do not necessarily appear in legal argument in sequential order; *ibid.*, 27.

[29] *Ibid.*, 17.

[30] *Ibid.*, 25.

rectitude or justice", but again "what ought to be done" is limited to the "given situation or subject matter" defined by a statutory context rather than by any vague morally-conceived standards.[31]

In other words, substantive arguments in law have to become "special cases" of general practical arguments.[32] And how they are made special differs, at least ostensibly, for MacCormick as compared to Dworkin. Where Dworkin had suggested (supra) that "we accept the adjudicative principle of integrity as sovereign over law", MacCormick appears to reverse the relation:

> The special sort of reasoning is one which leaves aside any general and abstract deliberation on what in a given context it would be best or would be all things considered right to do or not do. Where law is appealed to, all things are not considered. Rather, *the law's requirements* (and, perhaps, enablements and permissions) are considered, and decision focuses on application of, or compliance with *these* requirements, or "norms" more generally.[33]

Again it is arguable that Dworkin would also endorse the judge's decision as effecting law's requirements, but the rhetoric is quite different. What makes legal argument "special", and how it is special, is not the same for MacCormick as it is for Dworkin. Law's image of community and, indeed, law's image of itself, is different, and that difference is the one Cotterrell is drawing attention to between community and *imperium*.

A final caveat: Cotterrell himself admits that these differences do not fall neatly across an Anglo—or British—American divide, nor do they capture the full subtlety of each approach. Still it ought to be clear there is a difference. The *ratio* of the community image provided the "element of unifying moral authority in law", but that rhetoric is not openly present in the interpretative concerns of the *imperium* image. Cotterrell suggests the parallel element in the latter is that of *voluntas*, though I would prefer to see it as an alternative *ratio*, since both images (and here I agree with Cotterrell) must have both *ratio* and *voluntas*. His point is, though, that in the *imperium* image, "the dominance of *voluntas* over *ratio* celebrates political authority at the expense of moral authority in legal doctrine" (at 323); and moreover, that, though again only as a matter of degree, order and systematicity provide a greater force in the judicial mind, albeit often for moral reasons, in the *imperium* image, than they do in the community image, which relies on a much more explicit use of the language and determinacy of public morality.

[31] MacCormick, above n. 25.

[32] Cf. Robert Alexy, *A Theory of Legal Argumentation* (Oxford, Clarendon Press, 1989).

[33] MacCormick, n. 26 above, 19, emphasis added.

Some Preliminary Issues

(i) *Whose Community?*

First let me suggest that the community image is ostensibly more problematic for a radical liberal theory than is the *imperium* image. The problem can be reduced to one key concern: who are "we"?; that is, what constitutes the "we" of "the community"? The difficulty in asserting this is exemplified in the light-hearted story of the Lone Ranger and Tonto one day riding through the country when they are surrounded by a group of apparently hostile Indians. The Lone Ranger, realising a danger, turns to his trusty side-kick and asks, "What are we going to do?", to which the astute Tonto responds, "What do you mean 'we', white man?"

While both Rawls and Dworkin give their support to a reading of community in which the individual (and for the latter particularly his/her rights) is given clear prominence, they nevertheless resort to a notion of community that appears unacceptably homogenous in its construction of who "we" are. Rawls's problem is arguably an extension of the Kantian one identified by Berlin: that, in practice, not everyone can be asked all the time whether they consent to all enactments. So, when Rawls suggests that "our exercise of political power is fully proper only when it is exercised in accordance with a constitution the essentials of which all citizens as free and equal may reasonably be expected to endorse in light of their common human reason" (supra), we face precisely the pragmatic problem of how and by whom that expectation is constructed.[34] As Berlin warned, with this "the door was opened wide to the rule of experts". It has been suggested that this issue is particularly acute in America: the "United States of Anomie", as Hutchinson remarks.[35] More positively, it has been made acute where, according to Chantal Mouffe, "new political subjects have emerged, new forms of identities and communities have been created", and where Rawls's

[34] One can detect a similar slippage even in Habermas's abstract discourse principle: "[o]nly those norms of action are valid to which all possibly affected persons could assent as participants in rational discourse": see Jürgen Habermas, *Between Facts and Norms* (trans. W. Rehg, Cambridge, Mass., MIT Press, 1996), 459. The gap opens with the "*could assent*" and the "*may reasonably be expected to endorse*" (Rawls).

[35] Allan C. Hutchinson, "The Last Emperor?" in Alan Hunt (ed.), *Reading Dworkin Critically* (New York, Berg Publishers, 1992), 60.

notion of an "overlapping consensus" (amongst other things), "is unlikely to capture the imagination of the new social movements".[36]

The issue of who "we" are thus becomes susceptible to the question of who asserts the meaning of, in Rawls's phrase, our "common human reason". In terms of constitutional politics, room is opened up for a split between who decides that meaning and those for whom, and in whose name, it is decided. As Benhabib puts it:

> The republican formula of autonomy ["We the people decree as a norm . . ."] disguises the *differend* in politics, insofar as what is heterogenous, incommensurable, other and irreducible to a common denominator is here tied together via a formula of identity. . . . [This] logic of identity does violence to those whose otherness places them beyond the homogenising logic of the "we".[37]

Now if this is true in terms of the community at large, the problem is magnified rather than reduced when we come to the legal realm. The Supreme Court, said Rawls, "must appeal to . . . values that they believe all citizens as reasonable and rational might reasonably be expected to endorse" (supra). While it is no doubt true that it is more acceptable to appeal to such shared standards than to those, say, of one person in the community, the doubt is again twofold: first, whether such standards and values can reasonably be found and, secondly, who it is who decides on such standards and values as are found.

As to the first, we return to the problem MacIntyre identified with law and, in particular, the courts in liberal societies. In the four-level breakdown he used, his argument was that at level four (the legal system) the problem of referring to shared standards—or, as he put it referring to Dworkin, our shared moral first principles—was that "our society as a whole has none". Now I have gone into his reasons for this and do not need to repeat them here. What is worth mentioning, however, is why the problem becomes magnified when focused in on the legal realm, and in particular on the practice of the courts.

It is magnified, I suggest, because the community image of law must make a tremendous sacrifice of its proclaimed liberal premises of toler-

[36] Chantal Mouffe, "Rawls: Political Philosophy without Politics" in David Rasmussen (ed.), *Universalism and Communitarianism: Contemporary Debates in Ethics* (Boston, MIT Press, 1990), 230.

[37] Seyla Benhabib, "Democracy and Difference: Reflections on the Meta-Politics of Lyotard and Derrida" (1994) 1 *The Journal of Political Philosophy* 6, 10. For an interesting historical reconstruction which sees this issue at the heart of the founding of the American Republic see Elizabeth Mensch, "The Colonial Origins of Liberal Property Rights" (1982) 31 *Buffalo Law Review* 635.

ance to diversity in order to produce a single meaning for the values of the community. Dworkin's language is startlingly clear on this. As was noted earlier, Dworkin argues that the value of integrity is paramount for law because "we want to treat ourselves as an association of principle, as a community governed by a single and coherent vision of justice and fairness and procedural due process in the right relation" (supra). As Kerruish and Hunt, amongst others, have pointed out, however, what this fails to acknowledge—and even where we do not take the extreme position MacIntyre adopts in suggesting that there are no such shared visions never mind a single one—is that:

> [Dworkin's] simple unitary conception, epitomised by his unexplored category "we", has the effect of universalizing the interpretive perspective of one constituency, namely of lawyers and judges . . . [and] leaves unexamined the sociologically important question of the complex coexistence of interpretive consensus and "dissensus" between constituent groups and classes within any concrete community.[38]

Since Dworkin's judge must discover the right answer to the question of who has the legal right in any case, it becomes impossible for the judge to run with any possibility that does not produce a single answer. The "community's morality" must therefore be homogenised sufficiently to produce the single standard from which the right follows. He denies that any majoritarian principle can do this work; only the "best light" that judges can shed is capable, or justified, in doing so. Of course, Dworkin admits the possibility that judges might get it wrong sometimes, but even here his response is telling. That they may err, he suggests, should not lead us to abandon the present institutions or techniques of judging; "[t]here is no reason", he maintains, "to credit any other particular group with better facilities of moral argument; or, if there is, then it is the process of selecting judges, not the techniques of judging that they are asked to use, that must be changed".[39] Change the judges if necessary, in other words, but there is nothing wrong with *how* they do what they do, nor with the fact that they do do it.

Why might this be most problematic for a radical liberal theory? There are several reasons, most of which I will cover more systematically in the following sections. But immediately prominent is that, even where the community image has in its focus the guaranteeing of

[38] Valerie Kerruish and Alan Hunt, "Dworkin's Dutiful Daughter: Gender Discrimination in Law's Empire" in Hunt (ed.), n. 35 above, 209–39, at 227. These authors also suggest Dworkin's work has become progressively conservative in this regard.

[39] Ronald Dworkin, *Taking Rights Seriously* (London, Duckworth, 1979), 130.

individual rights, how these are justified seems to rely on an intransigent process which must assume both that the community in any particular case of determining such rights can be deemed to speak with one voice, and that there is one method and group of people—the judges, law's princes—who are to carry this out. On the surface, this already suggests a doubt expressible through two central concerns identified by Berlin. That is, the twin dangers inherent in assuming a unity of perspective toward conflict-resolution (the *a priori* commitment to commensurability), and of giving over that power of resolution to a single group of "experts".

The construction of a single standard, which Benhabib addressed at the level of constitutional politics in terms of the "logic of identity [doing] violence to those whose otherness places them beyond the homogenising logic of the 'we'" (supra), is both replicated and concentrated at the level of the court's decision, and is augmented in those legal systems where a constitutional court sits to review the legitimacy of acts passed by the legislature. This is of prime importance where there may be questions of constitutive values and identities at stake. Here the radical liberal theory argued that sensitivity toward the construction of disagreement and the danger of overriding potentially incommensurable values meant that particular attention had to be paid to the settling and the setting of such conflict.

The question therefore is whether or not the single vision of community to which this image refers is capable of paying such attention. Or, alternatively, how much this process depends, as MacIntyre suggested, on the production of "verdicts". This is of particular concern in those cases where clear results do not seem immediately readable from the construction of the relevant legal texts. For, arguably, what makes a case hard is usually precisely that there is a conflict between strong and deeply held convictions in the first place; that is, that there *is* no easy answer to be found. Yet the idea that such difficult cases *do* have an answer if only the judges look hard enough, and that they can and do construct what the community's morality actually requires, goes against the very reasons why it is a hard case at all. Surely, the degree of difficulty in the case is inversely proportional to the degree to which common standards exist.

Moreover, a worry remains that the reading of a historical understanding of the community "in its best light" remains fixed within the institutional bounds of the legal system and its personnel, and I will address this issue specifically later. But Dworkin is correct in noting also that it does matter *who* tells this story about what "we" are and are required to do in a particular case. And, as we might expect, this is by no means a new problem. The seventeenth-century common lawyers were opened to the same critique, in particular where their notion of the authority of law was bound up with such vague notions as custom and immemorial practice. So, for example, in a discussion between Sir Edward Coke and James I and VI about what was reasonable as defined through adherence to legal precedent, the King had asked Coke to bring him a precedent on a particularly disputed point of law. When he did, the wise King's response is reported to have been that he wished "that he would bring precedents of good kings' times"![40]

What this example shows is that it does indeed matter who reads the institutional history's meaning into the present, but it also perhaps hints at something more—that Dworkin might be wrong to suggest simply that where we worry about judges getting the decision wrong, it is the selection of judges rather than their method of judging that is really at issue. We would be hard pushed to imagine the conflict between King James and Coke as a fight over the meaning of liberal justice. Yet Coke's technique, as Cotterrell pointed out, of arguing in a similar community-bound vein to Dworkin, might suggest that where a liberal theory was to take seriously the existence of potentially intractable conflict, then such a technique of judging which relies on asserting the "community's constitutive morality" to answer questions of serious moral conflict might well need to be rethought in light of this apparent contradiction.

I should emphasise that Dworkin's possible response that the courts do uphold the rights of individuals and show "equal concern and respect" for them does not singularly rebut the point. For again what may be read into a legal solution productive of a right will to some extent depend on the attitude and expectations of those who construct the "we" within which the right makes sense. Arguably feminist jurisprudence has been most innovative and effective in making this clear. For example, Catharine MacKinnon's complaint about the law's attempts to deal with sex discrimination is made precisely on these grounds. For her, "sex equality" in the way in which it has conventionally come to be defined in law appears as something of an oxymoron. The reason for this is that where gender is defined initially as difference and equality as equivalence, it is inevitable that there remain a tension, even a contradiction, in attempts set up in this way to remove discrimination. What this

[40] See Christopher Hill, *Intellectual Origins of the English Revolution* (Oxford, Clarendon Press, 1965), 254.

"difference approach"—that women are the same, only different—neglects to account for is, she says, that its supposed gender neutrality in fact masks its use of a highly particularised single standard. According to MacKinnon this is plain from the very vocabulary employed: in the use of "different from" and "the same as", the "referent for both [is] unspecified".[41] Left unstated is that both are measured by or against a male standard, and the issue is never even considered as to "why maleness provide[s] an original entitlement, not questioned on the basis of *its* gender".[42]

But this is precisely what this perspective cannot see. In typical forthright style, MacKinnon writes, "[i]f gender is an inequality first, constructed as a socially relevant differentiation in order to keep that inequality in place, then sex inequality questions are questions of systematic dominance, of male supremacy, which is not at all abstract and is anything but a mistake".[43] What this "dominance approach" seeks to show therefore is that, in so far as law and legal regulation attempt to fit the broader picture of how the world is, and presumably visions of how it ought to be, they will merely reproduce features which are implicitly based on masculine standards. That is, if, for example, in order to gain equal treatment under the law, it is required to demonstrate how similar women are to the set standard (again, that equal to is equivalent to "the same as"), then where this standard has been defined by men to maintain difference in the first place, it now becomes very clear that sex equality is something that is "conceptually designed never to be achieved".[44] Or, more forcefully, that there exists a "legally sanctioned inequality".[45]

One example, amongst many, MacKinnon gives in support of this reading is a case where a woman applied for a contact job in an all-male prison. It was held she could be excluded on the ground that she was a woman. The reason for this was her very womanhood, the possibility being that she might get raped. On quasi-paternalistic grounds the issue of protection was defended as an issue of difference between the sexes. However, for MacKinnon this was merely indicative of wider male dominance throughout society, in that the court could be seen to be "taking

[41] See her *Feminism Unmodified: Discourses on Life and Law* (Cambridge Mass., Harvard UP, 1987), 33.

[42] *Ibid.*, 37.

[43] *Ibid.*, 42.

[44] *Ibid.*, 44.

[45] *Ibid.*, 42.

the viewpoint of the reasonable rapist on women's employment opportunities".[46] Furthermore, were we to follow this logic through, MacKinnon asks whether, if a court were to realise that the damage done to women as the result of sexual harrassment was as vicious as rape in an all male prison, women could be excluded from the workplace altogether?[47] So for MacKinnon, it is only once such categorisation is seen in terms of dominance, not as difference transparent of substance, and therefore initially as a question of power, that the political struggle to make law gender neutral can properly begin.

Now I do not want to suggest that MacKinnon's practice of empowering law through instituting legal changes in the United States is necessarily one with which I agree, nevertheless as an example of how the "we" of legal discourse in the community vision can and does mask heterogeneity, and can and does do damage as a result, her argument is particularly forceful. What makes this insightful for any radical liberal reading is the way in which the judge's or court's position nevertheless remains the apogee of the settler of the community's morality: for Rawls the Supreme Court was the "exemplar of public reason", for Dworkin, "the courts are the capitals of law's empire". But that construction of the singular voice of the community, spoken in the language of its judges, raises a doubt for the radical liberal which eschews the "*a priori* commitment to commensurability", and queries—as a matter of course—the terms on which the institutional setting of conflicts occurs. I will return to these points more directly in the following chapter.

Yet the argument put forward by Dworkin here is precisely the legalism that Shklar identified, and we have now asserted one significant problem with it, at least in the community image. That is, the construction of the "we" is deemed to take place in the "social paradigm, the very epitome" of legalist morality, the court of law. But that "we" is constructed in and by law, in and by lawyers and their "artificial reason", and this raises doubts for the radical liberal position which constantly seeks to be alert to the possible masking of heterogeneity and genuine conflict through a postulated uniformity. Peter Goodrich, writing of the ideology of the classical common lawyers of late sixteenth- and seventeenth-century England, has noted precisely the dangers, and they seem fully apposite to the present discussion:

[46] Catharine MacKinnon, *Toward a Feminist Theory of the State* (Cambridge Mass., Harvard UP, 1989), 226.
[47] *Ibid.*, 318.

> The judges take the role of custodians of a peculiar and antique "spirit of the law," of the *arcana iuris*, which is to be defended as axiom, maxim, and judicial declaration, against all secular, imperite, or vernacular forms of knowledge. Legal reason, in short, is conjoined with judicial power, tradition with authority, source with truth . . .[48]

As a consequence:

> There is an absolute force to the word of law as the expression of the totality, a marriage of authority and reason that precludes from the very start the possibility of any member challenging or even legitimately questioning the reason of the whole . . . the unity of reason is antithetically directed against the possibility of its fracture or fragmentation.[49]

Finally there is an irony which, if it was perhaps less pressing in the time of Coke and Richard Hooker, should concern us more where the notion of popular sovereignty has ostensibly become the governing principle of contemporary liberal democracies: "the authority of law in general, and of the judges in particular, is predicated upon a concept of law as the proper form of a public reason which is paradoxically neither accessible to the public nor open to public dispute".[50]

Here we have, I suggest, an example of the "incipient threat" that comes with the legalism of the community image. Berlin had talked of the tendency to reduce problems to the point where the expert can set them right, and this reduction recurs, and indeed as I have suggested is magnified, in the community image of liberal legalism. The inability for the "public reason" of law to fragment, or, where it seems to begin to, for the expert to set it right, is endorsed by Dworkin's suggestion that if Herculean judges err it is not their method that is at fault; that there is nothing wrong with postulating the community "personified" in a single vision as stated by a court. The consequence is that those "partial reasonings" which I identified in the Introduction need to be made uniform in law's reasoning, and it is only the quasi-mystical insights of the judges to produce single answers to deeply divisive and often constitutive (as, say, MacKinnon argues) disputes that can be the measure of resolution. Little wonder that, in Coke's words, "it is an act which

[48] Peter Goodrich, *Oedipus Lex: Psychoanalysis, History, Law* (Berkeley, University of California Press, 1995), 79.

[49] *Ibid.*, 92. This last point seems strikingly similar to Dworkin's argument against "internal skepticism" in *Law's Empire*, n. 20 above.

[50] Above n. 48 at 93.

requires long study and experience, before that a man can take to the cognizance of it".[51] For it is indeed a mighty task!

Liberal legalism in the community image encounters the mass of constitutive conflicts but fails to do other than evade the potential radicalism of this encounter by shifting terrain to the singular, aristocratic artificial reason of law. Administered by the judicial elite, at the crowning moment of liberalism's claim to value pluralism, that claim is dropped in favour of "one right answer" given by the judges' perception of the community's constitutive morality in its best light. The Supreme Court will have to answer the question, say, whether abortion is legal or whether it is murder. The promise of pluralism, of tolerance, is sufficiently cloaked in the language of principle such that deep division in such a hard case means that not only can a decision be given, but the fact that it is a genuine or real disagreement means that there is a right answer to the question. In this sense, law's empire arguably colonises the very landscape—moral and political—on which its radical sources are supposed to be founded.

Once again, therefore, the issue of legitimacy raises its head. Of course, it is answered in the community image in terms of an assumed single vision, or of a "common human reason" that "all citizens as reasonable and rational might reasonably be expected to endorse". Indeed they might be so expected, but then it is unlikely that if such was the case it would be in court at all, never mind in the Supreme Court. The stunning and stubborn question that Hobbes asked hypothetically of Coke remains: that the law is to decide according to reason "our lawyers are agreed . . . but the doubt is, of whose Reason it is, that is to be received for Law".[52]

There are points relating to this position that I will develop later, and do so not solely with reference to this model. However, suspicion has been aroused, I believe sufficiently, to query whether liberal legalism's promise of community in these terms is suitable for the radical liberalism I have outlined. For now though I will turn to the other "image", the *imperium*, to formulate some more opening concerns.

(ii) *Contested Rationalities*

The model of legal reasoning that does not appeal to the community personified, the singular moral voice of the "we", also faces the problem

[51] *Prohibitions del Roy* (1607) 12 Co.Rep. 63.

[52] See the Introduction to this volume.

of how to construct legal decisions in cases where competing visions of what ought to be done conflict. Cotterrell noted the openness of this model to a genuine plurality of moral values, and it is this which makes me suggest, at least initially, that the radical liberal thesis might be more sympathetic to it. That is, such a model seeks to allow for disagreement in the moral realm, and to acknowledge that no singular morality can emerge from this to define a legal decision. However, I want in this section to explore the idea that the logic of the production of decisions may impact on the rationality of decisions that are reached when this model is used. I will suggest subsequently that the contingency of expecting and demanding a court to reach a decision is something that is seldom realised. Yet when such contingency is brought into how we think about the role of law, particularly in hard cases, it arguably re-sensitises us to what goes on in contemporary liberal legal structures, what extensive impacts this might have, and how the radical liberal theory might respond to it.

Earlier I noted how the imperium model was seen to take a more focused approach to legal decision-making by concentrating on the valid sources of law rather than appealing to vaguer notions of community morality. It is unlikely however that such a model will see itself as completely isolated from broader arguments or concerns. One way in which this relation has been stated concentrates on what has been called the "special case" thesis. That is, that legal argumentation is a special case of general practical argument. In this section I focus on this as it appears in the work of Robert Alexy, though he is not alone in making this argument.[53] But to the extent that it exemplifies legalism in Shklar's sense (and I think it is quite clear that it does) I want to test the consequences of it for the radical liberal theory.

Alexy makes the point, as did MacCormick, that when it comes to the legal sphere, "all things are not considered". For Alexy, legal discourse is limited in a way that is emblematic of the "*imperium*" model. As he notes, "legal discourse can be distinguished from general practical discourse in that the former is, in short, restricted in its scope by statute, precedent, legal dogmatics, and—in the case of actual judicial proceedings—by procedural legislation and regulations" (at 18–19). And again,

[53] See Alexy, n. 32 above. Note that page references in this section are to this text. Other writings sympathetic to this argument include Neil MacCormick's *Legal Reasoning and Legal Theory* (Oxford, Clarendon Press, 1978), e.g. chap. X. Indeed I should note that though I use Alexy's discussion here I assume that as a theory of legal reasoning it is appropriate in common law reasoning as well.

"legal reasoning is characterised by its relationship with valid law, however this is to be determined. This highlights one of the most important differences between legal reasoning and general practical reasoning. In the context of legal discussion not all questions are open to debate. Such discussion takes place under certain constraints" (at 212).

There are a variety of such constraints, some pragmatic (for example, constraints of time), others more technical (such as procedural and evidentiary rules). Nevertheless, the special case thesis allows for, or promotes, the idea that legal reasoning is "infused" with conditions of general practical argument. Thus the norms of legal reasoning are not simply "subordinate" to conditions of general practical argument (i.e., that "legal discourse is nothing more than general practical discourse behind a legal facade"), nor are they merely a "supplement" to them (in the sense that general practical argument kicks in when the limits of legal argument are reached) (at 20).

For Alexy, therefore, discourse conditions operate in both spheres, though in the legal arena there are institutional constraints which may not operate in general practical argument. For example, there may be no obligation on an accused to say anything, their participation in the institutional setting will usually be involuntary, parties in civil litigation may pursue their own interests exclusively, not all statements may be admissible, etc. (see 212–20). As such, Alexy notes, claims to correctness in legal argument are "not concerned with the absolute rationality of the normative statement in question, but only with showing that it can be rationally justified within the framework of the validly prevailing legal order" (at 22).

However, the point I want to consider here is structurally similar to a point raised in the previous section. But it concerns the question why recourse to the legal institution is seen as necessary under this model, and what this says about the reflexive relation between legal and general practical argument. Alexy argues that:

> The need for legal discourse arises out of the weakness of the rules and forms of general practical discourse. This weakness consists in the fact that these rules and forms define a decision-making procedure which in many cases leads to no result at all and which, when it does lead to a result, in no way guarantees conclusive certainty [at 287].

He gives three reasons why this might be so: first, "the actual normative convictions, which are often mutually inconsistent, form the starting point of discourse"; secondly, "not all the steps in argumentation are fixed", and finally, "since . . . there are several rules of discourse that can only be approximately satisfied, there always remains the possibility of not reaching agreement" (*ibid.*).

Now it strikes me there is a tautology here. To suggest, as Alexy does, that the need for recourse to the legal institution lies in the "weakness of the rules and forms of general practical discourse" is tautologous. Of course there would be no need for such recourse if the rules were "strong" enough; if they produced a solution there would be no need for legal institutions at all. The problem, in other words, does not lie with the weakness or strength of such rules, but with the effectiveness of reaching or imposing a solution.[54]

Alexy is however correct in saying that the real issue is that "the actual normative convictions . . . are often mutually inconsistent"; or, more colloquially, people disagree about what is the right thing to do. Yet it is not the adequacy of rules that causes this failure to resolve a dispute, but the fact that the "inconsistency" cannot be resolved by such rules alone, no matter how good they were. The so-called "inconsistency" may potentially be a matter of a clash of genuinely held normative convictions; if there existed a discourse rule productive of a solution the clash would be merely ostensible, not real, and therefore resolvable.

And I think Alexy might agree with this last point, at least to some extent. Indeed, he goes so far as to admit that there "would appear" to be something contradictory in the special case thesis in this sense. In his terms, "how can [legal reasoning] achieve these outcomes [results unattainable in general practical reasoning] if in the last analysis it is after all dependent on general practical reasoning?" (at 292). Now this is an extremely important question. But I think Alexy's response to it puts, as it were, the cart before the horse. He suggests that there is a "structural correspondence between the rules and forms of legal discourse and those of general practical discourse" (at 289). Yet, as he admits, the correspondence is not exact, otherwise legal discourse would be just as potentially unyielding of solutions as general practical discourse. What, then, does legal discourse offer? In essence, one thing: it provides a solution. And how can it do so? Because its institutional setting means that a solution can be enforced.

[54] Habermas follows a similar line on this and is therefore susceptible to the same criticisms I make of Alexy. As he says, "[l]aw, as it were, compensates for the functional weakness of a morality that, from the observer perspective, frequently delivers indeterminate and motivationally unstable results." Habermas, n. 34 above, 452–3. I concentrate for present purposes specifically on Alexy.

But here is Alexy's reading:

> If one were always inclined to fill in this area of uncertainty [left by legal norms] by no other means than recourse to general practical reasoning, the weaknesses of general practical discourse would be transmitted to a considerable degree into legal decision-making. *So it is only rational* to introduce special forms and rules of legal argumentation and to institutionalize it as legal science . . . In this way it possible further to reduce the range of discursive possibilities in the area of uncertainty left by legal norms [at 288, emphasis added].

But "only rational" according to what? It cannot be the rules of general practical discourse since their "weakness" has led to failure. It cannot be "rational" according to legal discourse since rationality requires something *of* legal discourse. It is "only rational" therefore to introduce such forms, since *a decision* is needed. Such forms "reduce the range of discursive possibilities" clearly, but only because it is rational to demand of the legal system to do so in order to effect a decision.

However, Alexy suggests, "[i]t is not the generation of certainty which constitutes the rational character of jurisprudence, but rather its conformity to a number of conditions, criteria, or rules" (at 293). It is this that seems to me to put the cart before the horse. Yes, it may be rational within legal discourse to follow rules, but "rationality" in the previous paragraph did not refer to that, but to a requirement being placed *externally* on the legal system. What was rational in that sense was that, as general practical argument could not necessarily produce a solution, the legal system could be used to do so. But that is different from saying that procedures internal to the legal system produce a valid solution within the system. So when Alexy writes that "[t]he only question to be asked is what it means to decide rationally in the framework of a valid legal order" (at 289), I would suggest that there is a question which comes before this, namely, whether or not it is rational in the first place to ask the legal system to produce a solution.

This is a separate question but it is not often considered. As Gunther Teubner has noted (discussing the role of conflicts between subsystems of society), "[h]ere the major problem is whether a translation of the conflict into the legal code is desirable at all. We do not always see this as a problem because of the ban on the denial of justice."[55] Yet no matter how much the "special case" thesis produces appropriate rules

[55] Günther Teubner, *Law as an Autopoietic System* (transl. A. Bankowska and R. Adler, ed. Z. Bankowski, Oxford, Basil Blackwell, 1993), 109.

within legal discourse, it cannot seem to avoid the conclusion that what makes law special, and different from general practical argument, is that it can effect a decision. Whether or not it should do so does not seem to be opened to critique, and this is something I will develop in a moment.

This, arguably "*imperium*", function of law is noted more boldly in some arguments that I think it is in Alexy's. So, for example, we have seen how MacCormick draws on the difference between moral and legal argument to show how the latter can produce relatively determinate and common norms of action. He is quite clear about this authoritative role and the fact that the legal system has to be backed by power to make its decisions and its setting of standards effective. And, again, he notes that problems arise when the reading of the legal texts is not immediately conclusive of a solution, that is to say, in hard cases. There, he notes:

> We have a simple conflict of legal prima-facie rights or duties. But the law does then require deciders to have recourse to general practical reasoning. What that means is that only certain kinds of arguments have rational persuasiveness here. There is no reason to doubt that quite often the relative weight of the arguments may be such as to close the legally open issue. If in a given case they do not, the issue is then one of pure decision (subject to any presumptions that are applicable in case of uncertainty) at the best intuitive judgment of the authorized decision-maker. That the decision has been refined through so many levels of argument makes it arbitrary only in a Pickwickian sense. That it is also political is what no one can or should doubt.[56]

This seems to me similar to Alexy's argument. That is, within the legal system decisions have to be reached and legal discourse provides a way of cutting down on the number of norms available so that ostensibly intractable conflict can be levelled to produce a solution. Now I agree that to suggest the process, internally, is arbitrary would be inappropriate. What I want to question is, in what sense is recourse to law here rational? Elsewhere, MacCormick has written that, in cases of "speculative disagreement" in law (in hard cases, unlike in general practical argument), "[j]udges who disagree still have to decide . . . 'Non liquet' is not an available judgment; the Court must rule on the law and decide for one party or the other, and all concerned must live with the result."[57]

[56] Neil MacCormick, n. 13 above, 555.
[57] MacCormick, n. 53 above, 248–9.

This is where I think structurally the same argument that was made against Dworkin's right answer can be brought in. Neither Alexy nor MacCormick make the open use of the community's "constitutive morality" as did Dworkin, but they rely instead on valid arguments and sources of law even though in the end an *imperium*-type decision must be made. The difference then, as Cotterrell noted, was that the "*imperium*" model (though non-arbitrary) depends upon a reference to institutionalised politics, rather than the more vague construction of the "we" of the community as a whole. Nevertheless both models seem to rely on a "special" form of legal argument which is neither "common public reason", nor general practical argument. Both or either of these are seen to be insufficiently determinative of a solution. Only the "special rules and forms" of legal reasoning can be so determinate.

But what is going on here? MacIntyre argued that the legal system, as it cannot rely on shared standards, is used in liberal societies to effect a decision, a "verdict", and that this constituted a capitulation of philosophical argument, rather than its embodiment. That is, the reason of law was not a shining example of the highpoint of liberal philosophy, nor could it be, since such argument was necessarily inconclusive. As such, liberal legal argument was a way of channelling conflict within the legal institution so that a "verdict" could be effected. Law and legal discourse provided the only means whereby "resolution" of deep conflicts could be carried out.

Now this, despite the rhetoric of rational legal argument, does seem to underlie the special case thesis: legal forms are required to "reduce the range of discursive possibilities", since "all things considered" will not produce a result. This has become particularly clear in the "*imperium*" model (though not only in it). In the end the court must decide, and must produce a winner, and must do so by reference to norms that can produce determinate answers. My question is, in what sense is it rational to do this, and how would the radical liberal reading respond? This will be the subject of the next section. But in so far as the law's "artificial reasoning" works in this model, it is arguably susceptible to similar critiques as were made of the "community" image. In particular, issues recur concerning: who decides what the institutionalised politics of the legal system requires?; how and on what terms radical disagreement has to be homogenised to make a solution reachable?; what does it mean to "reduce the range of discursive possibilities" and what effects does this have?, etc. In other words, if in the *imperium* image, the courts are again the special place where legalism is exemplified in community, how does the fixing of the meaning of institutional politics and principles affect the claims to moral diversity for which it is supposed to allow?

6: Law, Conflict, and Consensus

Deeper Concerns

(i) A Note on Decisions

As I have suggested, the structural concern is the same for the *imperium* model as it was for the right answer thesis. That is, as a case becomes more and more difficult (either the community's morality is contested or the legal materials are still inconclusive) we reach a point where a decision still has to be made. Now, as MacCormick suggests, we may reach that point for reasons. But the issue seems to me that, as the case gets harder, it becomes *less rational* to decide it. As I noted earlier in relation to the community image, the degree of difficulty in the case is inversely proportional to the degree to which common standards exist. The more the law is unclear, or the more the community's morality is contested (perhaps often the same thing in difficult cases), the more the "verdict" will indeed appear as merely an exercise of power. But it will also appear as an increasingly illegitimate use of power as the degree of difficulty increases. When the cases on either side are so "finely balanced" why should it be reasonable just to decide it?

To explore this I need now to go into what I termed the institutional features of legal reasoning, rather than internal justificatory arguments. The first deals with what Shklar calls the "ideology of agreement" and the second with the contingency of decision production.

Shklar argues that both natural lawyers and positivists agree about one thing: that justice is a matter of following the right rules. This is what makes their respective positions, according to her definition, legalist, and the debate between them, she says, a "family quarrel". Their essential difference is "about what to do when a conflict between rules occurs",[1] but what they share is the devotion to rules themselves. As such, the judge will:

> call for *some* rule, *any* rule, even if statute and precedent have failed . . . Either he will convince himself that some set of social facts, some set of

[1] Judith N. Shklar, *Legalism: Law, Morals, and Political Trials* (Cambridge, Mass., Harvard UP, 1986), 106.

> expertly developed "is" conditions, yields a rule for him automatically, or he will appeal to a higher law, or he will rely on what he hopes is the majority view of his fellow citizens. In all three cases it is obviously of greater importance to him that the rules he relies on be based on universal agreement among either the experts, the wise, or the whole people.[2]

This view also underpins the two views of law—community and *imperium*—as I have discussed them above. The similarities and differences of the two positions are replicated in this description by Shklar. What I have been hinting at though is what the, as Shklar puts it, "ideology of agreement"—of the "community's constitutive morality" or of the judges' conclusions of what valid law requires—means and signifies beyond the internal realm of legal justification. I have suggested, *contra* for example Alexy who noted that it was "only rational" to cut down on discursive possibilities, that as cases become more difficult it becomes less rational to decide them. However what made it "only rational" for Alexy—and for both models generally—was precisely what Shklar calls the ideology of agreement. Yet this has certain assumptions and implications that make this form of legalism unattractive for the radical liberal position. Here are three aspects drawn from Shklar and elsewhere that begin to explore why.

The first is an assumption and relates to how the need to decide impacts on the process of reasoning. As Shklar notes, "[a] situation calling for a decision is already the mental construction of the observer, rather than something that presents itself to him "there" and ready-made . . . the act of deciding implies estimating the character of a situation and following the rules applicable to it".[3] Here the need for agreement is directed towards the fact that unless a single rule (or principle-embedded rule) can in the end be found, a decision cannot be made. Thus the need to direct the understanding of the situation into a form in which a decision is reachable requires viewing the conflict in a particular way. In MacCormick's terms, "the Court must rule on the law and decide for one party or the other, and all concerned must live with the result". In order to do so, the court must produce a rule by which that result is justified. And there must be agreement on what that rule is, even if it is the minimal requirement of a majority of the court. If there was no such agreement (regardless of how it was reached) the decision could not justifiably follow.

[2] Judith N. Shklar, *Legalism: Law, Morals, and Political Trials* (Cambridge, Mass., Harvard UP, 1986), 101 (original emphasis).

[3] *Ibid.*, 61.

The second aspect is that this assumption produces an in-built implication. As Marshall has put it, "it is difficult to separate the idea of an issue from the procedure by which it is settled, and difficult to define a deciding agent without reference to an implied mode of action".[4] In other words, the construction of the issue itself as in need of a decision draws into play both the way in which the rules are set and how the judge ought to act. That is, acting with a view to producing a decision infects or constructs how the issue is to be viewed. As Marshall continues:

> No dispute or issue is *inherently* justiciable or suited to judicial solution. The supposition that it might be involves the assumption that a dispute can be clearly contrasted with its methods of settlement and described independently. But once an issue or contest of interests is defined it is impossible to avoid mentioning or implying at least some indication of what constitutes winning or losing . . . once the description of the issue is filled out the contrast between the issue itself and its mode of settlement crumbles.[5]

This last point is most significant. What it draws out is that the assumption of the need to agree on a rule means that the issue has to be transformed in such a way as ultimately to make such agreement realisable. But, as Marshall rightly notes, this transformation means that the (re-)constructed issue cannot be separated from what is being demanded of the process, namely a single solution, a winner and a loser. This is a point I will return to in more detail subsequently, for it directly relates to the concern we saw in the radical liberal position over the *a priori* commitment to commensurability.

The third aspect concerns what effects this has *back* on the source of the conflict itself. Shklar notes that because legal conflict has been preset to require and produce agreement, one effect of this is that "legalism may in practice make people especially *uncompromising*".[6] That is, if the logic of the legal system is aimed at producing winners or losers, then as well as preforming alternatives there is a clear incentive to strengthen one's case as far as possible under legal procedures to produce the best chance of winning. Now Alexy noted this difference between legal argumentation and general practical argument, but failed to notice properly how this would in turn reflect back on general practical argument. When he suggested that part of the need for legal

[4] Geoffrey Marshall, "Justiciability" in A. G. Guest (ed.) *Oxford Essays in Jurisprudence* (First Series) (Oxford, Clarendon Press, 1961), 269.

[5] *Ibid.*, 278 (original emphasis).

[6] Shklar. n. 1 above, 105 (emphasis added).

argument was that there were inconsistent values or norms conflicting at the level of general practical argument, he did not appear to acknowledge as significant that the "infusion" might work in reverse. That is, that the determinacy achievable through the "rules and forms" of legal discourse might impact both on how and on what occasions recourse to legal argument was thought necessary or desirable, and that the influence of legal expectations might be partly responsible for inconclusiveness of general practical argument. The "structural correspondence" between legal and general practical argument may thus be more reflexive than Alexy seems to allow. For it is not simply the case that legal relations mediate disputes in the legal realm, but further that such relations as it promotes often become in part constitutive of social or political relations themselves. This is why I suggested that the question whether it was rational to have recourse to law was so important; dependency on the determinacy of law may itself predispose the construction of normative conflict at the level of general practical argument in a particular and potentially intransigent way. As Shklar correctly notes, given the expectations that legal argument constructs, it may lead people to become particularly uncompromising at the level of general practical argument.

This pushes us towards thinking about sociological dimensions of the role of law, and again I will develop this subsequently. But the deeper point Shklar is making here is that legalism as an ethical attitude, exemplified in the practice of the courts, tends to exclude, ignore or misdescribe other forms of moral understanding that do not correspond to the model of legalism and its ideology of agreement. Perhaps ironically, this is particularly true of the positivist or *imperium* model; ironical because of its supposed tolerance to moral diversity. The prominent position of the legalistic court tends, she says, in extreme form, to force legal argument to "seal itself off" from political conflict:

> The uncompromising character of justice [as rule following] as a virtue militates against any latitudinarian view of social morality . . . to maintain the contrast between legal order and political chaos and to preserve the former from any taint of the latter it is not just necessary to define law out of politics; an entirely extravagant image of politics as a species of war has to be maintained. Only thus can the sanctity of rule following as a social policy be kept from compromising associations.[7]

[7] Shklar. n. 1 above, 122.

Corresponding to the "*imperium*"—and its special case thesis—and the "community"—the construction of the singular "we"—models I have been using, Shklar notes that it will be the case that "[e]ither rules for their own protection must be magically lifted out of politics, or society itself must be made safe for justice by imposing a unity upon it, which will make possible a consistent policy of justice according to universally accepted rules".[8] The point is therefore that *both* models, and not just the community one in which it was most clear, have a converse impact on the terms in which law and legal argumentation construct and expect moral debate to be. So even when MacCormick rightly notes that the ultimate decision is a political one, it is political in a particular sense only, namely one that has been channelled in a specific way in order to make it amenable to the reaching of a legal decision. A diverse range of moral-political possibilities must be institutionalised in such a way that what is political for law abstracts itself from the realm of conflict to produce the conflict-immunised possibilities of settled institutional meaning. It is in this sense that Shklar points out, "[a]ll politics must be assimilated to the paradigm of just action—the judicial process".[9] The ideology of agreement thus infuses the understanding of political and moral conflict in a way that means that it is or becomes amenable to "resolution". And there is no doubt that this expectation is projected back on to the original realm of such conflicts: if one wants to be a winner, one's case must be presented accordingly.

As I have said I will delve more deeply into these three aspects shortly. But let me counter one argument that may be presented at this point. I am suggesting that an ideology of agreement operates in the legalist model and that this has certain, perhaps hidden consequences. These include the idea that conflict has to be understood in a specific way in order to produce a conclusion, and that this becomes more problematic the more difficult a case becomes. But what of the argument that this is a necessary price to pay for the production of a decision? That judges are expected to decide and if they did not do so there would be chaos; that we need authoritative common rules, someone has to provide them, and that is what judges are there to do? That "non liquet", as MacCormick noted, is not an available solution?

My response here is to say that it was not always thus, nor need it be. The contingency of the decision-making function of the legal system is something I have said is seldom realised. Interestingly,

[8] *Ibid.*, 122–3.

[9] *Ibid.*, 122.

J. H. Baker has noticed that in an earlier period of English legal history and due in part to institutional differences, judicial *indecision* was a prominent feature of the legal system. "Courts", he writes, "were simply not perceived as having a strong decision-making role . . . judges were very much less inclined to reach decisions at all if the law was unclear."[10] In a process where the appeal system did not operate in such a clearly defined manner as it does today, "[e]very opportunity for exploring doubts was therefore given before judgment was entered".[11] In cases where the point of law was particularly disputed, public consultation amongst judges and different benches was expected. "If after all that", says Baker, "they still had qualms—they did nothing. Judicial inaction was not seen as a dereliction of duty, as it would be today, because it encouraged and helped parties to settle their differences when the merits were balanced."[12]

Now there may be more likenesses here with our present system than we initially expect. For example, most of the time people act according to the law—in public acts or private arrangements—without the intervention of a judge. Yet what is most strikingly different is that when it does come to litigation under the system Baker describes, the possibility of "non liquet" *is* an option. And as Baker says, "[t]hat is by no means less wise or fair than our system, under which—even if the law is doubtful at the outset—the winner takes all".[13] It might, I suggest, if worked through, be *more* wise and more fair, especially when the law is unclear not simply at the outset, but towards the conclusion of the legal process.

I should note that this is not simply an issue of being concerned about the setting in place of a retrospective decision; that is, of a legitimate worry about creating "new law" in hard cases. Nor is it about the courts refusing to set in motion the power of the law's sanctions, for example when it refuses to enforce gambling contracts or "immoral" or "illegal" pacts. It goes instead to the theoretical point that the current decision-making function of judges is more contingent than is often assumed. Structurally, there is no necessity for judges to decide cases, particularly when they are hard. Of course, our legal system is built upon the assumption that there is, but the question arises whether that is more or

[10] J. H. Baker, "English Law and the Renaissance" in J. H. Baker, *The Legal Profession and the Common Law: Historical Essays* (London, Hambledon Press, 1986), 472.

[11] *Ibid.*, 473.

[12] *Ibid.*

[13] *Ibid.*

less fair or wise. At the very least however, we might consider it to be an available option rather than an impossibility.

I do not want it to appear that I am recommending that judges should never decide cases. Not at all. What I am proposing is that, given the "ideology of agreement" required by contemporary processes of legal reasoning, and given the varied assumptions, implications, and effects that the model of legalism rests upon and produces, there might be strong arguments in favour of exploring alternative models of the court to its present one as "exemplar of legalistic morality". As Baker's historical sketch shows, the court's role can vary depending on the expectations placed upon it in society. Of course, it might be said that in these times of which Baker writes a more homogeneous society was taken for granted, or even imposed, than would be acceptable today. This is probably true, but it does not in itself constitute an argument in favour of the currently dominant ideology of agreement of the legalism that operates in liberal communities.

Indeed, if anything, it points in the other direction. The more legalism has to postulate the reduction of radical conflict to the place where decisions can be reached in terms of winners and losers, the further it gets from the premises of a liberal theory that endorse in practice the possible incommensurability of ultimate values. For, as Baker suggested, part of the rationale for the judicial indecision was to encourage parties themselves to settle differences, in light of the fact that the institutional hearing had allowed the airing of disagreement in a more or less formal public setting and, as such, could not therefore be dismissed as time-wasting. Yet where the legalism of the contemporary court requires the production of winners and losers, this inevitably also affects the channelling of tactics, arguments and expectations in the realm outside the formalistic legal setting. And where this is so, we might wonder whether or not the commitment to commensurability that this ostensibly requires runs contrary to the radical liberal position which treated with suspicion the channelling of conflict into pre-ordained forms.

(ii) *Reasonable Men and Persons in Law*

Another aspect of the "ideology of agreement" resurfaces when we turn our attention to the place of legal personality in the process of legal decision-making. Consistently, it would seem, liberalism's conception of the legal person has come under attack from critics of liberalism generally.

In this section I want to look briefly at why this is so, and to consider whether such critique is justified. I then want to ask how the radical liberal position would respond. For it is my contention that even though liberalism's critics have misconstrued what they take to be an essential element of liberal argument, it is nevertheless the case that the radical liberal approach ought itself to be wary of certain aspects of legal personality as they are endorsed by liberal legalism. Here however, rather than delving fully into the subject of legal personality, my example will look at a different construction of the person used in legal reasoning, namely the "reasonable man", in order to see what role this figure plays and what issues it may raise for a liberal theory.

Some of the most trenchant criticisms of liberalism in recent years have come from feminist scholars. In particular they have concentrated on the political and legal construction of the individual as an isolated, self-seeking, masculine-biased figure. Perhaps ironically, this figure is seen to be at once unrealistic, even non-existent, and yet remarkably powerful. Its roots are usually taken to lie in the contractarian theories of Hobbes and his heirs. Here the individual is taken to be a pre-social being, whose problems begin when "he" encounters other equally egoistic individuals, and must find some way of making arrangements to curtail the potential for constant war that exists in the state of nature. (I should say, it always strikes me as odd that Hobbes is taken to be the founder of this social "war of all against all" scenario; it seems to neglect the fact that he was writing in the context of a bloody civil war, where individuals appeared to require no theory of liberalism to justify their aggression.) So, for example, Alison Jagger writes that one of the underlying foundations of liberal thought is "the metaphysical assumption of abstract individualism . . . According to this assumption, each human individual has desires, interests, etc. that in principle can be fulfilled quite separately from the desires and interests of other people".[14] And, as Val Plumwood adds in a similar vein, "[f]or such a lone, self-sufficient wanderer in the woods, he who encounters the other only accidentally and occasionally, the well-being of others is merely a contingent, mutual arrangement of convenience, not an essential part of his well-being".[15]

Now these kinds of arguments are familiar, though different in focus, from our analysis of MacIntyre. It should be clear by now that such

[14] Alison Jagger, *Feminist Politics and Human Nature* (NJ, Rowman & Allanheld, 1983), 30.

[15] Val Plumwood, *Feminism and the Mastery of Nature* (London, Routledge, 1993), 152.

atomism has been overstated, and the arguments from Berlin's liberalism have gone some way to showing how the social construction of values and individuals' relations within (broadly-defined) social institutions negate the very possibility of such a pre-social being. Even Adam Smith, it was seen, rejected out of hand the notion of an atomistic morality rooted simply in the desire for individuals to have their interests satisfied. Nevertheless, as I also noted, the individual still plays a prominent role in liberal theory, whose rational ability to choose ought to be acknowledged as an integral feature of such a theory. So, as Jaggar correctly points out, "liberalism's central moral belief [is] the intrinsic and ultimate value of the human individual",[16] and the radical theory I have outlined from Berlin would certainly have little difficulty endorsing this. What I want to concentrate on here, however, is what happens to the approach to individual worth when it appears in the legal realm, for it is here, arguably, that the radical liberal theory, and critics of liberalism generally, may have something in common.

In line with the perceived contractarian assumptions of liberal individualism, Benhabib has argued that law comes to play a specific though supporting role for liberal theorists. As she has written:

> The law reduces insecurity, the fear of being engulfed by the other, by defining mine and thine. Jealously is not eliminated but tamed; as long as each can keep what is his and attain more by fair rules of the game, he is entitled to it . . . The law contains anxiety by defining rigidly the boundaries between self and other, but the law does not cure anxiety. The anxiety that the other is always on the look [sic] to interfere in your space and appropriate what is yours; the anxiety that you will be subordinated to his will; . . .[17]

In this description law plays, in theory, the role of setting the rules for social interaction, without favouring one side or another, and the court's role is to adjudicate impartially on any disputes that should arise. Of course, and again as Jaggar has noted, the theory behind this was remarkably powerful in a historical context of countering state- or Crown-sanctioned privilege: "[c]ompared with medieval political philosophy", she writes, "which interpreted the social hierarchy as the god-given natural order, this basic egalitarianism in liberal theory was extremely radical".[18]

[16] Jaggar, n. 14 above, 33.

[17] Seyla Benhabib, "The Generalised and Concrete Other", in S. Benhabib and D. Cornell (eds.), *Feminism as Critique* (Cambridge, Polity Press, 1987), 85.

[18] Jaggar, n. 14 above, 30.

My contention, of course, is that arguably it still is. However, the uses of the person in law present problems for a liberal theory such as the one offered here. So in what follows I will argue that it is not liberalism that fails law, but that it is law that fails liberalism—that liberal law, in other words, is insufficiently liberal.

Ngaire Naffine has argued that the liberal conception of the legal person is not gender-neutral, but is best represented as "the man of law". In this form, she says:

> For the law to be regarded as a fair, impartial, non-arbitrary and universal system, it is essential that it invoke a universal person. The fiction of the equality and essential sameness of all before the law, the idea that the man of law is in fact a human prototype, is thus the very basis of the ideal of the Rule of Law. The legal person's very abstractness, his very paradigm quality, serves to show that the legal approach is not an approach in fact but an inherently neutral way of organising and arbitrating relations between human beings.[19]

According to the critique Naffine develops, the problem with this model is the assumption that all people are deemed to be a particular type of person in law. That is, they are expected to correspond to the image of the "liberal individual" who is atomistic, self-sufficient and self-seeking. The problem she identifies, however, is that this is merely a fiction, that not everyone can, nor is indeed allowed to, live up to this image. As such, the abstraction that constitutes the capacities of the legal person (or the "man of law") represents a supposed universality, but in effect involves abstraction from a particular type of person.

This is not a novel insight, and has been around at least since the writings of Marx. But the issue I want to raise, is, I think, more fundamental. It concerns the relation between the ideology of agreement (as just discussed) and what law requires of the person in law. We saw in the discussion of Berlin's liberalism the problems associated with postulating a "true self", the notion that the strong sense of reason (delineating uniformity and ultimately justifying "rational" imposition by the benign legislator) could only operate where "man's true nature" was identifiable. As was noted then, there were two elements to the logic of such a position: one, without a true self reason will not command an objective morality; and two, "it is up to those who *do* accurately perceive the dictates of reason to make sure that those "poor, ignorant,

[19] Ngaire Naffine, *Law and the Sexes: Explorations in Feminist Jurisprudence* (Sydney, Allen and Unwin, 1990), 123.

desire-ridden" others who do not properly grasp such dictates, are shown the path to enlightened, rational behaviour".[20]

The reason for rejecting these assertions was two-fold; they relied on the notion that all values could ultimately be made to conform to a harmonious pattern, and, that the consequences of holding this to be true involved an unwarrantable imposition upon those deemed to have an insufficient grasp of what reason required. The fundamental issue now, therefore, is to what extent does legal personality assume the same kind of logic—that which follows the assumptions and dicates of the "real self"—in effecting the dictates of its own impositions? As we have just seen, the need for contemporary law to produce single determinate answers to hard questions relied on the ability of law to formulate single standards, standards moreover that fitted or cohered with the overall pattern of law. Given that one of the responses to MacIntyre's diagnosis of liberal morality—as the mere lining up of preferences of the form "I want it to be the case that such-and-such"—was that it misconstrued the construction of moral disagreement, how can a radical liberal theory deal with a concept of law which appears ostensibly to rely upon a notion of singular personality in order both to justify its pronouncements and to legitimise its own authority? How can a theory committed to the idea of incommensurable values and the collapsing of the distinction between the right and the good be at ease with a legal theory that assumes a detailed harmony of standards and legal personality in order to effect a "weighing and tallying" of putatively commensurable claims?

One of the problems the radical liberal theory will have with contemporary liberal legal conceptions of personality concerns the possible input into defining the features of the identity of such a person. This is not a problem merely with liberal law, but with notions of legal personality that have long pre-existed liberal theory. However, the problem becomes particularly acute for a radical liberal theory that does espouse a commitment both to incommensurable values and to the realisation of the constitutive link between such values and self-identity. When we recall what I termed Berlin's distinct view of rationality, namely that when it comes to conflicting values then, that the choices are made by those concerned is the key to acknowledging their moral capability, we must ask to what extent this can be upheld in relation to the legal person.

[20] Above.

When it is recognised that legal decisions are productive of political outcomes and involve choices that constitute moral and political expectations, it is clearly of importance that the rationality of actors is not completely superseded by the defining of characteristics by the legal system. Yet how far is this the case with personality in law and legal reasoning? The "reasonable man" is often taken as a focus of critique, as he is deemed to represent the predominantly atomistic features of liberalism and the problems embodied in the "man of law". He will therefore provide a good test for our current concerns and will, I propose, come to suggest problems for a radical liberal theory of law.

Consider a part of the construction of a duty of care for negligent acts. In ascertaining whether a particular act ought to be considered negligent, the common law invokes a standard that is ostensibly general and objective: "[n]egligence is the omission to do something which a reasonable man, guided upon those considerations which ordinarily regulate the conduct of human affairs, would do, or doing something which a prudent and reasonable man would not do".[21] The "reasonable man" test may be seen to work in this way: it will help to determine what the law regarding a particular claim for damages is, and it will do so by providing a standard through which to judge how someone (the "reasonable man") should act in a situation like that of the defender's. In other words, it is used both to construct the general norm and to particularise it in the case at hand. However, even though particular features of the instant case may be taken into account in, say, assembling the knowledge expectations of the "reasonable man", the law will not judge until it has universalised the obligation that it will eventually find. The law will not invoke and judge by the particular. As Samuel Weber has noted, "[t]he first and foremost act of the law, then, is to prohibit itself from using proper names to define the object of its pre- and proscriptions. The more "proper", i.e., the more individual and particular, the name, the less lawful the law."[22]

In creating the norm to judge the case at hand, the law must move up to a standard that is not that (at least in principle) of any particular person. Until the last moment when the defender must be named ("you, defender X, are/not liable") the law's particularisation cannot announce in justification this particular name (X). Justification comes only in the

[21] Alderson B in *Blyth v. Birmingham Waterworks Co.* (1856) 11 Exch. 781.

[22] S. Weber, "In the Name of the Law" in D. Cornell, M. Rosenfeld, and D. Gray (eds.), *Deconstruction and the Possibility of Justice* (New York, Routledge, 1992), 247.

name of the "reasonable man", not "this man" or "that man". As Weber continues, "[t]he law, in short, must be anonymous".[23]

But here of course is an irony. For anonymity is no name; not just no particular name, but no name at all. Conventionally, then, the "reasonable man" assumes an anonymous voice, and speaks in law for no-one in particular, but instead for "all men". As Brennan J has put it, "once the facts are proved all that remains for the court to do in determining the standard of care is to apply community standards—the standards of a hypothetical person in the defendant's position".[24]

Commonly there is much debate whether this "hypothetical person" is an objective determination of what "community standards" require, or an inevitably subjective imposition of what some particular group (the judges) thinks is the best decision according to law, given that the community as a whole may have no single standard on which it could reasonably agree. What I want to suggest, however, is that the "reasonable man" is both subjective and objective, but, and I will come on to this, that stopping at a recognition of this alone is insufficient given our current concerns.

But, to begin with, consider that the process of assessing negligence, say, can on the one hand only take place in the particular terms that are already pre-set by legal forms, legal forms which, as we have seen, must reduce the possible range of normative input to produce a decision. Subjectivity might be thought to enter therefore in two forms: one, the creation of a single norm from a mass of potentially available norms and, two, the application of a legal, as opposed to any other normative, decision-making framework. Here Alan Norrie has noted the issue precisely:

> In order that the "language of equality" may be heard and obeyed it must be tied to its opposite: a general and omnipotent power source which, while presenting itself as representing the general social interest, in fact embodies particular social-political interests and points of view.[25]

On the other hand, however, the connection between the universal (the legal standard to be applied) and the particular (the alleged wrong being addressed and the finding of fault or not in the instant case) cannot be severed. The very reading of the instant case as one involving a legal issue to be resolved involves formulating the particular in such a way that it becomes "prepared" to receive the legal decision; that is, to

[23] *Ibid.*

[24] Brennan J in *Gala* v. *Preston* (1991) 172 CLR 243.

[25] Alan W. Norrie, *Law, Ideology and Punishment: Retrieval and Critique of the Liberal Ideal of Criminal Justice* (Dordrecht, Kluwer, 1991), 184.

receive the application of the universal. It provides, therefore, an opportunity for an objectification according to a legal rule. As Wietholter has noted, "[l]egal relations . . . are always premediated general decisions about the way facts [and, we can add, questions of fault] are assigned to a particular law in the process of being introduced as a qualification of the legal response to social questions".[26] The law therefore objectifies through an assessment of the requirements of the "reasonable man" (in order that it be, in Samuel Weber's term, anonymous), and thus makes objective that which has been underdetermined. But in doing so it cannot relinquish the fact that a subjective determination is nonetheless required both to produce the general norm and to subsume the particular as an instance of the application of that norm, a process which can only ultimately be done as each case presents itself to the court.

Still, the argumentative force provided by the "reasonable man" remains objective in its appeal to legitimacy. The sense of objectivity that this gives comes also to signify, in Cohn's terms, "the premise that the difference between right and wrong is a question of derivability" from a pre-existing rule; that "the case is not new, it was known already to the norm and has thus been disposed of".[27] And here we have a formulation that is essentially the same as the one taken from Erskine in the Introduction to this book: the law must "speak the same uniform language to all individuals" instead of leaving them to their own "partial reasonings". But the radical liberal's problem is not that that element of the law's subjectivity cannot be eliminated, that it cannot but promote one set of partial reasonings as the one with which to answer the case, nor that this presents itself as objective, but instead relates to the question of how and by whom the issue is determined. A point of great importance, it is this that is often overlooked in assessing the meaning and significance of legal decisions in cases of moral conflict. So when, for example, Collins suggests that "[w]e must reject the pessimism which preaches that law necessarily involves a scheme of ranks and entitlements imposed from above by the established elites . . . The law is an open system, capable of receiving and endorsing any standards which have proved acceptable to the community",[28] it is precisely the dubiety of this latter phrase that is at issue. The real concern for the

[26] Quoted in Günther Teubner, *Law as an Autopoietic System* (trans. A. Bankowska and R. Adler, ed. Z. Bankowski, Oxford, Basil Blackwell, 1993), 108.

[27] Georg Cohn, *Existentialism and Legal Science* (New York, Oceana Publications, 1967), 119, 78.

[28] Hugh Collins, "Democracy and Adjudication" in N. MacCormick and P. Birks (eds.), *The Legal Mind: Essays for Tony Honoré* (Oxford, Clarendon Press, 1986), 82.

radical liberal position is the suspicion that the legal mechanisms available in the production of legal decisions such as the "reasonable man" test make it unnecessary to engage the rationality of the actors themselves at all. As Farmer has suggested, it is possible that the "reasonable man" "is not the ideal legal subject but *the means by which the object of legal regulation is conjured up*".[29] This may be the true functioning of an anonymity geared to the pursuit of administrative ends—and one from which attention is displaced by focussing overly on the issue of subjectivity and objectivity—and so the question becomes, how far do the parties themselves contribute to defining, assessing, and deciding, the conflict?

The constraining issue in the legal construction of the requirements of the "reasonable man" is again its determination, as Shklar put it, to find *some* rule, *any* rule, by which to legitimise its decision, even if that rule is as vague and talismanic as a "reasonable man" test. Yet as Cohn puts it, the consequence of this is that, "[t]he concrete cases must be homogenised by a process which fits them into the rule whenever they occur. The law chooses from the concrete situation those elements only which seemingly co-respond to the rule. All else is rejected as irrelevant."[30] Yet in order to retain the rationality of actors themselves (to retain *their* reasonableness), how much significance should be placed on the uniqueness of the instant case "which never existed before and will never exist again"?[31] Is there not the danger here that requirements for "correspondence to the rule" treats the conflict as something that those involved are really not responsible for dealing with?

Even those who would seek to bring more "voices" into the discourse as it takes place before the court fail properly to acknowledge that the "ideology of agreement" required by the model of liberal legalism precludes a multiplicity of voices from being heard in their own terms. For the structural and institutional teleology of law and its mode of determination cannot, as we saw in the previous section, be separated from the construction of the issue itself. So when Martha Minow writes that "[d]ialogue in courtroom arguments can stretch the minds of listeners . . . [and] inventive approaches can bring the voices of those who are not present before the court . . . The introduction of additional voices may enable adversary dialogue to expand beyond a stylized either/or

[29] Lindsay Farmer, "The Obsession with Definition: The Nature of Crime and Critical Legal Theory" (1996) 5 *Social and Legal Theory* 66, emphasis added.

[30] Cohn, n. 27 above, 111.

[31] *Ibid.*, 113.

mode, prompting new and creative insights",[32] this neglects fully to account for the way in which the legal voice speaks, in Erskine's terms, "the same uniform language to all individuals", and that it must therefore translate multiple voices into the one language; that there is, in other words, a limit to the possibilities available in legal decision-making in the institutional setting in which legal standards are formulated and applied.

Reversing a metaphor I used in an earlier discussion of MacIntyre, for liberal legal reasoning, dreams of Babel lead straight back to Esperanto. But, like the would-be global language itself, such law is not *no* language, but involves its own grammar, its own predispositions to particular solutions, and assumes, worryingly for the radical liberal thesis, that everything *can* be translated into that language. Law, then, to vary and push a metaphor one last stage, is more akin to—and indeed even more demanding than—the French language council which stands as a gate-keeper against the corruption of the genuine form. The question remains what the price of entry entails.

The construction of a personality in law, then, is one way in which law sets a grounding for the comparison of what may be incommensurable values. This might be seen to be the true functioning of concepts such as the reasonable man—and perhaps of legal personality more broadly – and in this sense it cannot be opened to just any set of values where what is often significant about those values is their conflicting nature. Again, we can note the telling difference between a trade-off and legal verdict, and see that it is not of itself the subjective determination of content that is problematic. For in doing the commensurating work, sources of descriptive and normative input have to be re-channelled to effect the legal translation. Jan Broekman has stated this case in perhaps its strongest terms:

> those elements of social reality which are under the grip of legal thinking are *structurally altered*. Transformations have occurred. This simply means that the one reality is not the other. Legal provisions form a unique whole of its own kind which is a special category of human experience. One cannot understand a contract or a delict unless one recognises one's being as *de iure*.[33]

[32] M. Minow, "Justice Engendered" (1987) 101 *Harvard L Rev* 88–9, quoted in E. A. Christodoulidis, "'A New Constitutional Reality for Civil Society'?", R. Bellamy *et al.* (eds.), *Democracy and Constitutional Culture* (London, Lothian Foundation Press, 1995).

[33] Jan Broekman, "Revolution and Moral Commitment to a Legal System" in N. MacCormick and Z. Bankowski (eds.), *Enlightenment, Rights and Revolution: Essays in Legal and Social Philosophy* (Aberdeen, AUP, 1989), 323.

The inability of law to sever the connection between the norm-to-be-applied and the instantiation of that norm in the particular case means that the particular has to be presented in a way that is already conceived of as legal. It has therefore "structurally altered", or even ignored, other normative or descriptive realities where they do not match the law's requirements, in the process itself severing what may be the constitutive relation between values and identity presented as so important by the radical liberal theory. Again Broekman puts the case forcefully: "[t]he first word that the jurist utters to me by way of his typical manner of speech already transforms me into a legal subject. I am not a legal subject. I am not a legal subject by nature but nevertheless I must be such because it is the price that I have to pay for being in society and enjoying my rights therein."[34]

I asked earlier in this section whether or not Berlin's distinct view of rationality—that when it came to conflicting values, then, "where choices must be made in such [concrete] circumstances then the ability of the choice to be made by individuals or groups themselves, is part of being rational or capable of moral judgment"—was compatible with the notion of the use of the person under liberal legalism. The question now is just how much input do people have into the descriptive and normative meanings of their being represented in law and legal regulation? Or how much, in the words of Roland Barthes, do law and its construction of personality exemplify a case of "the spectacle of a terror that threatens us all, that of being judged by a power which wants to hear only the language it lends us"?[35] If the latter, then no number of "different voices" will generate a sought after authenticity, just as no number of reminders about the exclusions necessarily involved will allow an opening up of law's structures, particularly where neither position challenges the institutionalised settings and presuppositions of an ideology of agreement specifically from the point of view of the incommensurability of values.

When we think of the criticisms earlier made against—in Dworkin's phrase—"law's princes", is it still not a valid question to ask just who is that "person" who "speaks" in law? At the level of identity, just where do the descriptive and normative inputs into "personality" come from in the strictures of currently institutionalised legal reasoning? But more importantly, what chances are there within such structures of reasoning for meaningful dissensus? It is this point we must now consider.

[34] *Ibid.*, 321.

[35] Roland Barthes, *Mythologies* (London, Vintage, 1993), 46.

(iii) *Legal Conflict*

A third concern with liberal legalism therefore needs to be addressed, though it draws on elements of the arguments in the preceding sections. This deals with the way in which values conflict in law. I suggested earlier that what MacIntyre's critique of liberalism and my reading of the radical liberal position shared was the importance of recognising the way in which moral disagreement occurred. Where MacIntyre had correctly drawn attention to the way in which "socially effective" means were available for "weighing and tallying" preferences, I noted that the radical liberal theory would be equally wary of overarching frameworks which tended either to reduce the possibility of meaningful dissensus by postulating a single norm according to which conflict would simply disappear (the *a priori* commitment to commensurability) or where conflict was not picked up on at all. The reason meaningful dissensus was so important for the radical liberal theory was partly its recognition of the constitutive relation between identity and values, and partly that the consequence of this recognition entailed the ability to participate in social forms that were themselves constituted by their incommensurability with other values. Since MacIntyre's attack on liberalism rested in part on the claim that liberalism tended to stifle debate by pushing it into pre-ordained forms, my defence of the radical liberal position therefore rested (and rests) on the possibility that any trade-offs which occurred between conflicting values took place without any *a priori* commitment to commensurability.

And this is where such a thesis encounters problems in the institutional vesting it might receive at the hands of the legal system. If we think back to MacCormick's definition of legalism, we find that his apparently uncontroversial statement nevertheless contains concerns for the radical liberal theory.

Why? The first is the point raised above by Broekman; that to attract legal solutions requires that the conflict be read in such a way as to abstract it into the form of legal rights *v.* legal duties, and the question is to what extent this works to "structurally transform" the meaning of the conflict. Now this is precisely the query Berlin raised about expertise. There he considered the problem to be whether an issue was dealt with by focussing on, in his words, "the logical implications and elucidating the meaning, the context, or the relevance and origin of a specific problem", or whether instead a solution was reached by "altering the outlook which gave rise to it in the first place".

The problem with liberal legalism's focus on rights arguably works against the full attention being paid to the original location of specific problems. As Lyotard has written, the formulation of conflicts and differences in terms of rights has precisely this drawback: "[n]ow, completely occupied with the legitimacy of exchanges with others in the community, we are inclined to neglect our duty to listen to this other; we are inclined to negate the second existence it requires of us. And thus we will become perfect ciphers, switching between public and private rights without remainder."[36] It is that last phrase that is so important; the notion that there are "rights without remainder" as perceived by the legal system works to preclude in law possible sources of different *types* of reasoning that do not match up to those recognised by law.

Now it may be objected that this is indeed the case, but that this is merely the price to be paid for entering legal discourse. A further objection is that rights are and have been historically an essential element in liberal thought. Thus it could be argued that all groups or individuals will benefit equally, assuming they have a right or duty to be protected. Yet this does not fully take into account the effects of channelling the conflict in this way. Here are two examples.

First, one need only think about the way in which, for example, Anglo-Australian common law reasoning has worked consistently to deprive indigenous populations of the ability to assert "land rights" by refusing to acknowledge different forms of relations with land that did not conform to the property conceptions of the dominant legal system.[37] Doctrines such as "*terra nullius*" were thus employed to negate the possibility that native land relations amounted to something recognisable as "genuine" property rights. Moreover, even when, as has happened in recent years, the doctrine of *terra nullius* has been overruled, it still remains the case that the implementation of "rights without remainder" provides the dominant system itself with the legal and political means to define what will and will not count as valid "native title" claims, since it still retains control over the (legal) techniques of legitimising recognition. In other words, even though conflict has been picked up here,

[36] Jean-Francois Lyotard, *Political Writings* (transl. B. Readings and K. P. Geiman, London, UCL Press, 1993), 111.

[37] For a good overview, which also argues that this problem, despite recent legal acknowledgment, is ongoing in Australia, see Valerie Kerruish and Jeannine Purdy, "He *Look* Honest—Big White Thief" (1998) 4.1 *Law/Text/Culture* 146. In the North American context, see for example Robert A. Williams Jr., "Documents of Barbarism: The Contemporary Legacy of European Racism and Colonialism in the Narrative Traditions of Federal Indian Law" (1989) 31 *Arizona Law Rev* 237–78.

the inability of the common law legal system to do other than negate different sources of reasoning (or, more fundamentally, of world view) on its own terms seems to sit uneasily with a radical liberal theory which aspires to recognise the genuine incommensurability of social forms and values. There seems to be no better example of a case where, rather than looking to the "meaning, the context, or the relevance and origin of a specific problem", the role of law has been to alter "the outlook which gave rise to it in the first place". In this sense, the difference I pointed to earlier between a possible "trade-off" being required in a pragmatic sense (in terms of dealing with conflict in a way meaningful to those involved), and a "verdict" as the result of the legal decision seems to be strikingly clear.

If this shows a case of tangible harm being done through dispossession legitimised through the form of rights, the second example is more symbolic. In parallel with earlier arguments, the legal regulation of conflict in terms of rights has effects, in turn, back on the expectations and possible presentation of moral and political issues. This goes more to what Lyotard identified as the tendency to "neglect our duty to listen to this other", and has been suggestively enunciated by Milan Kundera:

> The world has become man's right and everything in it has become a right: the desire for love the right to love, the desire for rest the right to rest, the desire for friendship the right to friendship, the desire to exceed the speed limit the right to exceed the speed limit, the desire for happiness the right to happiness.[38]

The institutional dependency on law and the legal form of rights-claim has the potential to cut swathes across social forms. Arguably it constitutes a case of Raz's suggestion that, at least in certain cases, "success might mean failure"; a justiciable right to happiness, or love, or friendship (or realistically in America to good parenting, say) would make those most elusive of social and individual pursuits "unrecognisably different" from the hopes and desires we may painfully, though rewardingly, grasp for.

I do not want to press this point too far, but instead merely recall Berlin's opening lines as I quoted them, and suggest that the symbolic, and sometimes real, dimensions of legal intervention potentially constitute another example of what he called "a world stiff with rigid rules and codes", where the individual's choice and "capacity to cause mental stress and danger and destructive collisions, is eliminated in favour

[38] Milan Kundera, *Immortality* (transl. P.Kussi, London, Faber and Faber, 1991), 153.

of a simpler and better regulated life". It may of course appear as a paradox that I suggest that this diminishes conflict, when the common criticism of the increasing dependency on law and general litigiousness is that it increases conflict. But the point here is that how such conflict is constructed, channelled and resolved tends to obfuscate the notion of meaningful dissensus, particularly when it comes to conflicts of values; that such conflict as does occur in law is singular in terms of its construction in a way that cannot fully grasp the complexities of social forms, and works in fact to mask or distort genuine problems and in particular to reduce the difficult responsibilities required in understanding such varied social forms.

It may be then that the historical liberal mantra of the sanctity of private property rights—as Locke put it, that "property is the bulwark of liberty"—needs to be re-thought in the light of the radical liberal thesis. For not only is the relation between the rights-discourse of law and the premise of tolerance to incommensurable values problematic, especially where rights in law are lifted out from the input of various and diverse forms of good, but also where today the expectations placed on private property rights in particular no longer do the work earlier liberalism required them to do. As Nedelsky has cogently argued, "[p]rivate property was, for 150 years, the central and defining instance of the boundary between governmental authority and individual autonomy. Property can, however, no longer serve this function because it has lost its original political significance."[39] This is not to say that private property has lost *all* useful functions, but instead that it has lost its original *political* significance.

Where in the late seventeenth and eighteenth centuries private property may well have had the function of challenging the vested and intrusive interests of the Crown, we might wonder how those same rights can, again to quote Nussbaum, ask "society and politics . . . [to] respect the liberty of choice, and [to] respect the equal worth of persons as choosers".[40] To respect people's private property is only to respect one very small part of their liberty of choice, and *a fortiori* what people's human worth might be. It is a consistent confusion exemplified by the conservative Right to assume that "liberty of choice" means simply liberty to dispose of and acquire private property. Even, I suggest, a

[39] Jennifer Nedelsky, "Reconceiving Autonomy: Sources, Thoughts and Possibilities," in A. C. Hutchinson and L. J. M. Green (eds.), *Law and the Community: The End of Individualism?* (Toronto, Carswell, 1989), 233.

[40] Introduction to this work, p. 2.

radical reading of Berlin's negative liberty, requires no *a priori* commitment to private property as a definitional element. Respecting the moral autonomy of individuals is in fact unacceptably homogenised to a "single overarching principle" when that principle is the property right. Attention to the detailed and contextual conflicts that we face seems, as the land rights example tends to show, to be overridden when law's reconstruction of the conflict is in terms of rights and duties, winners or losers. Here we may have the clearest of examples of an incompatibility between the radical liberal view, and the logic and power of the institutionalised decision-making role of the courts in the liberal legal system.

This forces us to think about the role law itself may have come to play as a strategy in dealing with conflict, a meta-role, so to speak, that may not often be picked up on. I quoted Marshall earlier as saying that when the contest is set, it involves formulating how to ascertain the winner, and it may be important that reliance on legal conflict-resolution can be seen as a way of attempting to cut off or stem other forms of conflict. So here it is important to consider the effects of the way in which law *stages* conflict. As Christodoulidis has shown in a critique of Dworkin's thesis of law as integrity, what is most often neglected in arguments which see law as providing the means for pursuing political debate in community is that "taking the conflict to law . . . becomes a strategic move in the situation of conflict, an ideological move aiming to conceal what the conflict is really about". That is, "by taking the law as a neutral forum for conflict, one loses sight of the position of law itself within the grander framework of conflict".[41] In parallel with the argument we have canvassed already, this oversight and the ideological position of law which it masks are, he notes, largely attributable to a disregard for the way in which law treats conflict as having "an inbuilt tendency to resolve itself".[42] In other words, attention needs to be paid to the fact that where the conflict is staged in law, there is a presupposition that that conflict *can* be resolved, and this alone may provide a reason for having recourse to law. But, as we have seen however, this necessarily overrides the broader political *question* of its irreconcilability.

The production of verdicts may, in this sense, not merely be a capitulation of moral and political argument, but a deliberate attempt to refuse to engage in finding a trade-off solution. While we might think

[41] Emilios A. Christodoulidis, "The Suspect Intimacy Between Law and Political Community" (1994) 80 *ARSP* 16.
[42] *Ibid.*

of this in terms of a failure of private parties to negotiate solutions to particular problems, it is perhaps most commonly recognisable as a tactic of governments who refuse, for ballot-box reasons, to work towards and instigate a political solution and instead rely on the solution being provided by a court. In such instances, the reliance on the court's function and abilities exemplifies a complicity with rather than a dependence upon the forms of conflict-resolution that only the court can provide.[43]

One final aspect of legal conflict needs to be considered, and that deals further with some sociological significations of the problem. If conceptually it seems to be the case that conflict is suspiciously channelled and potentially distorted by entering the legal arena, as a matter of professional legal practice these suspicions are amplified. As Christie argued some years ago, legal professionals in both official (or state) and private practice roles contribute to the loss of conflict as property that might be shared. As he says, "[l]awyers are particularly good at stealing conflicts. They are trained for it. They are trained to prevent and solve conflicts."[44] Here once again the appearance of a conflict as such is not at issue, but the *way* in which it appears is. For Christie and others the effect of legal professionalism is to take conflicts out of the hands of those with whom they originate, and present them to a court system that duplicates and depends on this process. This depersonalisation is best represented when he considers that (writing of Scandinavia) "the symbol of the whole system is the Supreme Court where the directly involved parties do not even attend their own court cases".[45] The ethos of expertise thus functions to remove the conflict from the context in which it originated and present it such that only the applied expertise in the legal institutional setting can reasonably resolve it.

Again this has broad-ranging implications. For not only does the legal system control conflict in this way, but this has once again a reflexive effect on the initial contexts from which the disputes or conflicts came. As I noted earlier, the effects of the content of legal relations play a wider constitutive role. So, for example, one of the effects of the power

[43] Interestingly this feature has been noted by commentators on societies in recent transition, particularly Eastern Europe in the 1990s, where in the new liberal democracies constitutional courts were drawn on to decide divisive moral questions which the new politicians feared to deal with. It is clear here that legal verdicts were being used in a functional way to avoid endangering nascent democratic systems. But it is also indicative, I suggest, of an early slippage into a certain style of (party) politics, and the functional use of the courts' role here attests to their operating in precisely the ways I am identifying.

[44] N. Christie, "Conflict as Property" in C. Reasons and R. M. Rich, *The Sociology of Law: A Conflict Perspective* (Toronto, Butterworth, 1978), 298.

[45] *Ibid.*

given over to expertise is that there is instituted a dependency on seeking that type of solution; the more unavoidable the resort to experts, the more it is seen to be the natural way of dealing with conflicts. Moreover, and crucial for the present context, where only experts can truly evaluate the strength of (legal) arguments it may, as Christie points out, lead to the "destruction of certain conflicts even before they get going".[46] In other words, appropriation of conflicts by experts and the legal system not only defines the terms in which legal arguments may be presented, but potentially reduces the possibilities for self-expression in the wider setting where law is instrumental in defining (and allowing) what counts as a political or moral argument in the first place. And if this is the case, then the ideological role that law as resolver of conflicts may indiscernably have come to play must become of paramount concern to the radical liberal theory.

Law and "Other" Problems

I have said in a few places that there appear to me to be certain similarities with the radical liberal theory as I have taken it from Berlin, and certain postmodern writings on difference and the ethic of alterity, of responsibility to "the Other".[47] In this section I consider one such approach, but do so in a critical way in order to apply the insights from the preceding sections, but also to draw attention to the pitfalls in assuming that such an ethic can easily be brought into current structures of law and liberal legal argument. Once again, I suggest that the problems an ethic of alterity has with the institutional dynamic of liberal legalism—and to the extent that the radical liberal position shares these concerns then that too—need to be addressed in a broader manner. To that end, in this section I will draw on some arguments from the prominent postmodern theorist Jean-François Lyotard to work through what I see as the implications for the postmodern theory as presented, and also address how the radical liberal theory might use such insights to challenge current legal assumptions. This will involve considering how Lyotard's more powerful political arguments need to be worked through in the context of law.

[46] N. Christie, "Conflict as Property" in C. Reasons and R. M. Rich, *The Sociology of Law: A Conflict Perspective* (Toronto, Butterworth, 1978), 301.

[47] In line with the texts quoted I use here the term "ethics" from these sources, though, perhaps unconventionally, make no claims as to differences to "morality".

While certain postmodern thinking about law seeks to reinstate ethical concerns at the core of its jurisprudence, it nevertheless tends too easily, I suggest, to replicate several of the assumptions of a modernity it claims to move beyond. Concentrating in particular on the ethics of alterity, itself not a novel focus, it falls prey to several of the dichotomies and categories of liberal legalism. As such it is not surprising that it is often accused of a conservative inertia. To hold to the insights of difference which postmodernists espouse requires not simply attention to the form of law, but, as I have argued in terms of the radical liberal theory, to its relative positioning and role as a source of obligation, as well as to a rethinking of the law-ethics relation as part of an institutional critique of law.

Attempting to challenge and rework what is perceived as the obsessive modern distinction between law and ethics, a postmodern jurisprudence faces three problems: its conception of law, its conception of ethics and its conception of the relation between the two. As a constructive effort, the task of reinvigorating ethical debate within and about law may be thought to be timely. Yet hostility to postmodern thinking generally comes equally from all directions. One of the most pressing complaints is that of inertia, the apparent ability to say much but suggest little. The more one hears about "deferring the undeferrable", of "conceiving a justice that cannot but must be conceived", of "saying what cannot be said" and "listening to what cannot be heard", the more one is tempted to produce a charge not so much of relativism (for what values *do* these espouse?), but of serious fence-sitting. I suspect that part of the problem here is the way in which postmodern jurisprudence (of which I will give an example shortly) conceives of law and its relation to ethics still in a way that condemns it to the modernist dichotomy it seeks to overcome. I will argue therefore that in order to treat seriously the political claim that an ethic of alterity or difference be invoked, the structural positioning of law as ambiguously protector and enemy of justice needs to be reviewed. In particular, and drawing on the arguments made earlier, both the constitutive and the destructive roles of law within a broader context of the creation of normative meaning require attention. For what has been said of the prescriptions and conflicts of morality applies equally to law: that they make us what we are as much as we make them what they are. As such, in this section, it is the relative positioning of law as a source of obligations that must be addressed as much as the form of its deliberation and judgment.

In what follows I treat, and make, the charge of inertia as a serious one. As I have suggested I will argue for a relocation of some of Lyotard's political arguments about the role of the differend in state politics in the (to be contested) legal arena. By doing this I hope to draw attention to a few of the problems that jurisprudence ought to consider if it wants properly to champion either an ethic of alterity or, for my concerns, the values of the radical liberal theory. Before that, however, I want to look at three problems that can be identified in a recent version of postmodern jurisprudence. They develop from, successively, the problems that crystallise around the meaning of ethics in the law-ethics relation; the issue of form in legal reasoning; and, finally, what is called here the problem of information.

(i) *The Problems*

To begin with here is a formulation of some of the central concerns and presuppositions of a postmodern jurisprudence:

> The law is necessarily committed to the form of universalisation and abstract equality; but a just decision must also respect the requests of the contingent, incarnate and concrete other, it must pass through the ethics of alterity in order to respond to its own embeddedness in justice. In this unceasing conjunction and disjunction, this alternating current between the most general and calculating and the most concrete and incalculable, or between the legality of form and legal subjectivity, lies the ethics of a critical legal response to the material legal person, law's morality of the contingent.[48]

Consider three problems with this.

The first concerns the consequences of replicating the structural distinction that is seen as integral to the initial problematic of modernity. Thus justice is dependent on the particular, the contingent, is fleeting and momentary, while law is constructed as its opposite: abstract, dependent on form, with an eye to existence over time and to co-ordination. Yet this same construction in another guise has been identified with part of the failure of a modernity we have traced which has seen the retreat of individualised or particularised judgments—into an inscrutable, private realm leaving them ostensibly immune from shared public evaluation or justification—impact on the expectations placed upon law. Historically bound up with part of the liberating potential of

[48] Peter Goodrich, Costas Douzinas, and Yifat Hachamovitch, "Introduction" to C. Douzinas, P. Goodrich and Y. Hachamovitch (eds.), *Politics, Postmodernity and Critical Legal Studies: The Legality of the Contingent* (London, Routledge, 1994), 24.

modernity, the effect of this retreat is most profound where the viability of meaningful agreement or disagreement on ethical issues is seen to have been largely excluded because of the way in which moral expressions are conceptualised. We noted this at length in the analysis of Alasdair MacIntyre's work, and the danger here is of reproducing what he saw as one of the failures of liberal societies. We recall, for example, that such "emotivism" worked to preclude rational discussion and resolution of ethical and political controversies which liberal societies face. The difficulty was this: where "moral assertions are seen as mere expressions of approval or disapproval, there can be differences, but no contradictions".[49] In turn this was deemed to have consequences for how the role of law is characterised, as well as the demands subsequently placed upon it. For MacIntyre, one of the defining features of the contemporary liberal order was its inability to do other than refer its conflicts to the legal system where verdicts could be produced. The question then arises whether an ethic of alterity has sufficient critical ability to go beyond this abdication to the legal system of debate and resolution, which effectively leaves law as the sole fixer of any coherent values.

The response to this has been ambiguous. On the one hand it has been said that "postmodern justice cannot follow the protocols of a theory, it is not a concept and does not apply a principle, value or code".[50] Even if we accept this as a non-nihilistic position, though one admittedly "dedicated to failure", there would seem to be insufficient articulation here alone to challenge law's hegemony of staging or resolving contradictions or conflicts. Where an ethical response lacks a coherent theoretical basis then, given the structural opposition in place between law and ethics, the force of MacIntyre's criticism of law in liberal society would still appear to be applicable. On the other hand, and despite the admitted "dedication to failure", the position the same postmodern writers adopt is not, however, deemed nihilistic, for one reason: that "ethics precedes law". Consequently, if apparently contradictorily, and despite the claim that ethics requires "a judgement without criteria",[51] the aspiration of that ethics is indeed defined, defined as an embracing of a responsibility "for the other, the stranger, the outsider, the alien or underprivileged who needs the law".[52]

[49] Robert Wachbroit, 'A Genealogy of Virtues' (1982–3) 92 *Yale LJ* 564–76.

[50] Goodrich, Douzinas, and Hachamovitch, n. 48 above, 24.

[51] C. Douzinas and R. Warrington, "The Face of Justice: A Jurisprudence of Alterity" (1994) 3 *Social and Legal Studies* 405–25 at 419–20.

[52] Goodrich, Douzinas, and Hachamovitch, n. 48 above, 22.

But here again, the problem MacIntyre identified with contemporary morality and the role of law in the liberal order cannot be fully addressed merely by expressing this temporal dimension ("ethics precedes law"). As I have tried to show, the ethics-law relation may be both more dynamic and fluid than this suggests, and the power of law more constitutive (or destructive) in the ethical realm than either the postmodernists or, for that matter, MacIntyre would seem to acknowledge. Moreover the location, as well as the imaginative construction, of the solidarity that the responsibility for the other would require is critical. Championing a radically indeterminate ethic may be different from the failed moral emotivism of modernity, yet the case remains to be demonstrated how this is so. It is potentially little short of disingenuous to suggest on the one hand the occurrence in modernity of "the final accomplishment of MacIntyre's 'moral catastrophe' ",[53] and on the other the uncertain certainty of the ready existence of an ethic of alterity. That "the other comes first. (S)he is the condition of the existence of language, of self, of law"[54] needs to be translated into a set of coherent if revisable terms that themselves transcend the structural oppositions and prompt explicit consideration of the varied meanings and significance of the social forms (as I have called them) within which these moral understandings might be expressed. Without this, the "unceasing conjunction and disjunction" of abstract and concrete, calculating and incalculable, appears essentially to replicate the liberal legal predicament rather than fully confront it. The unwillingness however, albeit for what are taken to be sound philosophical grounds, of postmodern jurisprudence to put any such thing on the line in terms of a developed critique, might then turn out to be hollow comfort for the alien or underprivileged lined up in the sights of the law.

Part of the difficulty identified here links to a second problem. This concerns the "critical legal response to the material legal person". At issue here is the apparently uncritical placing of the person in the relation between law and justice already in legal terms, the easy assumption of how "the other needs the law". The aspiration in this instance is to see "the legal subject in terms of differences, of lives composed or built up of accidents, contingencies and errors".[55] Of course, not only does such a suggestion appear to sit uneasily with the form which law is given

[53] Douzinas and Warrington, n. 51 above, 405.

[54] *Ibid.*, 414. See also, by the same authors, " 'A Well-Founded Fear of Justice': Law and Ethics in Postmodernity", *Law and Critique* Vol. II, no. 2 [1991] 115–47.

[55] Goodrich, Douzinas, and Hachamovitch, n. 48 above, 23.

as one which is antithetical to disorder and contingency, but more importantly, as we have seen, it fails properly to challenge the giving over to law of the means through which difference is to be asserted. Yet to do so is to foreclose certain issues.

First (and this is acknowledged) it allows legal categories to define what is to count as the same and different. This is the first and crucial step in the process of legitimating legal judgment, and raises similar concerns to those brought out when we considered aspects of the role of personality in law. As Valerie Kerruish has written, "if law is seen as giving an objective or right answer to questions of how different individuals are the same, then its generalities are legitimated".[56] Thus only where sameness can be constructed through law will it be possible for the law to claim authority to compare competing assertions and in turn weigh them. Yet this process of abstraction from a wealth of potential normative and descriptive possibilities can only be opened to critique where the role of law in defining sameness is itself put in question. To attempt to assert difference through law in the manner suggested is already to have cut off certain vocabularies and self-descriptions, and to have taken a stance on certain specific issues. Therefore the suggestion that the demand of an ethics of alterity requires that the "other be heard as a *full person*" in the "interpretation and application of the *relevant legal rules*"[57] appears as a contradictory aspiration. And the expressed justification of postmodern jurisprudence that "injustice is the inescapable condition of all law"[58] is the consequence of a failure fully to recognise this as a contingent feature of the ideology of agreement of liberal legalism.

This latter point is intimately related to a second, which concerns the selection or abstraction of issues themselves. This deals principally with the type of question, "what is this conflict *about*?" Again, to formulate an answer to this in terms of how law should respond is already to endorse the technique of a liberal legalism which requires that the question be located within one or other of the categories of issues or set of principles that law already understands. As we have seen, this is necessary for law so that the conflict, which is of course never natural or given but always constructible within a variety of possible milieux, be seen as a "genuine" disagreement and thereby made to appear resolvable. Beverley Brown has considered this effect, writing of the way in which

[56] V. Kerruish, *Jurisprudence as Ideology* (London, Routledge, 1991), 111.

[57] Douzinas and Warrington, n. 51 above 422, emphasis added.

[58] *Ibid.*

liberal legal debate responds to and prejudges the construction and issue of pornography by forcing its location within categories and principles that it can already recognise, such as harm or free speech. But, as she notes, this technique of setting a legal test functions merely to present "a way of determining the choices between available, preconstituted alternatives . . . It is thus the perfect mechanism for asserting and deferring issues".[59]

Nevertheless the aspiration of postmodern jurisprudence here is one that maintains that the "openness of the concrete materiality of the other arguably enables postmodern ethics and justice to resist the totalising influence of politics and law".[60] Admirable as this sentiment may appear from the point of view of the radical liberal theory, it remains the case that where that materiality is already constructed as or geared towards (the question of) *legal* materiality—the person constituted in law or in need of law—the choice of descriptions of both identity and issue is, as I have suggested, already in a strong sense predetermined. Again a part of the problem for postmodern jurisprudence here is to define the relation of law and ethics as oppositional, such that the legal form is conceived as being "committed to the form of universality and abstract equality". Yet this neglects to take full account of the consequences of such a position.

As Pierre Bourdieu, for example, has argued, in a sociological dimension, "the force of the form . . . is that properly symbolic force which allows force to be fully exercised while disguising its true nature as force and gaining recognition, approval and acceptance by dint of the fact that it can present itself under the appearances of universality".[61] In other words it is to overlook the fact that this force of form "is a force which is both logical *and* social", and that the "legality of form" the postmodern position accepts, "unites the force of the universal, the logical, the formal, of formal logic, *and* the force of the official".[62]

We have seen already how feminist jurisprudence has identified the significance of this feature of law which "presents itself under the appearances of universality". Combining, in varying degrees, a critique of both the form of universality itself and the practical presuppositions and distortions it entails, it has sought to expose the particularity of the

[59] B. Brown, "Debating Pornography: The Symbolic Dimensions" *Law and Critique* Vol. 1 no. 2 [1990] 131–54 at 140.

[60] Goodrich, Douzinas, and Hachamovitch, n. 48 above, 23.

[61] P. Bourdieu, "Codification" in *In Other Words: Essays Towards a Reflexive Sociology* (Cambridge, Polity Press, 1990), 85.

[62] *Ibid.*, emphasis added.

values of universalism within a social and historical context. It has shown how manifestations of such would-be universality recognisable in liberal legalism support and uphold very specific qualities, as well as the importance of the link Bourdieu identifies between the image of form and its manifestation in relations of power. Thus, and this is the important point, any attempt to enhance a responsibility to the other comes up against not just the posited universal form itself, but that universal as "another other", as another set of identifiable interests that may or may not be open to the other's reception. Bringing the full person before the law, it seems to have been demonstrated, is what the form of law, through its partiality, precludes.

So again, maintaining the descriptive opposition here both masks and leaves in place the relations of power that may be discerned, and also works *against* the possible re-ethicisation of law through awareness of the other. The best it may hope for, and this perhaps its true dedication to failure, is the replacement of one set of "universals" with another. But then in this instance, the problem of the relations of power—the force of the form of law and its personnel—is reproduced, never addressed.

There is one final issue implicit in the original formulation, which I have termed the problem of information, that I wish to consider. The difficulty here is with whether law, or even an ethics of alterity, has sufficient information of the concrete other to make viable judgements at all. The acknowlegment of this comes in these terms:

> There is always a difference which exists between what we know of a phenomenon in advance, even before being confronted with it, and what we are to learn from it *a posteriori*, what we could in no circumstances have foreseen, anticipated or judged *a priori*.[63]

In the view of a postmodern jurisprudence, this is taken as indicative of the "fraction or fracture of things", the "remainder that escapes the concept", the inevitable existence of an epistemological gap. Not itself a novel realisation, what is problematic with this formulation is the similar lack of an understanding of its potential political implications.

For this is the very problem Hayek identified and used as a justification against state intervention and planning. Like the postmodernists on the application of laws, he argued that:

> general rules, genuine laws as distinguished from specific orders, must be intended to operate in circumstances which cannot be foreseen in detail, and,

[63] Goodrich, Douzinas, and Hachamovitch, n. 48 above, 24.

therefore, their effects on particular ends or particular people cannot be known beforehand.[64]

Drawn into a dichotomy between the rule of law and coercion and discretionism, the issue takes the form of a double bind: if there is insufficient *a priori* knowledge of personal details and values, then to be impartial the government must accept that it has "no answer to certain questions"; yet only through this acknowledgment will government actions be predictable. But if the government does presume to know such information it asserts its control in such a way as to make any sense of individual responsibility (to self or other) largely meaningless because of the imposition of its own evaluations of what is best for those individuals; as such, the required action here demands a detailed response to "the full circumstances of the moment" and, as a consequence, government action will in this case be unpredictable.

Hayek's own resolution of this issue is familiar, and uses both economic and moral arguments in treating the problem of information as a justification for opposing state planning. But what is noteworthy in the current context is not so much that this argument is one which is conclusive in itself (which it is not), but that the dichotomy it suggests is apparently inevitable for postmodern jurisprudence given the similar way in which it poses the issue. I am not suggesting either that Hayek is correct or that postmodern jurisprudence has to take one or other side here, but simply that the consequences of the stance adopted be explored in a way that goes beyond the simple assertion of an epistemological gap. For it is (ethically?) irresponsible to expose, perhaps even exult in, the gap, without thought to the way in which it will or ought to be filled in practice.

A more detailed, informed response would seem to be required. For the radical liberal theory, such a response would again require a closer analysis of the input into, as I have termed it, the information available for decision-making. What I have addressed in the previous sections goes some way to suggesting that the techniques of liberal legalism might well make the legal institution an uncertain ally in attempts to hold onto an ethic of alterity. As such, it is again an insufficient response to bask in the "fraction or fracture of things" without due attention to how the form and power of contemporary legal institutions will, so to speak, mend that fracture. The fact that not everything can be known in advance becomes merely trite when the sensitivity sought in relation

[64] F. A. Hayek, *The Road to Serfdom* (London, Routledge, 1944), 57.

to the ethical awareness of the other is not addressed as a matter of challenging the institutional requirements and expectations of liberal legalism.

These three criticisms I have identified have been largely concerned with the difficulties I perceive with the attempt of postmodern jurisprudence to reinvigorate the law–ethics relation, mainly because of the ways in which it fails to acknowledge and work through the implications of its premises. Thus while it does in fact recognise some of the issues I have addressed, it does not do enough to situate the ethic of alterity within a broader critique. As such, this potentially allows it to be subject to a charge of collaboration since it appears to leave intact the thought it seeks to overcome.

(ii) Perspectives on Law

Let me suggest then that there may well be insights from certain postmodern theorists on political debate that could usefully be brought into the legal context in a way that could also provide important insights for the radical liberal theory. To draw these out I will use a part of the work of Jean-François Lyotard.

To begin with, take one of Lyotard's central definitions:

> As distinguished from a litigation, a differend would be a case of conflict between (at least) two parties, that cannot be equitably resolved for lack of a rule of judgement applicable to both arguments . . . However, applying a single rule of judgement to both in order to settle their differend as though it were merely a litigation would wrong (at least) one of them (and both of them if neither accepts the rule).[65]

This is, I suggest, remarkably similar in formulation to the arguments about incommensurability we considered in Part Two. There we saw how, in the example of comparing monetary value and friendship, the *a priori* commitment to commensurability not only failed fully to understand the complexity of the clash of values, but also how, to use Lyotard's term, damage may occur to those social forms when commensurability was assumed either possible or desirable.

But we now also see in this formulation by Lyotard a clear problem with situating conflict within law. If Lyotard's aim is to "bear witness to the differend", to "think justice in relation to conflict and difference",

[65] Jean-François Lyotard, *The Differend: Phrases in Dispute* (Manchester, Manchester UP, 1988), p. xi.

we have seen how law has the potential to distort both issues and consequences. That is why I have suggested that a political response to the position of law within structures of normative reasoning is required. In a previous section therefore I argued for the importance for the radical liberal theory of pressing the question whether or not it was rational to have recourse to the processes of law at all, as a question that was prior to the rationality of law's decision-making procedures themselves.

To ask such a question clearly involves giving a full consideration to political and moral issues, but it should also be made clear that the notion of "politicisation" does not mean simply "getting the state involved"; for this too is potentially to eliminate types of self-description and modes of reasoning. As such, the state itself may be as much part of the problem as the solution. As Readings has suggested in a way that the radical liberal position might endorse, for Lyotard, "[r]ather than the political question being what kind of state can establish the just society and realise human destiny, the positioning of the state as the unifying horizon for all political representations becomes the stumbling block for a just politics".[66] In other words, the tendency to allow the state to colonise political or moral conflict ought to be seen as—in Roberto Unger's phrase—a false necessity that must itself be challenged in any attempt to overcome the inertia that sets in when there is a failure to question the overarching institutional structures within which the vesting of conflict presently occurs. The state arguably, with its own dynamics and logic, provides a way in which the openness to meaningful dissensus might be curtailed. While this might sound a dramatic suggestion, it is nevertheless the case that where we are now witnessing the potential breaking down of nineteenth-century statist assumptions today, we are confronted with the need—and the opportunity—to rethink new (and indeed in some cases old) political associations and groupings formerly suppressed by the strong nation state.

Leaving this at the level of suggestion, the more detailed point is that if the state's hegemony in these issues is to be challenged, so too must the law's. For, as should have become clear, the perceived need for the legal institution to decide to give its verdict implies that it must take a stance with a view to *legal* action (or inaction). The force of the linking of "form and official" deems that law is bound to resolution, and this presupposes that the conflict be understood in a specific way. While it has been noted that this provides a way of asserting and deferring issues,

[66] Bill Readings, "Foreword", in J.-F. Lyotard, *Political Writings* (trans. B. Readings and K. P. Geiman, London, UCL Press, 1993), pp. xix–xx.

the importance of reaching a decision might further be seen to operate in tandem with the institutionalised politics of the state without due regard for the alternative sources of normative commitment that could be opened up as an integral part of the radical liberal theory.

In order to pay full attention therefore to the constitutive incommensurabilities that may be in danger of being overridden, or, in Lyotard's terms, the danger of the unacknowledged suppression of the differends, it becomes necessary at the institutional level to explore ways in which the practice of judicial decision-making can be made susceptible to an external critique; that is, one in which the issue of whether the power to decide should be given to the legal system at all is seen as just as important as how decisions are justified within that system. As Amy Gutmann has suggested, such a notion would "justify judicial decision-making on the basis of the legitimacy of judicial authority in deciding certain categories of cases rather than the rightness of its decisions or its special decision making technique".[67]

For where it is otherwise, we might usefully introduce a parallel with an interpretation Lyotard has given of Kafka's law machine in "In the Penal Colony"[68]: in that well-known story, the cruelty of the machine is that "guilt is never to be doubted"; yet its ghost reappears even in the use of a "humane law" as "resolvability" is never to be doubted. What Lyotard's interpretation of Kafka draws our attention to is that—in the first case, as well, I would add, as the second—law's "inscription of the prescription" attests not to the prisoner or person who comes before the law, but to law's own instantiation. The fact that resolution may bask in the logic of justification as consensus—"we the people", or the "reasonable man"—as opposed to a machine-like instrumentalism, does not affect the fact that the sovereignty of decidability is never relinquished. But this necessarily overrides the broader political and moral question whether, and on what terms, a decision should be made by the legal system at all.

To be consistent, then, with Lyotard's wariness of any "machines"—be that state politics, the means and pretence to speak in the name of others, the systematic violation of the differend—of any *machines* that *generate commonality*, the use of the force of law must be questioned itself as an issue of demarcation about which sources of obligation we

[67] Amy Gutmann, "The Rule of Rights or the Right to Rule" in J. R. Pennock and J. W. Chapman (eds.), *Nomos XXVIII: Justification* (New York, New York University Press, 1986), 165–77 at 172.

[68] Jean-François Lyotard, "Prescription" in R. Harvey and M. S. Roberts (eds.), *Toward the Postmodern* (NJ, Humanities Press, 1993).

ought to promote and which we ought to reject. Thus the political requirement to raise questions, so to speak, of jurisdiction, of law's interests and our interest in law; questions that—and this is the most important point—should not be answered by law itself.

Conceiving the person as in need of law, as did the postmodern jurisprudence which I have discussed, is always to prejudge certain consequences and issues, and to go beyond the dichotomy of "universal law/fleeting justice" therefore requires a rigorous challenge to the mindset of a pervasive legalism. But it thereby also demands an informed moral response to the pressing question of how to go about considering what differences should count as making a difference. Yet this can only be approached, as I suggested from the outset and as should now be clear from my analysis of Berlin, from the point of view of an understanding of moral disagreement and conflict which is attentive to the relation between values and identity as expressed in the liberal theory I have outlined.

If law is to be relieved in large part of the framing and answering of those issues, for some of the reasons I have been suggesting, then the approach to disagreement remains a central concern of any ethical or political enquiry. This is why the task is too important to be left to law and current legal structures, but also why some coherent and committed moral premises, in the full light of an understanding of conflict and its relation to identity, need to be explored and articulated, and their consequences for law tested. As the much-quoted Dylan line put it, to live outside the law you must be honest. While this may well involve appeal to a development of the kind of consensual norms Berlin drew attention to, it would also, in particular, require fuller attention to the role of what Raz called "constitutive incommensurabilities" as prominent elements of moral and political reasoning.

For it is insufficient to talk of decentring justice merely by promoting our responsibility to the other through legal means; the alien or underprivileged or victim of "justice miscarried" is perhaps unlikely to be content with the idea that justice is momentary, fleeting, without a "principle, value or a code", while all the while law's machine grinds on. It is because legal norms come at least in part to constitute how people come to and are allowed to relate to each other that we must ask questions about the institutional setting of law itself, its limitations and prejudices, the functions it serves or should serve and its position in current hierarchies of normative thought. In the end, this suggests more focus on the concerns raised by the radical liberal theory, since there we saw the demand, not for a rejection of norms as such, but an enquiry into their source as a function of their authority. And while this does not require a redemptive narrative, it does require facing up to hard moral questions, without the easy fall back onto either exclusionary reasons or epistemological gaps. To attempt simply to reinvigorate with a different, newly sensitive ethic, the ossifying, bureaucratised, professional legalism with which we are confronted is inadequate. For all that could be hoped for then would be the option of choosing to replace within that system one "reasonable man" with another. But even then the problem is merely replicated: for the question which remains is that even if this is a choice, whose choice and on whose terms, is it going to be?

CONCLUSION

These problems are, I suggest, indicative of the broader concerns of a theory which seeks to put moral conflict at the core of its analysis. Yet, despite the specific problems with liberal legalism which have been identified, I have argued that the concerns and insights of the radical liberal theory I have brought out here go some way to challenging the bleak picture of liberalism drawn by MacIntyre and other detractors. Such a theory's focus on the worth of the individual makes sense, I have suggested, only when that worth is seen to exist within shared forms of social life which are in part constitutive of individuals themselves and the "partial reasonings" through which they live their lives. But such worth is compromised by contemporary legal structures where both images of law—as community and as *imperium*—work against the instantiation of a truly agonistic liberalism of the form delineated here, and do not, perhaps cannot, follow through the implications of such premises. Internal and external demands on legal structures suggested dictates and confines that the radical liberal theory would see as deeply problematic.

Perhaps most problematic of all is the compromise that liberal legalism makes to a form of moral conflict that is as susceptible to the critique of emotivism (and of its role within the four-level analysis) as MacIntyre makes out. Liberals can little afford to continue in shoddy practices, given the critiques they are up against.

Berlin himself championed an unusual, maybe even nostalgic, form of liberalism. Yet he was not naïve. "It is true", he said, "that the cry for individual liberty has often disguised desire for privilege, or for power to oppress and exploit, or simply fear of social change".[1] The social costs of recent resuscitations of laissez-faire economics are in their way as much a reminder of the effects of these desires masquerading as a craving for individual liberty as were their nineteenth century counterparts. But in the way that I have read it, what Berlin's theory and the radical liberal thesis I have set out here do not lack is a political dynamism

[1] Isaiah Berlin, "Introduction" to *Four Essays on Liberty* (Oxford, OUP, 1969), p. lii.

which rests uneasy with easiness, with the comforts of a disguised consensus that seeks to replace genuine moral conflict. And so the caveat, from Berlin, remains as I have said, that we ought to be wary that these forms never become too common; that people's worth is itself prominently concerned with respecting individuals themselves as choosers, but choosers not merely amongst pre-set preferences, including those offered up by law, but among ways of being, together and separately. This is the meaning of autonomy—non-dogmatic yet insistent—I suggest flows from this kind of liberalism.

In the context of moral conflict, and recalling Hobbes's question about whose reason it is that is to count for law, we might consider a curious role Hobbes has come to play in contemporary theory. For the opponents of liberalism, and essentially of much of the last couple of hundred years of western intellectual history, he is the starting point for the critique of male bourgeois individualism. For proponents of liberalism, and in particular that variety of revamped, updated, sensitised, though always, ultimately, conservative, liberal constitutionalism, he is the sensible fanatic who prophesies what politics beyond liberal institutions would look like; that is, an unacceptable mess.

I have tried to show how neither grasps fully either the meaning of liberalism in the sense I have drawn out here or the implications of this for a liberal theory of law. Of particular concern is how moral and political conflict comes to be emaciated where the Hobbesian scenario is adopted as either reality or dark prediction. A sustainable, yet precarious, version of the meaning of moral conflict and its institutional settings challenges these, but only where the role of law and legal mechanisms is rethought. In particular, constitutional liberal lawyers still do not fully grasp the problems inherent in the notion of politics they support, which ends up only in fact as an anti-politics, since it never fully engages with the contradictions of the position. If anything, the reliance on law and legal structures promotes, as Shklar predicted, a reduction of agonistic conflict over values, to the version of interest politics which MacIntyre's critique identified. This is perhaps the strongest sense in which liberal legalism supports a view of social relations which should be seen to be incompatible with the liberal theory I have outlined here.

I have suggested instead that what is seen as the Hobbesian abyss misconstrues the nature of moral conflict, but also that law is itself implicated not only in the misconstrual but in its necessary perpetuation. Both images of law which conform to the strictures of liberal legalism work, together with the ideology of agreement, to force a particular view of moral and political conflict that depends upon and in turn reproduces a constitutive relation that emaciates the meaning of such conflict. Law's centripetal force makes it much harder to say, "no, that's not it, that's not what I meant, at all"; and the reinforcement of a professionalised cultural dependency only serves to augment this. Liberals, of all people, should be attentive to this, as well as to seeing that the use of law's instrumental authority may not always be a response to the perceived needs of the relations of a society of strangers; it may signal an official capitulation to the pedlars of paternalism and a formal embodiment of what the merchants of distrust would have us buy.

The effect of this is that the institutions of our social and legal systems continue to form channels along which selective amnesias can run, and has two important consequences. First, it neglects the broader insights, by Foucault and others, that the exercise of power can no longer be seriously conceived of simply in terms of legal sovereignty. To concentrate on the public arena of "rights without remainder" constitutes a forgetting of the minutiae of the practices and locations of power which, nonetheless, continue despite their being ignored. This tends to allow for an optimism—a kind of Dworkinian fantasy—about the coherence of community and its values, but in practice, and legal mechanisms are complicit in this, it allows political and moral debate to be swamped by a technocracy and professionalism which acts *as if* political and moral values were *not* at stake.

This paradox reminds us of what Berlin saw as an end of politics scenario; where means, not ends, are seen to be all that is legitimately at stake, and where opposition is seen to be not only illegitimate, but irrational, even disloyal. What Berlin saw clearly—as does McIntyre in his own way—about the working of contemporary democracy was its expert ability to disguise major forces of homogenisation at work which jointly operated through the appeals to comfort and inevitability, and to the denigration of the independently disloyal. Combating these would, I suggest, not call for more sensitivity; quite the opposite in fact.

This links to the second point, and it is perhaps the most significant in this connection. That is, that the channelling of morality and politics through legal categories is not challenged by simply attempting to revamp legal institutions to make them more sensitive to calls to different stances. My approach to moral conflict has suggested something more fundamental, and this is what I meant when I suggested earlier that law was part of the problem (as exemplified in my criticisms of postmodern jurisprudence), rather than the solution. But as today the benign aspects of rights culture within the liberal legal community are applauded, key sources of homogenisation come, without coincidence, to be systematically forgotten, including among these the role of economic structures to which Berlin in his day sought to draw attention.

Today Lyotard perhaps best captures this when, in line with Berlin's concerns about conflict being reduced to the "approbation of the official auditor", he writes that, "the economic genre of capital in no way requires the deliberative concatenation, which admits the heterogeneity of genres of discourse. To the contrary, it requires the suppression of that heterogeneity. It only tolerates it to the degree that the social bond is not (yet) entirely assimilated to the economic phrase alone . . . If this is one day the case, political institutions will be superfluous."[2] Lyotard's insight is important because it forces us to consider the relation between identity, self-definition and the preservation of values in forms of social life, and what the stakes of challenge to these imply: namely, that the reduction of conflict in this sense may appear—in MacIntyre's terms—as another instance of the obliteration of the distinction between manipulative and non-manipulative social relations and would, as I have shown, be of just as prominent concern to the radical liberal theory as it is to MacIntyre. But what it also implies is the need for such a theory to address and challenge forms of homogeneity that goes far beyond what can be dealt with either in liberal legal structures or in the championing of a postmodern localism or simplistic ethic of difference. For, as Lyotard continues, "[t]he resistance of communities banded around their names and their narratives is counted on to stand in the way of capital's hegemony. This is a mistake . . . this resistance fosters this hegemony as much as it counters it."[3]

It is precisely such forms of diversion that seeking difference through law help to sustain, and explains why a postmodern jurisprudence may be susceptible to the critique of inertia in the face of greater forces. I mention this example in part since other forms of theorising, such as putative forms of republicanism—always problematic if, as I believe to be the case, we are genuinely "after virtue"—and versions of legal pluralism, for example, do seek to "band around the name", but usually refuse to engage with their (to put it oxymoronically) resistant complicity in structures and practices of legal and economic power which, in

[2] Jean-François Lyotard, *The Differend: Phrases in Dispute* (trans. R. Harvey and M. S. Roberts, NJ, Humanities Press, 1993), 178.

[3] *Ibid.*, 181.

the end, leaves everything in place and thus perhaps constitute among the most insidious sorts of theorising as seen from the radical liberal point of view.

The liberal theory I have advanced here seeks, therefore, to lay open a challenge to this. Putting conflict over values at its core and following through the implications of this require, I suggest, a more rigorous approach to assessing the role of law for a liberal theory. The forms of community and autonomy which it then may seek to defend will cut across easy claims to localised commonality which would inhibit an engagement with a host of often less visible commensurating mechanisms, including those of the law, but which will not be limited to them. This is the defence of liberalism but one which is also at once the defiance of liberalism, that I have sought to delineate here.

I will end on that note. I have shown how the current role and structures of reasoning which make up liberal legalism's practices fall short of such an aspiration. The sometimes hidden assumptions of such practices, and the attendant consequences of these, may work to inhibit or distort the genuine moral conflicts which we face, and in that process reduce the possibilities for meaningful dissensus. In this sense, the incompatibilities between liberalism and liberal legalism need to be addressed in particular by liberal lawyers, who should not seek refuge behind the legal institution when the premises of a liberal theory are coming under threat across a range of social practices, and when legal mechanisms are themselves implicated in this.

It is better, I suggest, paraphrasing Berlin, to face up to these conflicts, and the agonising choices they bring, rather than be offered the choice in terms which so many will find alien and alienating. Only then might we, in a last, beautiful tension, expressed by Iain Crichton Smith, become attuned to the "unpredicted voices of our kind".

BIBLIOGRAPHY

ROBERT ALEXY, *A Theory of Legal Argumentation: The Theory of Rational Discourse as Theory of Legal Justification* (trans. R. Adler and N. MacCormick, Oxford, Clarendon Press, 1989).

PERRY ANDERSON, "England's Isaiah", *Times Literary Supplement* 20 December 1990.

J. H. BAKER, "English Law and the Renaissance", in J. H. Baker, *The Legal Profession and the Common Law: Historical Essays* (London, Hambledon Press, 1986).

ANNE BARRON, "Ronald Dworkin and the Challenge of Postmodernism", in Alan Hunt (ed.), *Reading Dworkin Critically* (New York, Berg Publishers, 1992).

ROLAND BARTHES, *Mythologies* (London, Vintage, 1993).

SEYLA BENHABIB, "The Generalised and Concrete Other" in S. Benhabib and D. Cornell (eds.), *Feminism as Critique: Essays on the Politics of Gender in Late-Capitalist Societies* (Cambridge, Polity Press, 1987).

——"Democracy and Difference: Reflections on the Meta-Politics of Lyotard and Derrida" (1994) 1 *The Journal of Political Philosophy* 1–23.

ISAIAH BERLIN, *Four Essays on Liberty*, (Oxford, OUP, 1969).

——"Does Political Theory Still Exist?" in P. Laslett and W. G. Runciman (eds.), *Philosophy, Politics and Society* (Second Series) (Oxford, Basil Blackwell, 1969).

——*Against the Current: Essays in the History of Ideas* (ed. H. Hardy, Oxford, Clarendon Press, 1981).

——*The Crooked Timber of Humanity* (London, Fontana Press, 1991).

——and BERNARD WILLIAMS, "Pluralism and Liberalism: a Reply" [1994] *Political Studies* 306–9.

RICHARD BERNSTEIN, *The New Constellation: The Ethical-Political Horizons of Modernity/Postmodernity* (Cambridge, Polity Press, 1991).

C. BEVERIDGE and R. TURNBULL, *The Eclipse of Scottish Culture: Inferiorism and the Intellectuals* (Edinburgh, Polygon, 1989).

PIERRE BOURDIEU, "Codification" in *In Other Words: Essays Towards a Reflexive Sociology* (trans. M. Adamson, Cambridge, Polity Press, 1990).

JAN BROEKMAN, "Revolution and Moral Commitment to a Legal System" in N. MacCormick and Z. Bankowski (eds.), *Enlightenment, Rights and Revolution: Essays in Legal and Social Philosophy* (Aberdeen, AUP, 1989).

BEVERLEY BROWN, "Debating Pornography: The Symbolic Dimensions" *Law and Critique* Vol. 1, no. 2 [1990] 131–54.

NILS CHRISTIE, "Conflict as Property" in C. Reasons and R. M. Rich, *The Sociology of Law: A Conflict Perspective* (Toronto, Butterworth, 1978).

EMILIOS A. CHRISTODOULIDIS, "The Suspect Intimacy Between Law and Political Community" (1994) 80 *ARSP* 1–18.

——"'A New Constitutional Reality for Civil Society'?" in R. Bellamy *et al.* (eds.), *Democracy and Constitutional Culture in the Union of Europe* (London, Lothian Foundation Press, 1995).

GEORG COHN, *Existentialism and Legal Science* (New York, Oceana Publications, 1967).

SIR EDWARD COKE, *Prohibitions del Roy* (1607) 12 Co.Rep. 63.

HUGH COLLINS, "Democracy and Adjudication" in N. MacCormick and P. Birks (eds.), *The Legal Mind: Essays for Tony Honoré* (Oxford, Clarendon Press, 1986).

——*The Law of Contract* (London, Weidenfeld and Nicholson, 1986).

ROGER COTTERRELL, *Law's Community: Legal Theory in Sociological Perspective* (Oxford, Clarendon Press, 1995).

ROBERT M. COVER, "The Supreme Court 1982, Foreword: Nomos and Narrative" (1983–84) 97 *Harvard Law Review* 4–68.

GEORGE DAVIE, *The Crisis of the Democratic Intellect* (Edinburgh, Polygon, 1986).

COSTAS DOUZINAS and RONNIE WARRINGTON, "'A Well-Founded Fear of Justice': Law and Ethics in Postmodernity" *Law and Critique* Vol. II, no. 2 [1991] 115–47.

——and ——"The Face of Justice: A Jurisprudence of Alterity" (1994) 3 *Social and Legal Studies* 405–25.

SHEILA DUNCAN, "Law's Sexual Discipline: Visibility, Violence, and Consent" (1995) 22 *Journal of Law and Society* 326–52.

RONALD DWORKIN, *Taking Rights Seriously* (London, Duckworth, 1977).

——"Liberalism" in Stuart Hampshire (ed.), *Public and Private Morality* (Cambridge, CUP, 1978).

——*Law's Empire* (London, Fontana Press, 1986).

DAVID DYZENHAUS, *Judging the Judges, Judging Ourselves: Truth, Reconciliation, and the Apartheid Legal Order* (Oxford, Hart Publishing, 1998).

JOHN ERSKINE, *An Institute of the Law of Scotland*, (1773, 5th edn., Edinburgh, Bell and Bradfute, 1812).

LINDSAY FARMER, "The Obsession with Definition: The Nature of Crime and Critical Legal Theory" (1996) 5 *Social and Legal Theory* 57–73.

MICHEL FOUCAULT, "Two Lectures" (reprinted from his "The Juridical Apparatus") in W. Connolly (ed.), *Legitimacy and the State* (Oxford, Basil Blackwell, 1984).

ELIZABETH FOX-GENOVESE, "The Many Faces of Moral Economy: A Contribution to a Debate", *Past and Present* 58 (Feb. 1973) 161–8.

HARRY FRANKFURT, "Comments on MacIntyre", *Synthese* 53 (1982) 319–21.
NANCY FRASER, "Solidarity or Singularity?: Richard Rorty between Romanticism and Technocracy" in Alan R. Malachowski (ed.), *Reading Rorty: Critical Responses to Philosophy and the Mirror of Nature (and Beyond)* (Oxford, Basil Blackwell, 1990).
LON L. FULLER, *The Morality of Law* (revised edn., Newhaven, Conn., Yale UP, 1969).
H. H. GERTH and C. WRIGHT MILLS (trans. and eds.), *From Max Weber: Essays in Sociology* (1948, London, Routledge, 1991).
——and ——"Introduction", *From Max Weber.*
PETER GOODRICH, *Oedipus Lex: Psychoanalysis, History, Law* (Berkeley, Cal., University of California Press, 1995).
——COSTAS DOUZINAS and YIFAT HACHAMOVITCH, "Introduction" to C. Douzinas, P. Goodrich and Y. Hachamovitch (eds.), *Politics, Postmodernity and Critical Legal Studies: The Legality of the Contingent* (London, Routledge, 1994).
JOHN GRAY, *Isaiah Berlin* (London, HarperCollins, 1995).
CHARLES B. GUIGNON and DAVID R. HILEY, "Biting the bullet: Rorty on Private and Public Morality", in Alan R. Malachowski (ed.), *Reading Rorty: Critical Responses to Philosophy and the Mirror of Nature (and Beyond)* (Oxford, Basil Blackwell, 1990).
AMY GUTMANN, "The Rule of Rights or the Right to Rule", *Nomos XXVIII: Justification* (eds. J. R. Pennock and J. W. Chapman, New York, New York University Press, 1986), 165–77.
KNUD HAAKONSSEN, *The Science of a Legislator: The Natural Jurisprudence of David Hume and Adam Smith* (Cambridge, CUP, 1981).
JURGEN HABERMAS, *Communication and the Evolution of Society* (trans. T. McCarthy, London, Heinemann, 1979).
——*The Theory of Communicative Action* (trans. T. McCarthy, Boston, Mass., Beacon Press, 1984).
——*The Philosophical Discourse of Modernity* (trans. F. G. Lawrence, Cambridge, Polity Press, 1987).
——*Between Facts and Norms* (trans. W. Rehg, Cambridge, Mass., MIT Press, 1996).
HERBERt L. A. HART, *The Concept of Law* (Oxford, Clarendon Press, 1961).
ROGER HAUSHEER, "Introduction" to Isaiah Berlin, *Against the Current: Essays in the History of Ideas* (ed., H. Hardy, Oxford, Clarendon Press, 1981).
F. A. HAYEK, *The Road to Serfdom* (London, Routledge, 1944).
CHRISTOPHER HILL, *Intellectual Origins of the English Revolution* (Oxford, Clarendon Press, 1965).
THOMAS HOBBES, *Leviathan* (ed. C. B. Macpherson, Harmondsworth, Penguin, 1968).
——*A Dialogue Between a Philosopher and a Student of the Common Laws of England* (ed. J. Cropsey, Chicago, Ill., Chicago UP, 1971).

STEPHEN HOLMES, *The Anatomy of Antiliberalism* (Cambridge, Mass., Harvard UP, 1993).

DAVID HUME, *A Treatise of Human Nature* (2nd edn., ed. L. A. Selby-Bigge, Oxford, Clarendon Press, 1978).

ALAN HUNT (ed.), *Reading Dworkin Critically* (New York, Berg Publishers, 1992).

——*Explorations in Law and Society: Towards a Constitutive Theory of Law* (New York, Routledge, 1993).

ALLAN C. HUTCHINSON, "The Last Emperor?" in Alan Hunt (ed.), *Reading Dworkin Critically* (New York, Berg Publishers, 1992).

——*Waiting for CORAF: A Critique of Law and Rights* (Toronto, Toronto UP, 1995).

F. C. HUTLEY, "The Legal Tradition of Australia as Contrasts with Those of the United States" (1981) 55 *Australian Law Journal* 63–70.

MICHAEL IGNATIEFF, *Isaiah Berlin: A Life* (London, Chatto & Windus, 1998).

ALISON JAGGER, *Feminist Politics and Human Nature* (NJ, Rowman & Allanheld, 1983).

IMMANUEL KANT, *The Metaphysics of Morals* (trans. M. Gregor, Cambridge, CUP, 1991).

VALERIE KERRUISH, *Jurisprudence as Ideology* (London, Routledge, 1991).

——and ALAN HUNT, "Dworkin's Dutiful Daughter: Gender Discrimination in Law's Empire" in Alan Hunt (ed.), *Reading Dworkin Critically* (New York, Berg Publishers, 1992), 209–39.

——and JEANNINE PURDY, "He *Look* Honest—Big White Thief" (1998) 4.1 *Law/Text/Culture* 146–71.

STEPHAN KORNER, *Kant* (Harmondsworth, Penguin Books, 1955).

SAUL A. KRIPKE, *Wittgenstein on Rules and Private Language: An Elementary Exposition* (Oxford, Basil Blackwell, 1985).

MILAN KUNDERA, *Immortality* (trans. P. Kussi, London, Faber and Faber, 1991).

GENEVIEVE LLOYD, *The Man of Reason: "Male" and "Female" in Western Philosophy* (London, Methuen, 1984).

NIKLAS LUHMANN, "The Third Question: The Creative Use of Paradoxes in Law and Legal History", (1988) 15 *Journal of Law and Society* 153–66.

STEVEN LUKES, "Alasdair MacIntyre: The Sociologist versus the Philosopher" in Steven Lukes, *Moral Conflict and Politics* (Oxford, Clarendon Press, 1991).

JEAN-FRANÇOIS LYOTARD, *The Postmodern Condition: A Report on Knowledge* (trans. G. Bennington and B. Massumi, Manchester, Manchester UP, 1984).

——*The Differend: Phrases in Dispute* (trans. G. Van Den Abbeele, Manchester, Manchester UP, 1988).

——*Toward the Postmodern* (eds. R. Harvey and M. S. Roberts, NJ, Humanities Press, 1993).

——*Political Writings* (trans. B. Readings and K. P. Geiman, London, UCL Press, 1993).

NEIL MACCORMICK, *Legal Reasoning and Legal Theory* (Oxford, Clarendon Press, 1978).
——*Legal Right and Social Democracy: Essays in Legal and Political Philosophy* (Oxford, Clarendon Press, 1982).
——"The Ethics of Legalism" (1989) 2 *Ratio Juris* 184–93.
——"Reconstruction after Deconstruction: A Response to CLS" (1990) 10 *Oxford Journal of Legal Studies* 539–58.
——"Argumentation and Interpretation in Law" (1993) 6 *Ratio Juris* 18.
——"The Relative Heteronomy of Law" (1995) 3 *European Journal of Philosophy* 69–85.
ALASDAIR MACINTYRE, "How Moral Agents Became Ghosts, or, Why the History of Ethics Diverged from that of the Philosophy of Mind", *Synthese* 53 (1982) 295–312.
——"Moral Philosophy: What Next?" in Stanley Hauerwas and Alasdair MacIntyre (eds.), *Revisions: Changing Perspectives in Moral Philosophy* (Notre Dame, University of Notre Dame Press, 1983).
——*After Virtue: A Study in Moral Theory*, (1981), 2nd ed., London, Duckworth, 1985.
——*Whose Justice? Which Rationality?* (London, Duckworth, 1988).
——*Three Rival Versions of Moral Enquiry: Encyclopaedia, Genealogy, and Tradition* (London, Duckworth, 1990).
CATHARINE MACKINNON, *Feminism Unmodified: Discourses on Life and Law* (Cambridge Mass., Harvard UP, 1987).
——*Toward a Feminist Theory of the State* (Cambridge Mass., Harvard UP, 1989).
ALAN R. MALACHOWSKI (ed.), associate ed. Jo Burrows, *Reading Rorty: Critical Responses to Philosophy and the Mirror of Nature (and Beyond)* (Oxford, Basil Blackwell, 1990).
GEOFFREY MARSHALL, "Justiciability" in A. G. Guest (ed.), *Oxford Essays in Jurisprudence* (First Series) (Oxford, Clarendon Press, 1961).
KARL MARX, "On the Jewish Question" in Lucio Colletti (ed.), *Karl Marx: Early Writings* (trans. R. Livingstone and G. Benton, Harmondsworth, Penguin Books, 1975).
ELIZABETH MENSCH, "The Colonial Origins of Liberal Property Rights" (1982) 31 *Buffalo Law Review* 635.
——and ALAN FREEMAN, "A Republican Agenda for Hobbesian America?" (1989) *Florida Law Review* 581.
MARTHA MINOW, "Justice Engendered", (1987) 101 *Harvard Law Review* 10–95.
CHANTAL MOUFFE, "Rawls: Political Philosophy without Politics" in David Rasmussen (ed.), *Universalism and Communitarianism: Contemporary Debates in Ethics* (Boston, Mass., MIT Press, 1990).
NGAIRE NAFFINE, *Law and the Sexes: Explorations in Feminist Jurisprudence* (Sydney, Allen and Unwin, 1990).

JENNIFER NEDELSKY, "Reconceiving Autonomy: Sources, Thoughts and Possibilities" in A. C. Hutchinson and L. J. M. Green (eds.), *Law and the Community: The End of Individualism?* (Toronto, Carswell, 1989).

ALAN W. NORRIE, *Law, Ideology and Punishment: Retrieval and Critique of the Liberal Ideal of Criminal Justice* (Dordrecht, Kluwer, 1991).

MARTHA NUSSBAUM, "The Feminist Critique of Liberalism", Lecture at Oxford University, Feb. 1996, excerpted in the *Times Higher Education Supplement* as "The Sleep of Reason", Feb. 1996, 17–18.

TIM O'HAGAN, "Searching for Ancestors", *Radical Philosophy* 54, Spring 1990.

VAL PLUMWOOD, *Feminism and the Mastery of Nature* (London, Routledge, 1993).

JOHN RAWLS, *Political Liberalism* (New York, Columbia UP, 1993).

JOSEPH RAZ, *The Authority of Law* (Oxford, Clarendon Press, 1979).

——*The Morality of Freedom* (Oxford, Clarendon Press, 1986).

BILL READINGS, "Foreword" to Jean-François Lyotard, *Political Writings* (trans. B. Readings and K. P. Geiman, London, UCL Press, 1993).

THOMAS REID, *Essays on the Active Powers of the Human Mind* (1813–15, Cambridge, Mass., MIT Press, 1969).

RICHARD RORTY, *Consequences of Pragmatism: Essays 1972–1980* (Minneapolis, Minn., University of Minnesota Press, 1982).

——*Philosophy and the Mirror of Nature*, (Oxford, Basil Blackwell, 1989).

——*Contingency, Irony, and Solidarity* (Cambridge, CUP, 1989).

——"Postmodern Bourgeois Liberalism" in *Philosophical Papers: Volume I* (Cambridge, CUP, 1991).

——"On Ethnocentrism: A Reply to Clifford Geertz" in *Philosophical Papers: Volume I* (Cambridge, CUP, 1991).

——"Freud and Moral Reflection" in *Philosophical Papers: Volume II* (Cambridge, CUP, 1991).

——"Moral Identity and Private Autonomy: The Case of Foucault", *Philosophical Papers: Volume II* (Cambridge, CUP, 1991).

GILLIAN ROSE, *The Broken Middle: Out of our Ancient Society* (Oxford, Blackwell, 1992).

PHILIP SELZNICK, *The Moral Commonwealth: Social Theory and the Promise of Community* (Berkeley, Cal., University of California Press, 1992).

JUDITH N. SHKLAR, *Legalism: Law, Morals, and Political Trials* (Cambridge Mass., Harvard UP, 1986).

KENNETH SIMPSON, *The Protean Scot: The Crisis of Identity in Eighteenth Century Scottish Literature* (Aberdeen, AUP, 1988).

ADAM SMITH, *The Theory of Moral Sentiments* (6th edn., 1790), eds. D. D. Raphael and A. L. Macfie (Oxford, OUP, 1976).

BOAVENTURA DE SOUSA SANTOS, *Toward a New Common Sense: Law, Science and Politics in the Paradigmatic Transition* (London, Routledge, 1995).

STAIR, VISCOUNT (JAMES DALRYMPLE), *The Institutions of the Law of Scotland*, (1693, ed. D. M. Walker, Glasgow and Edinburgh, University Presses, 1981).

LESLIE STEVENSON, *Seven Theories of Human Nature* (Oxford, Clarendon Press, 1974).

WILLIAM M. SULLIVAN, "After Foundationalism: The Return to Practical Philosophy" in E. Simpson (ed.), *Antifoundationalism and Practical Reasoning: Conversations between Hermeneutics and Analysis* (Edmonton Alberta, Academic Printing and Publishing, 1987).

GUNTHER TEUBNER, *Law as an Autopoietic System* (trans. A. Bankowska and R. Adler, ed. Z. Bankowski, Oxford, Basil Blackwell, 1993).

ROBERTO MANGABEIRA UNGER, *Law in Modern Society: Toward a Criticism of Social Theory* (New York, Free Press, 1976).

——"The Critical Legal Studies Movement" (1983) 96 *Harvard Law Review* 563–675.

ROBERT WACHBROIT, "A Geneology of Virtues" (1982–3) 92 *Yale Law Journal* 564–76.

MARY WARNOCK, *The Philosophy of Sartre* (London, Hutchinson, 1965).

——*Existentialism* (London, OUP, 1970).

——*Existentialist Ethics* (London, Macmillan, 1974).

MAX WEBER, "Science as a Vocation" in H. H. Gerth and C. Wright Mills (eds)., *From Max Weber: Essays in Sociology* (1948, London, Routledge, 1991).

——"Bureaucracy" in H. H. Gerth and C. Wright Mills (eds.), *From Max Weber: Essays in Sociology* (1948, London, Routledge, 1991).

SAMUEL WEBER, "In the Name of the Law", in D. Cornell, M. Rosenfeld, and D. Gray (eds.), *Deconstruction and the Possibility of Justice* (New York, Routledge, 1992).

ROBERT A. WILLIAMS JR, "Documents of Barbarism: The Contemporary Legacy of European Racism and Colonialism in the Narrative Traditions of Federal Indian Law" (1989) 31 *Arizona Law Review* 237–78.

PHILIP WINDSOR, "Reason Becomes Contingent in History: Can History Become Reason?" in Philip Windsor (ed.), *Reason and History: or only a History of Reason?* (Leicester and London, Leicester UP, 1990).

LUDWIG WITTGENSTEIN, *Philosophical Investigations* (2nd edn. 1958, Oxford, Basil Blackwell, 1989).

INDEX

www.ingramcontent.com/pod-product-compliance
Ingram Content Group UK Ltd.
Pitfield, Milton Keynes, MK11 3LW, UK
UKHW020832290926
15470UKWH00009B/1863/J

9 781841 131085